Language, Mind and Computation

Language, Mind and Computation

Prakash Mondal
Indian Institute of Technology, New Delhi, India

First published 2014 by
PALGRAVE MACMILLAN

Palgrave Macmillan in the UK is an imprint of Macmillan Publishers Limited,
registered in England, company number 785998, of Houndmills, Basingstoke,
Hampshire RG21 6XS.

Palgrave Macmillan in the US is a division of St Martin's Press LLC,
175 Fifth Avenue, New York, NY 10010.

Palgrave Macmillan is the global academic imprint of the above companies
and has companies and representatives throughout the world.

Palgrave® and Macmillan® are registered trademarks in the United States,
the United Kingdom, Europe and other countries.

ISBN 978-1-349-49678-5   ISBN 978-1-137-44943-6 (eBook)
DOI 10.1057/9781137449436

This book is printed on paper suitable for recycling and made from fully
managed and sustained forest sources. Logging, pulping and manufacturing
processes are expected to conform to the environmental regulations of the
country of origin.

A catalogue record for this book is available from the British Library.

A catalog record for this book is available from the Library of Congress.

Typeset by MPS Limited, Chennai, India.

To Amrit Srinivasan,
for her boundless enthusiasm

Contents

List of Figures

Preface

This book is about human language – the language that we utter, understand and feel so close to us. But the title of the book conveys the impression that it is also going to say something about mind and computation. For readers who may misapprehend the title, I must emphasize at the outset that this book is not a collection of essays on topics covering various issues on language, something about the mind and a bit on computation. Rather, the book aims to explore and investigate the nature of language in an attempt to figure out how and in what sense language is *intrinsically* mental and/or computational. That is to say that this book will probe the relationship of language to mind and computation, only insofar as the relationship may be reasonably believed to unlock something deep about the intrinsic nature of human language. The reasons for the specific aim of this book may not appear to be tantalizingly clear. However this comes about, the following reasons seem to me to be significant.

First, with the rise of modern theoretical linguistics language has come to be studied as a formal object. That is, the mathematical and computational properties of natural language(s), as opposed to artificial languages like C or Fortran, have become a source of fascinating new insights into the form of language. But this has not been sufficient to independently project linguistic inquiry onto another plane where questions about the mental connection of language – way beyond the limitations of behaviourism, which jettisoned the mind altogether – could be asked and raised. The very idea of Noam Chomsky that natural language grammar has a mental organization aligned the study of language as a formal object with the study of language as a branch of psychology, or rather of cognitive science. Overall, this seems to bring a splendid harmony and a sense of marvellous order within the fabric of connections thus forged between language, mind and the computational properties of natural language. Far from it, this carries many hidden conundrums and quandaries barely recognized, let alone explored.

Second, the relationship between language, mind and computation has had the notion of computation most unconscionably tacked onto it. The notion of grammar as a kind of computing device that generates sentences with operations of grammar characterized as computations muddles, rather than enriches, the very conception of what it is for grammar to be mental. Clinging precariously to the trinity of language, mind and computation has its devastating consequences which can be uncovered only by careful scrutiny which current discourses on the foundational issues in theoretical linguistics seldom attempt. A lot is taken for granted when one talks about computations operating on mental constructs of grammar. Thus some of the orthodoxies are in urgent need of being dispelled. But then this requires an opening up never judged indispensable to the foundational questions and goals of linguistics.

Third, the overarching belief that the property of mental organization of natural language grammar wedded to the 'laws' of computation can be the basis of theoretical advances both in linguistics and in cognitive science in general appears to construct elegant solutions to many baffling problems at the interface of language, brain and cognition. Although this idealization is tempting enough to lull many theoretical linguists and cognitive scientists into a tranquillizing sense of theoretical security, it needs to be made clear that the exact nature of the relationship between language, mind and computation is far more convoluted and complicated than has been assumed or even realized. But this requires a demonstration which is what is presently absent.

Of course, I am not in a position to pretend to have laid bare in the most unequivocal manner the connection obtaining between language, mind and computation. This connection may not be simply taken to be something that is beyond our grasp. Rather, the vectors of complexity of the problems surrounding the connection between language, mind and computation cut deep into the theoretical machinery that we have constructed. This book merely attempts to show where the postulations have gone wrong, and in so doing, glimpses into the immensely tangled form of the riddles wrapped around the relationship between language, mind and computation. I must acknowledge that I have not been able to fully make sense of it all. I think there is indeed more to this topic than meets the eye. For those who may skim through the initial portions of this book, I suggest that they tread carefully because it may seem to them that I have uncritically accepted the accounts of linguistic structure proposed by theoretical linguists whose theoretical programme has been critiqued. Such readers are encouraged to read through these portions in order to figure out how the inconsistencies and paradoxes follow from the axioms of the theoretical programme which has been presented virtually in its entirety just with this purpose in mind.

With this as backdrop, I intend to open this book up for anybody and everybody. It is understandable that appraising the complexity of issues is not something everybody indulges in. Be that as it may, I must add that this has its own fruits. Walking through the complexities of the riddles and paradoxes a complex issue opens up can also be illuminating in a rather strange way. I ask for readers' indulgence in this matter. With this in mind linguists, philosophers, psychologists, computer scientists and cognitive scientists of all persuasions, and everybody else, are invited to see what the book can offer. I have made every effort to make this book as accessible as possible, but certainly not oversimplified it. If readers gain something from the book they can ruminate over, I shall be glad. I give it all to you, readers!

Acknowledgements

A substantial portion of this book was completed at the Indian Institute of Technology Delhi. I am enormously grateful to the institute for providing me with the necessary resources that have been extremely valuable for the completion of this work. The idea of writing a book of this kind was first instilled in me by my friend Ravi Shankar Mishra. Hence I thank him for understanding the felt necessity only adumbrated by my mind. I express my gratitude to Bijoy Boruah for all the discussions that I have had over myriad issues, many of which bear directly or indirectly on the contents of this book. I also thank him for the encouragement that I have received from him. In this connection I acknowledge the support of Rukmini Bhaya Nair as well. I take this opportunity to thank the audience at the Indian Institute of Technology Gandhinagar for their comments on the ideas presented in the book. I express my sincere thanks to Marcelo Dascal for his comments on the ideas expressed in this book. Thanks also go to Ray Jackendoff and Kyle Johnson for many interactions we have had on various issues over the years some of which have found a place in this book, although they do not fully agree with me in many ways. I also owe a lot to two anonymous reviewers for their thorough review reports.

I am especially – and perhaps in a deeper way – grateful to Avishek Chakraborty and Kiran Pala for their interactions, discussions and comments on the contents expressed in the book, and also for their unfailing support and unflagging enthusiasm for the book.

Given that I have articulated many of my views on language, cognition and computation in my articles published in various places, some contents from them have been adapted for the present book. Thus, Chapter 5 draws upon the following two articles of mine:

'Logical form vs. logical form: How does the difference matter for semantic computationality?' In Heather D. Pfeiffer, Dmitry I. Ignatov, Jonas Poelmans and Nagarjuna Gadiraju (eds) *Conceptual Structures for STEM Research and Education*, Lecture Notes in Computer Science, Vol. 7735, 2013, pp. 254–65 (Springer).

'Does (linguistic) computation need culture to make cognition viable?' *Procedia: Social and Behavioral Sciences* 97: 464–73 (Elsevier).

Chapters 6–8, on the other hand, have been written by borrowing ideas from the following article of mine:

'How does the faculty of language relate to rules, axioms and constraints?' *Pragmatics and Cognition* 21(2): 270–303 (John Benjamins).

I am immensely indebted to my editors Olivia Middleton and Rebecca Brennan of Palgrave Macmillan for their guidance, assistance and genuine interest in the project. This book would not have taken the form it has without them. Libby Forrest deserves special thanks for everything she has done to streamline things for me so as to make my task a lot easier than it would have been. Any remaining errors are mine. I hope to have kept the coverage of the literature within the reasonable and justifiable boundaries of the contents of the book.

Finally, I am thankful to P.A.S. for her tolerance of my obsession.

1
Introduction

Linguistic theory had its chief preoccupation with form and meaning in most of twentieth-century linguistics grounded in the Saussurean legacy of the pairing of the *signifier* and the *signified*. And with it came the division between *langue* and *parole*, the former being the abstract (but arbitrary) system of relations between *signifiers* (or simply, signs) and the *signified* (meanings), and the latter being the entire constellation of speech events. What Saussure bequeathed to the study of language influenced, whether in a linear or non-linear manner, much of the linguistic theorizing in the decades to come as well as in the subsequent century. A lot of what structuralism had to offer in the twentieth century was already inherited from the Saussurean legacy which posited, among other things, the primacy of *langue* over *parole*. But the relations between the signifier and the signified had by then captured the imagination of not just linguists but also philosophers, literary theorists and anthropologists, for the exact nature of relations between the signifier and the signified needed to be thoroughly understood in any sphere that has any purported liaison with language. As it turns out, if the relations between the signifier and the signified are arbitrary, this adds, rather than detracts from, the complexity of such relations between the signifier and the signified which have widely different and thus diverse manifestations in different languages across the world. Even if aspects of the Saussurean legacy have defined much of the progress in the emergence of modern linguistics as a science, it has not been at all easy to flesh out the intricacies involved in the relations between the signifier and the signified. When looked at in a mere formal fashion, it makes sense to the extent that one can treat the relation between the signifier and the signified as a pairing of form and meaning, but a rigorous formalization of the relation between the signifier and the signified has always been elusive since the signifier does not always go in a perfect lockstep with the signified, and worse than that is the fact that the signified is still poorly understood. This does not put an end to all worries. Questions regarding the grounding of the relation between the signifier and the signified have also erupted in that we still wonder where we need to place the relation between the signifier and the signified – whether in the ontological system of language itself, or in the psychological domain or in the Platonic sphere.

All this exegesis is not meant to suggest that the inheritance of the Saussurean legacy has had disastrous consequences for linguistic theory. Not at all. Rather, it has opened up an enormous space of possibilities and wide ramifications that are still discussed, debated in current studies on language, and encompass the very foundations of modern linguistic theory. The two fundamental aspects of the Saussurean legacy – the primacy of *langue* over *parole* and the relation between the signifier and the signified – have penetrated deep into linguistic theorizing. Whether it was in the structuralist tradition or in the period subsequent to that, these two aspects have configured and broadened the horizons of any serious thinking on aspects of language. However, it is all a story of an overall continuity that has prevailed over and above any breaks or cracks in the system of thinking on language. When structuralism flourished in the twentieth century with a heavy dose of analysis of forms over meaning, the attempt to purge linguistic theory of any association with the intentionality of humans as evoked in the earlier traditions of philology was solidified, though there was certainly some trade-off of ideas from behaviourist psychology as evident in the work of Leonard Bloomfield (1933). Perhaps it was the gradual spread of structuralism all over Europe and the Americas that was responsible for the converging threads of structuralism to consolidate the Saussurean legacy by way of shedding the humanized element in language and building the scientific basis of the linguistic endeavour (Joseph 2002). Again, we encounter another form of continuity that cuts across all traditions of linguistic inquiry right from the Saussurean period but this had a mark of a discontinuity too, as specified just above, in having thrown away the *diachronic* garb of language study along with the intentionality-laden linguistic methodology. But how is this continuity to be understood rather than explained away? This continuity needs to be deeply understood before we embark upon any exploration of the discontinuities that defined themselves against the stratified layering of patterns of such continuity. As we go on, we will see that it is the mutual tension and undulation between such continuity and discontinuities which constitute breaks, if not from such continuity, but from a palpable contour of continuity telescoped from the earlier tradition of linguistic theorizing, that characterizes the crux of issues surrounding language.

It is with the advent of Generative Grammar in the second half of the twentieth century that another discontinuity, greater in scale and significance, started to appear on the landscape of linguistic theorizing. Noam Chomsky posed questions about the nature of language with respect to how it is acquired, known and instantiated in the human mind. It is these questions that made the advent of Generative Grammar a remarkable break from the earlier continuity derived from the structuralist tradition. Though Chomsky's *Syntactic Structures* (1957) was targeted at the behaviourist essence of the structuralist tradition in linguistic theory, his later publications starting with *Aspects of the Theory of Syntax* (1965) began to erect the architectural foundations of Generative Grammar on *rationalist* principles. One of the central goals of a linguistic theory is to characterize the faculty of language in its form of growth, knowledge and perhaps use (Chomsky 2004, 2005) undergirded by the distinction between *competence* and *performance*, the former being the system of mental rules and representations and the latter denoting aspects of processing. Even if Chomsky (1965, 1980) has over the decades presented the faculty of language as a computational system with its own domain-specific cognitive structures which can be characterized as a system of rules and representations, the nature and form of rules, representations as conceived of within a system of principles of grammars, have then been questioned, reviewed and modified over the successive phases of development of the theory of Generative Grammar from the Government and Binding model to the Minimalist Program (Epstein and Seely 2002, 2006). The recent development in Generative Grammar has been the development of phase theory that partitions the computational space into smaller domains of operations called *phases* (Chomsky 2001), the goal having been to achieve formal elegance and computational parsimony. Beneath all this lie some of the deep-seated assumptions about the connection between language, mind and computation. We shall have a glimpse of this in the next section.

1.1   At the cross-section of language, mind and computation

It is the connection between language, mind and computation that the present book will try to investigate in a more fundamental and deeper way than has been possible so far. One of the ways of seeing the connection is this: linguistic representations are (internalized) mental representations, and operations on such representations by means of rule systems are computations. On the one hand, this connection between language, mind and computation has constituted or helped consolidate the plexus of assumptions underlying a whole gamut of linguistic theories which covers Generative Semantics (Lakoff 1971; Postal 1972), Head-Driven Phrase Structure Grammar (Pollard and Sag 1994), Lexical Functional Grammar (Bresnan 2001), Cognitive Grammar (Lakoff 1987; Langacker 1987) and so on, all under the broader canopy of the Saussurean legacy in continuity, although Autolexical Syntax (Sadock 1991, 2012) and the Parallel Architecture model of language (Jackendoff 2002) have split the signifier (that is, form) into smaller parts. On the other hand, this connection between language, mind and computation – whatever way it is framed – seems to be the least understood thing ever encountered in linguistic theorizing when juxtaposed with the conception of relations between the signifier and the signified in the system of *langue*. More significantly, the Generative tradition has made the whole relationship between language, mind and computation far more muddled and confounded, instead of teasing it all out. And this has been carried over into other linguistic theories as well. A part of the problem has something to do with the very nature of what language is, that is, a question about its ontology. Is language really abstract? It is not an easy question. Language may well be abstract, but then why do we feel that language is a concrete thing coming right out of our vocal apparatus? The other part of the problem is that something as nebulous as the human mind and something as spooky as computation have been linked to language. Ultimately, the triumvirate is not an easy combination. An example might give one a glimpse into the monstrosity of the problem. Let us look at the sentence below.

(1) Why does John laugh__?

Here 'why' is a *Wh*-phrase adjunct that is supposed to be interpreted in the gap shown in (1). This is the phenomenon of displacement which is also called *movement* in the Generative literature. But how does one know that 'why' has been displaced (or moved) from the gap shown in (1)? Well, the answer may come from one's interpretation of 'why' as a part of the predicate 'laugh'. If this is so, let us look at another example.

(2) Why does she wonder__ [how John laughs_]?

Here again 'why' seems to be interpreted at a place other than where it appears. But this time 'why' is a part of the predicate 'wonder', as indicated through the gap right after 'wonder' within the matrix clause, and 'how' is a part of the predicate 'laughs', as enclosed within the square brackets indicating the embedded clause. These two displacements are thus independent. But again the question is: how does one know this? The answer appears to be similar to what has been stated just above. If that is the case, one has to match 'why' with the gap at the appropriate place. But how does one know what an appropriate place is? One may well form a syntactic rule that states that 'why' must be matched in interpretation with the closest gap (in the local predicate). What is the nature of this rule? On the one hand, this rule cannot be formulated without any reference to the matching of an expression with the interpreted gap. On the other hand, the correspondence of an expression with the interpreted gap can only be possible if they are *mentally* represented as such. But how come such mental representations form part of a rule if rules are meaning-free operations running on in a mindless machine? To put it another way, how come such mental representations constitute a point to which rules make reference if rules are just operations devoid of meaning? This brings us nearer to the concept of computation, as we can see. But does it then mean that the matching or correspondence of an expression with the interpreted gap is a computation or is what drives a computation? If we say that the matching or correspondence of an expression with the interpreted gap is itself a computation, the process of interpretation involving meaning becomes a part of computation. The other possibility is that the matching or correspondence of an expression with the interpreted gap is *not* a computation per se; rather, it is what drives a computation. This too makes computation sensitive to the process of interpretation involving meaning. Either way we lose out. How to resolve this? To my knowledge, this issue has not been given the due attention it should have had.

However, this certainly does not complete the picture. There is more to it than meets the eye. Now let us assume that any syntactic rule for cases like (1)–(2) needs to make reference to the matching or correspondence of an expression with the interpreted gap. Now the question is: what do we mean when we say that the gap is interpreted? Are we referring to a process – a psychological process of interpretation? Or are we making a descriptive generalization which is (sort of) frozen as abstracting away from real instances (as in a case where we say the direction in which the sun rises is *generally* interpreted to be the east)? These questions are not trivial ones. They are intertwined with the issues of how language, mind and computation relate to each other in any linguistic theory that aims to take a stance on the relationship between language, mind and computation. Since these questions have arisen here, let us see how they bear on the issues to be discussed throughout this book.

Now if we pursue the first option – that is, when we say that the gap is interpreted we actually refer to a mental process of interpretation – this is going to put us in a vicious trap. If a syntactic rule is a syntactic rule only by virtue of appealing to a process of interpretation, this squeezes the entire mind into the syntactic rule! This is absurd. Each time a syntactic rule such as the one for cases (1)–(2) is formulated, one has to push mental processes into it by stipulating that this rule makes sense and operates only when all mental processes are part of it. This is awkward as long as one has to formulate valid syntactic rules for cases like (1)–(2). Otherwise, how do we account for linguistic intuitions that deliver linguistic judgements through inferences? If this takes us nowhere, let us explore the other possibility. Now if we say that the gap is interpreted, in fact we mean that it is a descriptive generalization which is *sort of* frozen from real instances. And that is what we mean when we say, for example, the colour red in traffic signals is *generally* interpreted to mean 'stop'. If this is so, a syntactic rule is defined with reference to a frozen or abstracted descriptive generalization. Hence we can understand a syntactic rule to be a syntactic rule only by appealing to an abstracted descriptive generalization. But then how does one know an abstracted descriptive generalization (about the matching or correspondence of an expression with the interpreted gap) to be what it is, if not by having it defined on the strings that syntactic rules generate? What this means is that we can understand an abstracted descriptive generalization about the matching or correspondence of an expression with the interpreted gap only when we make reference to the syntactic rule(s) a string or a set of strings is subject to. But how is this so? This is so because any interpretative generalization can be potentially defined in an arbitrary manner, but in any formal system for (natural) language interpretative generalizations are defined only with respect to the syntactic rule(s) a string or a set of strings is subject to. That is, for cases like (1)–(2) we cannot make any descriptive generalization (about the matching or correspondence of an expression with the interpreted gap) except by an appeal to the syntactic rule that is itself defined on the basis of such descriptive interpretative generalizations. This is circular. If one is still not convinced, here is a way of seeing through this circularity. In example (2) above, there are two predicates (in the matrix and embedded clauses) and 'why' can be a part of either of the two predicates as an adjunct. What is it about meaning taken by itself which prevents this? In fact, there is none. There is nothing wrong in having 'why' interpreted to mean what it will as an adjunct as part of the predicate 'laugh'. And this is what we see in (1). However, there is something about English syntax that does not allow 'why' to be interpreted through a long-distance dependency in (2). This is exactly the point at which we fall into the trap of circularity. We define syntactic rules on the basis of descriptive interpretative generalizations, and at the same time, we define descriptive interpretative generalizations on the basis of the very syntactic rules. What if we split this sentence and make a disjunction. That is, either we define syntactic rules on the basis of descriptive interpretative generalizations *or* we define descriptive interpretative generalizations on the basis of those syntactic rules. Is it going to be of any help? Perhaps not. If the requirement goes this way, there will be nothing left of syntactic rules because a sound descriptive interpretative generalization and nothing else will serve our purpose, on the one hand, or descriptive interpretative generalizations will turn out to be vacuous and thus not of much content, on the other. This does not give us any purchase on an understanding either of natural language syntax or of natural language semantics in any conceptually significant and/or empirically substantive sense.

One may also note that there is auxiliary insertion/inversion in (1)–(2), as in (3) below:

(3) Is the man who is a linguist__ home?

Cases like (3) have been marshalled to argue for the structure dependence of linguistic rules, in that the fronted auxiliary 'is' is interpreted with reference to the matrix predicate 'home' (at the syntactic level), but not to the embedded predicate '(is) a linguist'. Now suppose we need to have a rule that differentiates the cases in (1)–(2) from (3), for the sentences in (1)–(2) involve the displacement of a different *kind* of items (that is, *Wh*-phrases) which rides on the displacement of the auxiliary that underscores the commonality of all the three sentences. After all, we can have an echo question such as 'John laughs why?', but not 'She wonders why John laughs how?' How can a computation be sensitive to the differences in the *contents* of the syntactic rules that differentiate the cases in (1)–(2) from (3)? Another question also arises: what is it about computation that can make out the differences in the contents of the syntactic rules that differentiate the cases in (1)–(2) from (3)? Can the differences be phrased in such a manner as to lead one to say that the syntactic rule for (1)–(2) is *not* (syntactic) structure-dependent (given the dilemmas in the formulation of the *structural* generalizations for (1)–(2)), while the one for cases like (3) is? Our linguistic sensibility revolts and we ask: how can this be possible? How can some syntactic rules be structure-dependent and some not? Above all, it is structure dependence that gives us a licence to claim that syntactic operations are *systematic* operations which count as computations. One may note that the criteria that help make out the differences in the content of the syntactic rules differentiating the cases in (1)–(2) from (3) are second-order generalizations or rules. At which order does computation operate – at the level of first-order syntactic rules or at the level of second-order rules that differentiate one set of first-order syntactic rules from another? We have already run into fiendish problems in connection with first-order syntactic rules. So if computation operates at the level of first-order syntactic rules, one has to buckle under the problem of circularity with respect to the relationship between syntactic rules and interpretation/ interpretative generalizations. In that case, computation stagnates in a vacuum, and it does not make any sense for us to say that computations operate on linguistic representations, given that we cannot define, in a non-circular manner, what computations operate on. Nor can we say anything determinate about whether syntactic rules are mentally *instantiated* or whether computations operate on linguistic representations in the mind or whether such computations are themselves representations or instantiations. So no solid resolution for any of these issues has been arrived at (see, for a discussion, Langendoen and Postal 1984). What if we go for the other option? If we say that computation operates at the level of second-order rules that differentiate a set of first-order syntactic rules from another, we may need a set of third-order rules for a distinction between a set of second-order rules from other sets of second-order rules, and so on ad infinitum. Certainly neither such rules nor such computations – whatever they turn out to be – can be in the mind. But one should never forget that such first-order rules for (1)–(2) and (3) are learnt by children when they acquire English. So it must be the case that second-order rules that differentiate between sets of first-order syntactic rules are also learnt and so on – we encounter infinite regress again. There is no way we can escape this by arguing that all such syntactic rules are part of the Universal Grammar (UG), the genetic endowment for human language, since even our genome cannot encode, in any computational manner or otherwise, such an infinite regress of rules.

If the problems and issues raised above do not yet bother us and have us cudgelling our brains over what these problems and issues give rise to, let us then move over to something else. Thus what follows can perhaps offer one a sound justification required for an appreciation of the formidability of the problem(s).

(4) Either John bought a bottle of wine or he bought something else.

Now let us look at the example in (4). As far as the presupposition of this sentence goes, it will be a disjunction of the following:

(5) A seller sold a bottle of wine to John.

(6) John bought X (when X ≠ a bottle of wine).

Now, one can see that (5) and (6) may not be compatible with one another if one possesses the background knowledge that what the seller sold to John (in 5) and what John bought (in 6) are the same thing (such cases do arise in other contexts too, see Soames 2008). Are these presuppositions part of a rule – syntactic or semantic or otherwise and thus computed? Are these presuppositions mental representations derived from linguistic representations? These questions are not easy to answer given what we understand about the relationship between language, mind and computation. Still these issues deserve to be minutely probed. Let us go into them to see to how they fare in the light of the current discussion here. Let us assume that the derivation of such presupposition is part of a semantic rule since there does not seem to be anything in the structure of the sentence that determines the derivation of the presupposition in an *intrinsic* sense. This certainly does not mean that tweaking the sentence syntactically this way or that will not change the presupposition, but this is an *extrinsic* sense in which syntactic structure constrains the derivation of presuppositions. Thus, if we have the sentence 'Either John bought something else or he bought a bottle of wine' instead of what we have in (4), this will certainly change the relevant presuppositions. Now, one should also note that one does not need to go beyond the sentence in (4) to derive the presupposition; there is no need to appeal to pragmatic factors including background knowledge or worldly knowledge. If so, is the derivation of the presupposition conceptual and thus mentally derived from linguistic representations? If yes, it would appear to be easy to have computations operate on the syntactic structure in (4) and derive a disjunction of (5) and (6). This cannot be the case if computation is devoid of any conceptual content of the strings in (4). But if the set of presuppositions in (5)–(6) is not derived in any means other than by means of a reference to the syntactic structure of the sentence in (4), we have to ask whether conceptually derived presuppositions can be *computed* from syntactic structures at all. This is also because of the fact that 'something else' gives us (6) simply because 'something' will not lead to (6). This is problematic. On the one hand, it seems to be possible to derive the presuppositions from (4) in a conceptual or, say, logical manner without any appeal to pragmatic factors including background knowledge or worldly knowledge and thus computations can give us the desired output whenever it is true that X buys Y from Z, it is also true that Z sells Y to X. Similarly, if one gets something else (X), it is true that he/she has not got Y or Z. But on the other hand, computations cannot operate on the syntactic structure in (4) and derive a disjunction of (5) and (6) because computation is devoid of any conceptual content of the strings in question. This appears to be a dead end.

What if we say that computation operates on the mental representations of the linguistic strings/structures? This apparently gets us out of the dilemma, and it becomes feasible to state that presuppositions can be *computed* from syntactic structures. But this is not so since presuppositions do not need to be computed *from* syntactic structures; rather, presuppositions can be computed right from the computational space of mental representations as far as there are no syntactic rules/constraints defined on mental representations. And it would be really mysterious to explain how natural language speakers derive presuppositions from the syntactic structures of natural language sentences.

These and similar such issues have received very scant attention from theoretical linguists because one can just talk about lots of linguistic phenomena in an empirically faithful way backgrounding a specific set of vague and rarely defined assumptions hidden behind the theoretical paraphernalia. Thus one hardly becomes aware of the fact that the specific set of assumptions behind the theoretical machinery is what leads to the problems that are empirically recognized as such. This engenders further problems and so on. Ultimately, the theoretical machinery goes through a number of reformulations, but the specific set of assumptions behind the theoretical machinery are never questioned or scrutinized. Perhaps this is what has happened with the emergence of Generative Grammar with all its fundamental assumptions about the nature of the relationship between language, mind and computation. But does it then mean that one should stop talking about mind and computation when building linguistic theories? Perhaps there is no easy answer to this question. One has to be very cautious when one steps into this territory. The problems of the mind and computation are deeply perplexing, and they become compounded when adjoined to language. But from another perspective, after the advent of Generative Grammar, new connections between language, mind and computation have been forged, giving rise to viable enterprises like psycholinguistics, computational linguistics or even computational psycholinguistics. There is a lot more that we now know about the computational and psycholinguistic mechanisms underlying language processing than was possible before. But I will argue that this has come at a cost. And this is the burgeoning amount of confusion and vagueness regarding the relationship between language, mind and computation.

Controversies over the form of the interface between syntactic rules and semantic rules, as in the Generative Semantics tradition, or over the nature of the Universal Grammar (UG), seem to have devoured virtually the entire range of linguistic debates so much that one feels this is all there is to the fundamental issues in linguistic theory. There is already a huge literature on the issues covered in these debates. This book will present a lot of cases associated with some of the concerns not raised or at least peripheralized in any of these debates. The present work aims to bring them to the forefront with a view to telling one thing apart from another for an enriched appreciation of the vital issues at hand. This will not only broaden the base of one's understanding of what is at stake in linguistic theorizing and what is not, but also pave the way for an opening up of issues which, though otherwise related to the current debates on the syntax–semantics interface or on the UG, are crucially different too. One can take, for example, the case of intensionality in language. A sentence like 'John desires a blue car for his birthday' can have two different readings of the noun phrase 'a blue car ...'. It may mean a specific blue car that John has perhaps seen somewhere which he desires for his birthday. The other meaning is that John does not have any specific choice; any blue car for his birthday will do. So far so good. But based on these readings, one gets a difference in the *mental* structures underlying affect (a point made in Jackendoff 2007) – one mental structure directed at something specific and another at something non-specific. Now the question is: how does one go from the linguistic meanings right onto the *mental* structures of affect? This is more so because one does not get the two readings in 'He is happy to hire an engineer' (the specific reading is blocked and so is the mental structure directed at something specific), even though 'hire' is intensional and 'happy' is an emotive predicate. There seems to be something fishy going on between intensionality and the syntactic structure that blocks one of the *mental* structures of affect. This appears to be crazy. Again we have to look beneath what syntactic computations, if any, are intertwined with what mental structures. This is not an easy task as we will see in this book.

Another significant issue that this book will also devote some space to is to do with the nature and form of the faculty of language and its relation to the architecture of grammar. There is a lot of variation among different linguistic formalisms and the architectures of grammar they represent. Constraint-based formalisms like Head-Driven Phrase Structure Grammar (HPSG) do not comport well with precisely described architectural specifications; but Lexical-Functional Grammar, Autolexical Syntax, etc. may well have some commitment to architectural concerns. This relates to the issues, perhaps rather directly, with respect to the relationship between language, mind and computation. Linguistic formalisms are designed to often seek an optimal fit between the computational properties of natural language and formal economy/ elegance in describing natural language phenomena. Architectures of grammar, on the other hand, reflect the way the language faculty can be instantiated in the mind/brain. It is not quite true that we get transparent translations between linguistic formalisms and the architectures of grammar they represent. This issue has a direct bearing on the problems revolving around the relationship between language, mind and computation. This will be dealt with at length in the fifth and sixth chapters of this book.

Finally, this book will also try to explore whether the barriers to an understanding of the relationship between language, mind and computation can be overcome in a fruitful manner. The most important point has to do with whether the knots that have formed surrounding language, mind and computation can be disentangled. But the current approach of the book will be more oriented to a deeper delving into the reasons why the knots have formed in the first place, and also into the ways in which these have formed, thereby confounding some of the issues that could have otherwise eliminated some theoretical and foundational problems in linguistics. One may well argue that the issues surrounding the relationship between language, mind and computation are not substantial and empirically interesting at all. This is the kind of reaction that may come from many sections of theoretical linguists. The upshot is that one may well go about figuring out how certain generalizations accrue from the data linguistic phenomena offer, and then fashion woolly theories scaffolded by something the presence of which the theorist may deny. This certainly militates against the development of a scientific enterprise if linguistics is meant to be a science. If the entire network of assumptions regarding language, mind and computation forms the bedrock of the technical and even methodological paraphernalia employed in linguistic inquiry, steering clear of a readiness to examine that very network of assumptions is an indefensible exercise. This has made exceedingly complicated the relation of mind and computation with the signifier and the signified too. And there are strong grounds for this conclusion, as this book will argue.

Let us ponder over it for a while. Is the relation between the signifier and the signified just a representation? If so, what is the ontology of that representation? Is that a representation that obtains in the mind/brain? If so, is that representation a computation? What is it about the signifier, or for that matter, about the signified that leads to frequent mismatches between the signifier and the signified (form–meaning mismatches) and what do they mean for mind and computation? Are these mismatches mental? Or are they rooted in the way computation operates on representations? These questions have certainly preoccupied many linguists but the substantive problems that ensue from this have either been hardly addressed or at worst ignored. Suffice it to say for now that these problems constitute the crux of the issue at hand, regardless of whether or not they are acknowledged as such. Since there is no easy way to any resolution, no resolution is aimed at. What is desirable at this stage is, I believe, a bit of transparency in the assumptions that form the basis of linguistic hypotheses. Often flabby assumptions supporting a hypothesis generate more inquiry, which need not be taken to be the proof of the viability of the hypothesis concerned.

With this goal in mind, I would like to emphasize that this book is intended for anybody who wishes to seriously think about language and also about the issues that define the crux of language. The book will be semi-technical for reasons having to do with the subject matter dealt with. But the use of jargon will be kept to a minimum and clarified with examples whenever possible. I will first walk the readers through the material that tells us how and in what sense a linguistic theory is a theory of language. Then the relation of language to mind and computation will be explored with the goal of seeing how they have come to be keyed to one another. Then they will be viewed together in a more precisely crafted form. The emerging insights will then be spelled out with various connections to general issues in theoretical linguistics. A caveat is in order here. I would like to caution that the presentation of the theoretical analyses of linguistic structures should *not* be taken as implying a commitment to the axiomatic system constraining the theoretical analyses, since the axiomatic system has been presented as fully and faithfully as possible in order to demonstrate the inconsistencies hidden within. Importantly, it is about (re)presenting an axiomatic system from which some logically derived consequences by means of inferences are to be drawn in order to show that the axiomatic system is *logically* vacuous. I hope this can help readers assimilate what it is overall that I will make a space for.

1.2   Summary

This introductory sketch has provided a rough overview of the contents of this book. As we proceed to the next chapters, new insights into the puzzling and problematic nature of the relation between language, mind and computation will be projected so that the readers can gradually immerse themselves in the unfolding of layers of complexity in the issues this book will unpack. This book is divided into nine chapters. They are not self-contained as there will be a great deal of continuity, though I believe each of them may be read on its own, if some readers wish to do so. Be that as it may, there is a single story that I wish to tell. Readers can decide for themselves whether to pick up on the forest, or to figure out how the trees make up the forest.

2
Language and Linguistic Theory

As we ruminate over the aspects of natural language, we wonder what constitutes a theory of language given an understanding, at a certain level of inquiry, of the properties and features of natural language. And this is not a trivial issue though it may appear to be so upon a cursory observation. Natural language users have a certain level of understanding of a range of characteristics of language(s). But this does not necessarily equip them with a systematic body of knowledge constituting a theory that they can articulate when speaking of language(s). Nor do they readily build a theory of language(s) when they describe aspects of natural language. But linguists who build sophisticated theories of language are also users of language in some way or other. What is it about natural language that then enables them to understand natural language in a manner that may correspond to the way a theory of language is constituted? One may note that this question has a different flavour from what one may ordinarily ascribe to linguists who appear to gain a specialized expertise by way of training. To be clear, the question has a direction of fit from the properties of natural language to a theory of language, in that the question is of how to move from the properties of natural language to the construction of a theory of language. This issue is quite different from that usually raised in the context of determining what a theory of language has to account for when it accounts for natural language phenomena or aspects of natural language. To notice the difference, one can observe that the first question on how aspects of natural language lead to and fit a systematic body of descriptions of language arises from a natural inquiry into the nature of language independently of any concern or association with a putative theory of language, although the construction of a theory of language may well follow on from such an inquiry into the nature and form of language.

Whereas the second question having to do with how a constructed theory of language comes to provide an account of natural language phenomena stems from meta-theoretical considerations that involve musings on what a theory of language can do or actually does when it is employed to describe and explain properties of natural language phenomena.

So in a way, the significant question we started out with boils down to a question of understanding natural language in the barest possible form with an open eye on whatever natural language turns out to be. It is this concern that makes us ponder over what natural language really is. Thus we go about exploring diverse natural languages trying to figure out a bewildering spectrum of puzzling characteristics of natural language. Ultimately this is what helps us understand a lot about natural language(s) in all its variety enlivened with a converging order. But another related question crops up: what makes a linguistic theory a theory of language rather than of, say, stones or snow or cars? We can avoid giving an obvious and tautological answer by *not* saying that a linguistic theory is a theory of language by virtue of being a linguistic theory. That is certainly a trivialized answer which we want to put aside for the sake of unmasking the non-trivial issue lurking behind it. If this still barely scratches the surface of what it is that we bother to mull over, let us think it over for a while. In fact, it is not necessary that a linguistic theory should deal with language rather than with, say, quarrelling or debating. What this means is that we may well observe certain salient aspects of language deployed in quarrelling or debating which ultimately lead to our designing a linguistic theory as a theory of quarrelling or debating. What exactly precludes us from doing that? Above all, we can justify our approach by saying that is all there is to any rational observation of language use in pressing situations that unpacks the most crucial aspects of natural language which are thereby credited with such weight as to deserve incorporation into the heart of a linguistic theory. But at the same time there is a strong feeling that this leaves a lot of language out of the purview of such a linguistic theory. Even if certain properties of language come apart in certain domains of language use, this barely covers what a linguistic theory can be preoccupied with, although it is certainly true that in the earliest periods of Greek theorizing on language the development of a theory of rhetoric was perhaps a move in this direction. We have moved far beyond approaches that circumscribe the domain of language exclusively to its use in communication. Nonetheless, a linguistic theory can be considered to be a theory of language use or communication if there are aspects of language use in communication which demand a more precise and systematic formulation through stages of elaboration on what the theory in question aims to exemplify. It is quite clear that when speakers and hearers use language, what passes for communication between them is, in broad outline, a mapping from meaning(s) onto form(s) from the speaker's perspective on the one hand, and/or from form(s) onto meaning(s) from the hearer's perspective, on the other. This brings the Saussurean legacy – the duality of the *signifier* (form) and the *signified* (concept or meaning) – into a more focused perspective in the arena of language use. Even if it is true that we all succeed more often than not in our linguistic communication, that is, we are somehow capable of understanding what speakers (intend to) say, and at the same time, we produce what hearers comprehend more reliably than we may assume, the mappings from meaning(s) onto form(s) and vice versa are enormously complex. As was discussed in Chapter 1, such mappings are a precarious, albeit useful, simplification of a vastly complicated scenario. To come back to the issues raised in the context of the earlier discussion in this paragraph, a linguistic theory may well be a theory of linguistic communication on the grounds that the theory in question has to describe and perhaps explain the mappings from meaning(s) onto form(s) and vice versa.

Moreover, it needs to be emphasized that the mappings from meaning(s) onto form(s) and vice versa in themselves can yield up more than what they offer when they are incorporated into a linguistic theory that aims to be a theory of linguistic communication. It will be argued here that the complexity lying at the heart of the mappings from meaning(s) onto form(s) and vice versa can unravel a formidable gamut of properties and characteristics of natural language that make a linguistic theory a theory of language, but not *merely* a theory of linguistic communication. Thus a lot of variability enlivened with a complexity underlying the mappings from meaning(s) onto form(s) and vice versa can help us derive some of the most basic facts about linguistic phenomena. But the present work aims higher than that. Here it would be shown that even the fundamental architectural specifications of current linguistic theories can be derived from the complex properties of form–meaning mappings as we move through the chapters of this book. In fact, mappings between form and meaning may also be pivotal to the understanding of ontological differences between different components of language itself, that is, syntax, semantics, morphology, phonology (Jespersen 1924). Jespersen, the Danish linguist who made a number of contributions to the study of English grammar and linguistics, maintained that mappings between form and meaning would help us conceptualize what constitutes different components of language. So for example, in the domain of morphology the significant mapping can be in the direction from form to meaning schematized as F → M when F signifies form and M meaning (or concept). An example can be provided to clarify how this holds. The morpheme '-s' in English has various manifestations in English and thus is associated with various functions in different linguistic environments. It can be a plural morpheme (manifested in the form of three different plural allomorphs [s, z, iz] in the respective sets of plural nouns {cats, laps ...}, {boys, cows ...} and {roses, boxes...}); it can be a genitive marker as in 'Peter's car', 'John's house', etc.; it can also be an agreement marker as in 'He believes in ghosts'. All these different grammatical functions, or rather functional meanings, are associated with the same morpheme. Likewise, in syntax we again get a mapping between form and meaning; but the relevant mapping here is in the direction from meaning to form M → F, as has been emphasized by Jespersen. So the same grammatical function such as that of plurality can be encoded through different formal devices as diverse as the examples 'bats', 'sheep', 'women', 'stimuli', 'phenomena', 'us', 'these' etc., and in a similar manner the functional meaning of a nominal can be encoded through different forms such as 'Seeing is believing', 'That he swims ... is bad for his health', 'To see is to believe', 'His sight is poor' and so on.

2.1   Form–meaning correspondence and aspects of language

Overall, it appears to be the case that form–meaning mapping can itself curl inside other types of form. What this means is that form–meaning mapping is a higher-order description of the relation between form and meaning which are first-order entities; but from the phenomena described above, it transpires that form–meaning mapping as a second-order description of the relation between form and meaning can itself reside inside a first-order entity such as form (or perhaps meaning) when morphology or syntax is essentially construed as a type of form just as phonology is. Hence we seem to have derived a higher-order description from first-order entities. This is crucial for us as far as natural language is concerned. Since we aim to unfold the most fundamental aspects and features of language from form and meaning as well as from their relation, this observation will turn out to be of substantial significance as we will see. It looks like a case of recursively embedded

higher-order emergence in natural language in the sense that the structure of complex relations built on simple elements is inherent and
implicitly present in those simple elements themselves with possibilities of multiple such iterations. Thus we have come nearer to the key
to the vast possibilities form and meaning together open up. Form and
meaning can in fact be correlated with one another in innumerable possible ways with different grains of correspondence between them. This
is what has been crucial in linguistic theory and elsewhere, with some
approaches positing a closer coupling between them (as in Montague
semantics to be touched upon later in this chapter) and some others a
looser one (as in Generative Grammar). This issue is more substantial
in the current context, given that linguistic form does not seem to have
any atomic nature by virtue of the fact that linguistic form may well be
distributed across the components of grammar, that is, syntax, phonology and morphology. A reasonable assumption is that linguistic form is
not any sort of monolithic entity; it has its own complexities, idiosyncrasies and nuances in diverse sets of manifestations as evident in cross-
linguistic mismatches of form and meaning. Meaning has, on the other
hand, been restricted to the domain of semantics. This derives from the
observation that whatever is linguistically conceptualized can certainly
be represented at different levels – lexical, phrasal, sentential (and/or
even discoursal), but the differences between such levels of meaning,
regardless of how they are represented, are not as ontologically marked
as they are when syntax is contrasted with phonology (syntactic rules
cannot be reduced to phonological rules and vice versa), or when phonology is contrasted with morphology (phonological rules cannot be
reduced to morphological rules and vice versa). Thus we can proceed to
see how form and meaning can have widely diverse sets of correspondences as we zoom in and out varying the grain of (mis)match in myriad
possible ways.

2.1.1   Form and meaning pulled wide apart

Thus, in the weakest possible correspondence between form and meaning, one can have no possible correlation between form and meaning.
In such a scenario form and meaning run apart and go quite different
ways. Something can assume a form in language the meaning of which
will be nowhere nearer to a match with the form or which may have
no corresponding meaning. To be sure, there are certain areas within
which natural language throws this possibility open. For example,
most words in natural language have a form such that the meanings of
those words do not look like the form the words in question assume.

How on earth can one imagine that the meaning of the word 'airport' resembles the shape of the word 'airport' or any arrangement of the letters contained in the word 'airport'? The same goes for 'phenomenon', 'box', 'fight', 'establishment', 'integration', 'number', 'people', etc. and for innumerable words in any language. Apart from that, there is another sense in which a form may have no corresponding meaning. The expletive 'it', for example, does not appear to have any meaning when it is used in sentences like 'It is raining', 'It is clear that John has duped her', etc. This is true of many function words such as 'to' in the sentence 'John helped Mary to achieve her goals'. Similarly, there are many phrases in English that have meanings which cannot be traced to the constitution of the form(s) such phrases take. The verb phrase 'kick the bucket' means 'die', and this meaning cannot be attributed to any of the words or to any combination of them in 'kick the bucket', and it is also true of the phrase 'beat around the bush', which means 'to delay talking about something unpleasant/embarrassing'. The converse is also true of form–meaning mapping when meaning comes out in the absence of any distinguishably visible form, as in examples like 'Ron likes macaroni more than/as much as Sam does__ noodles' (an instance of pseudo-gapping – only the verb is elided), 'David will build a tower and Mary, __ a small house' (an instance of gapping – the verb along with the auxiliary/tense head is elided), 'Mary attends the lecture of the famous professor of computer science every Sunday and so does__ Peter' (an instance of verb phrase ellipsis – the entire verb phrase is elided). In all of these cases the gap is shown through '__', which indicates that the part of the form which is missing is interpreted the same way as the one (which is realized) in the matrix clause. Quite apart from these, there are other instances in which certain forms appear in constructions without the meanings the forms in question typically have. When the third person indirect object clitic in Spanish appears before a third person direct object clitic, it is realized as *se*, which is a reflexive form but does not lead to a reflexive meaning (Carlson 2006). The examples (7)–(8) make this clearer:

(7) Se   lo   mandas.
    REFL 3PERS.SG send.2PERS
    'You send it to him/her/them.'

(8) * Le/*Les   lo   mandas.
    3PERS.SG/3PERS.PL 3PERS.SG send.2PERS
          (REFL = reflexive, PERS = person, SG = singular, PL = plural)

A similar example may also be given from Bangla. Many verbs in Bangla combine with a fixed set of light verbs and the complex verb form (also called a *complex predicate*) thus constituted does not appear to carry over the meaning of the light verb (that is why it is a *light* verb, after all!). So, for example, in (9) below the imperative sentence contains the content verb 'phela' (to throw) but the sentence in (10) contains the complex verb form 'phele dao' combining 'phela' and the light verb 'daoa' (to give) with virtually the same meaning as 'phalo':

(9) pathor-guli phalo
    stone-PL   throw-PRES-2PERS
    'Throw the stones.'

(10) pathor-guli phele   dao
    stone-PL   throw-NONF give-PRES-2PERS
    'Throw the stones.'

But there seems to be a slight difference in the aspectual profiles of the corresponding verb forms – simplex and complex. The simplex verb 'phela' denotes an instantaneous event and thus looks like an achievement verb, but the meaning of the construction in (11) indicates that this is not quite true. The event in (11) is iterative in nature as part of the same single situation and thus points to the *semelfactive* nature of the verb in (11) since achievement verbs cannot be durative and do not take a *for an X* form (when X is a period). The complex verb form (the complex predicate) in (12), on the other hand, seems to behave like an achievement verb in barring iteration through a *for an X* form or otherwise. Ultimately, what turns out is that the light verb 'daoa' still does not contribute its original meaning (that is, 'to give') to the complex verb form, even though an aspectual configuration of non-durativity is projected by the light verb onto the eventive frame of the complex predicate.

(11)   se   pathor-guli ek   ghonta dhore phello
      he/she stone-PL   one hour   for   throw-PAST-3PERS
   'He/she threw the stones for an hour.'

(12) *se   pathor-guli ek   ghonta dhore phele   dillo
      he/she stone-PL   one hour   for   throw-NONF give-PAST-
      3PERS
    'He/she threw the stones for an hour.'
     (PRES = present tense, PAST = past tense, NONF = non-finite)

Instances of light verbs are also found in English in examples like 'He **keeps** writing letters', 'John has **got** a nice plan' and so on. However, the message to be driven home is quite clear. Here again, we encounter a case of form–meaning divergence. And this keeps on reminding us that this is what has driven many linguists to look deeper into the nature of intricacies and idiosyncrasies that language offers. So in a way, this aspect of the form–meaning convergence, or rather divergence, qualifies as an important property that may require incorporation into a linguistic theory. In fact, the Saussurean duality of form and meaning carries with it the feature of arbitrariness lying at the heart of the relationship between form and meaning, and this became the cornerstone of Saussure's structuralist theory. Most linguistic theories including Generative Grammar have since then also made this aspect of language an essential part of the architecture of grammar. Most functionalist systems of grammar including Systemic Functional Grammar (Halliday 1973) have stuck to a division of labour between form and a system of functions which encompass meanings language has evolved to convey or is used for. Mainstream Generative Grammar right from the *Aspects* model (Chomsky 1965) has reserved a separate semantic component (which is different from *Deep Structure*, a level of syntactic representation that makes explicit semantic uniformity across different syntactic forms) for possible form–meaning divergences. Lexical-Functional Grammar (Bresnan 2001), which emerged as an offshoot of Generative Grammar in the 1970s, has also partitioned the system of grammar into two different compartments called *c-structure* (constituent structure) and *f-structure* (functional structure), grounded in the understanding that form–meaning divergences may pull form too wide apart from meaning in the furthest direction on one end.

2.1.2   Form and meaning: a partial congruence

Now we can tweak the grain of correspondence between form and meaning a bit so that they come a bit closer to each other in a kind of what Jackendoff (2002) calls 'partial homology'. When the correlation between form and meaning becomes patchy, the relationship between form and meaning can become one-to-many or many-to-one in any direction. Thus, a single form can be mapped to many meanings and similarly a single meaning can be mapped to many forms. We have already seen some examples of this kind in the earlier part of this chapter. We can look more closely at this when we lock our interest in what comes up as the grain of correspondence between form and meaning varies. One of the most famous examples aimed at showing a patchy correspondence between form and meaning is by Chomsky (1957): 'Colorless green ideas sleep furiously'. The patchy correspondence between form and meaning emerges when one considers that this sentence has a perfectly fine syntax even though it is semantically odd. This is not the only case; there is a whole range of phenomena across languages that strongly point to a patchy correspondence between form and meaning in various manifestations. For example, there seems to be a residue of form in meanings of words like 'glitter', 'glister', 'glisten', 'gleam', or in the meanings of words like 'litter', 'scatter' or in 'slide', 'glide', etc. – a watered down version of onomatopoeia. Besides that, agreement in languages is one of the best examples of a patchy correspondence between form and meaning across languages. In English, for instance, the same functional meaning conveyed through agreement morphology may be spread over many forms or pieces of a form in a single sentence such as 'These houses have glass windows', 'Those boys are nasty players', etc., as Carlson (2006) points out. Another example is from Bangla. The word 'naki' has the meaning of both a question particle and a discourse particle. The sentences below make this clearer:

(13) tumi jabe   naki?
     you   go-FUT-2PERS Q
     'Will you go?'

(14) ebar   naki   tarai   jitbe
     this time DPTC   they-EMP win-FUT-2PERS
     'This time only they will win (showing disapproval)!'
                    (Q = question particle, DPTC = discourse particle,
                     EMP = emphatic clitic, FUT = future tense)

The first 'naki' in (13) behaves like a question particle and the second one in (14) has the force of modality in which the speaker, taking an epistemic stance on the proposition expressed in the sentence, expresses his/her doubt and thus questions the evidential basis of the state of affairs conveyed in the proposition.

In fact, the notion of Deep Structure is itself an outcome of theoretical ventures in the Generative paradigm that seeks to capture as much as possible the messiness lying at the syntax–semantics boundary. The concept of Deep Structure was not merely an artefact of grammar; but Deep Structure as a level of syntactic representation that structures and constrains semantic representations fringes the other side of Surface Structure, which emerges out of the application of a number of relevant transformations operating on the Deep Structure representations. Passivization was, for example, a phenomenon at the interface between form and meaning. So, for instance, the following pair of sentences needs to get a conceptually correct treatment flanked by Deep Structure and Surface Structure:

(15) John killed the snake.

(16) The snake was killed (by John).

Since both (15) and (16) are supposed to mean the same despite not being identical to each other in form, or rather in representation on the Surface Structure. Hence, there seems to be a need to start from a Deep Structure representation of (15) and then let the passive transformation apply on it, finally deriving a representation of (16) at the level of the Surface Structure. One may note that the presupposition underlying such a technical move is that passive transformations preserve meaning. But this has turned out to be illusory. Chomsky (1975a) has provided the following examples that reveal the fallacy:

(17) Beavers build dams.

(18) Dams are built by beavers.

Even if the sentence (17) means that *all* beavers build dams in a generic sense such that *all* beavers possess the capacity of building dams, the sentence (18) does not mean quite the same thing. The sentence (18) is about all dams which happen to be built by beavers. While (17) may be false, insofar as not all beavers *actually* build dams, (18) may be false on the grounds that not all dams are built by beavers. These problems arise in many quantificational contexts as well (but see Katz and Postal 1964). The following pairs illustrate this well:

(19) a. Everybody in this town speaks two languages.
     b. Two languages are spoken by everybody in this town.

(20) a. A student passes every mathematics exam that he takes.
     b. Every mathematics exam that he takes is passed by a student.

(21) a. All linguists visit a restaurant.
     b. A restaurant is visited by all linguists.

In (19a) we have an ambiguity depending on whether the universal quantifier scopes over the existential quantifier, or the other way round – which leads to two different readings: the former situation leads to the interpretation that for every x: x is a person in this town, x speaks two different languages y and z co-varying with each x, and the other interpretation is that two specific languages y and z (say, English and Spanish) are spoken by every x: x is a person in this town. The sentence (19b) only has the second reading. Similarly, (21a) has both readings emanating from the same kind of ambiguity but (21b), on the other hand, has only one, that is, the one in which a specific restaurant (say, Noma in Denmark) is visited by all linguists. Even if the sentence (20b) apparently has the same kind of ambiguity, (20b) does not seem to have the reading in which every mathematics exam is passed by some student or other. This may be due to the fact that in (20a) 'he' is bound by 'a student' while in (20b) 'he' may be bound by some other ante-cedent (that is, by somebody other than the student) or by 'a student'. These examples also raise questions about the preservation of meaning through transformations in that transformations such as passivization change meaning as shown in (19)–(21) and if this is the case, the map-ping at the form–meaning boundary becomes murkier than assumed.

There is also a host of other syntactic transformations like negation, question formation and generalized transformations such as embedding all of which change meaning. The reason why meaning-preservation or meaning-change is significant in the architecture of grammar is that the former but not the latter gives rise to a smoother mapping between syntax and semantics. And meaning-change gets into more complexities in the mapping at the syntax–semantics boundary. The stance taken by the approach called Generative Semantics (Lakoff 1971; Postal 1972) advanced the case for meaning-preservation by identifying Deep Structure itself with semantic representation, thereby eliminating the need for another level of mapping between Deep Structure and an independent semantic component. So cases in which meaning appears to change can be uniformly treated in a manner such that abstract categories are introduced at the level of the Deep Structure which syntactic transformations operate on to derive the Surface Structure representation by inserting items into the positions of those abstract categories. Thus question formation, negation, etc. will have their abstract categories at the level of the Deep Structure (such as NEG, Q (for questions), *Wh* (for *wh*-questions) etc.). And this architectural ten-sion between meaning-preservation and meaning-change was at the heart of the formidable conflict between *interpretative semantics* stand-ard in mainstream Generative Grammar and the approach adopted by Generative Semantics. The conflict was so deep as to intensify into what

Harris (1993) called the *Linguistic Wars*. In fact, the tension between meaning-preservation and meaning-change is symptomatic of a larger issue having to do with how on earth meaning maps onto form, and vice versa. Though the conflict between the two competing approaches has sort of subsided, the paralysing and deeply perplexing problem has not evaporated and is certainly aggravated by cases like the following:

(22) a. John gave/donated the book to Mary.
b. John gave/*donated Mary the book.

(23) a. Jim falls apart when he likes something.
b. Jim falls apart when something pleases him.

(24) a. Susan left everything she carried and ran off when something frightened her.
b. Susan left everything she carried and ran off when she feared something.

In (22) dative alternation, though not possible with the verb 'donate', appears to bring out the same meaning, and so do (23) and (24) through an alternation involving Experiencer–Stimulus verbs (such as 'like', 'fear', etc.) and Stimulus–Experiencer verbs (such as 'please', 'frighten', etc.). Apparently, this resurrects the problem of identical meaning with different representations at the Deep Structure; this is, however, a wholly different problem that evokes and fosters complexities nestling in the realm of semantic knottiness. The pairs of sentences in (22)–(24) are not in fact identical in meaning (Rappaport Hovav and Levin 2005; Rappaport Hovav and Levin 2008; Levin and Grafmiller 2013) since there seems to be a residue of information-structural content in such pairs (and perhaps also in (17)–(20)) that makes the interpretations of the sentences in the pairs different. Dative alternation in (22a) marks the focus on the book – the thing that is transferred – whereas in (22b) it focuses on the recipient, that is, Mary, who comes to possess the book. Alternations involving Experiencer–Stimulus verbs and Stimulus–Experiencer verbs have an irreducible perspectival component involving the agent that perceives/experiences something – which is scaled down when the focus drifts somewhat away from the experiential realm of the agent on to the world. The paradoxical situation this warrants is that the sentences in such pairs, on the one hand, have a roughly similar meaning, but, on the other, they do not mean exactly the same when a structural difference appears to be correlated with a semantic difference. Any linguistic theory that aims to have a mapping of form and meaning incorporated as part of the architecture of grammar has to grapple with this paradox. And that is why this has remained a problem for lexicon–syntax mapping, or rather for lexicon–syntax–semantics mapping.

However, *interpretative semantics* has survived through later theoretical developments in the Generative paradigm by being recast in a different format. What all these developments have kept intact is the general notion of mapping between form and meaning mediated through Logical Form (LF) whether in the Government and Binding (GB) tradition (Chomsky 1981) or in the current Minimalist framework (Chomsky 1995). Hence a need to pinpoint the design specifications of the relation between syntax and semantic interpretation in the overall architecture of the language faculty has been felt right from the dawn of Move α (which is the core transformational operation) in the earlier Generative tradition. Generative Grammar in the GB tradition incorporated LF into the GB architecture of grammar within which S-structure maps onto LF, apart from being mapped to PF (Phonological Form). LF is a covert syntactic component where syntactic computations make contributions to a characterization of the semantic interpretation. As May (1985) clarifies the role of LF in grammar, according to him, on architectural grounds LF represents whatever syntactic properties are relevant to semantic interpretations or those aspects of semantic structure that are expressed syntactically. So it seems that the relation of syntax to semantics has been built into the architecture of grammar.

But what are the conceptual and empirical motivations for positing such a level of syntactic operations that interfaces with aspects of semantic interpretation? As May argues, it all starts with Russell's and Frege's concerns with the relation of LF to the syntax of natural language, inasmuch as LF representing the semantic structure is not akin to the syntactic form of natural language (in fact, it goes back to the Greek thinkers including Aristotle who also mused over the problems such mismatch leads to, and later in the twentieth century this came to assume a greater significance in all thinking about language and logic). LF is concealed by the syntactic structure of natural language. This essentially underscores the incongruity between form and meaning, and can be illustrated with a simple example:

(25) Coffee grows in Africa.

From (25) one might be inclined to say that the grammatical subject is 'coffee' and the rest is the predicate. But logically, 'be in Africa' characterizes a property, and so it is the logical predicate, whereas 'the growth of coffee' is the logical subject (Seuren 2009). It can be written as:

(26) + **P** (Be in Africa) ([growth of coffee])

Given this difference, it may be stated that the LF of natural language and the corresponding syntactic structure(s) identify two different representational structures. Since LF is a syntactic level of representation, the question of representations and issues of meanings assigned to structures at this level are in a relevant sense entwined. In reality such a level gains its theoretical justification through the postulation of a number of independent descriptive levels each of which has its own well-formedness conditions and formal representations – which has remained the underlying thread through all mainstream versions of Generative Grammar. Chomsky (1957) himself was of the opinion that the syntactic and semantic components of grammar could be kept separate but there should be a way of keeping them properly aligned with each other so that they can be partially correlated as well. Needless to say, LF fills the bill for this requirement. Moreover, LF attempts to characterize the extent to which a class of semantic interpretations that can be assigned to syntactic structures at this level are a function of their grammatical properties, as May emphasizes. This need not be taken to mean that LF has any commitment to all possible semantic interpretations that can be assigned to syntactic structures as a function of their grammatical properties. This clarifies how LF is specified and what LF is designed to be.

As far as the empirical motivations behind the postulation of such a level are concerned, quite a few relevant points can be stressed. LF is reserved for movements which are covert rather than overt, that is, for displacements which are supposed to hold at a level more abstract than is observed on the surface. As May argues, QR (Quantifier Raising) is the 'central case' of LF movement, and hence quantificational scope is determined at this level. Quantificational scope in natural language is the epitome of the masking of the semantic structure by the syntactic form, as also seen in examples (19)–(21). But are there good reasons for claiming that QR represents the core of LF operations? May argues that we do have independent evidence to claim so. A crucial piece of evidence comes from *Wh*-movement which constructs an operator-variable configuration in overt syntax given the understanding that a *Wh*-item is an operator that links a variable corresponding to the gap from where the *Wh*-item is displaced. Quantificational scope also derives from a kind of operator–variable link construction but with the added proviso that it obtains in the covert component of grammar. Thus both *Wh*-movement and quantificational movement are examples of what is called Ā movement (A-bar movement), which is different from A-movement (argument movement). The following examples from May clarify this rather well:

(27) Who does he like?

(28) He likes everybody.

The trees in Figures 2.1 and 2.2 are the respective LF representations of (27) and (28). Given that Ā movement displaces items to a position not suitable for the thematic role assignment of arguments (and that thematic roles are roles that fit the participants in an event/state described by a verb), 'who' in Figure 2.1 and 'everybody' in Figure 2.2 are each in an Ā position as the thematic role (THEME/STIMULUS) for 'everybody' or for 'who' is to be interpreted in the position occupied by e in the figures below. Apart from that, May argues that ECP (*Empty Category Principle*) – which bans variables not bound by their binding operators – also holds true for LF representations. It may be noted that the covertly moved operator in Ā position ('someone') should, but does not in fact, bind the variable in the **A** position (e_1) in (29) because e_1 is not within the domain of the position occupied by 'someone' in the hierarchy. This is supposed to explain the ungrammaticality of (29).

(29) *[$_S$ e_1 believes [$_S$ someone$_1$ [$_S$ she is pissed off]]]

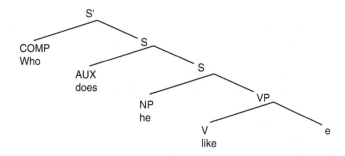

Figure 2.1   Tree diagram for *Wh*-movement in (27)

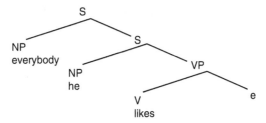

S = sentence, NP = noun phrase, VP = verb phrase,
V = verb, COMP = complementizer, AUX = auxiliary

Figure 2.2   Tree diagram for quantificational movement in (28)

It is ECP again that has motivated May to propose his *Scope Principle* which can actually derive two different LF representations from just one save when the two are independent.

(30) Every woman loves a man.

Two different readings for (30) can be represented in (31) and (32) below:

(31) [$_S$ a man$_2$ [$_S$ every woman$_1$ [$_S$ e$_1$ loves e$_2$]]]

(32) [$_S$ every woman$_1$ [$_S$ a man$_2$ [$_S$ e$_1$ loves e$_2$]]]

Given that (32) violates ECP since 'a man' blocks the binding of e$_1$ with 'every woman', May proposes that the two readings can be derived through a single principle. He calls it the *Scope Principle* which states that a class of operators ψ forms a Σ-sequence iff for any operators O_i, $O_j \in \psi$, O_i governs O_j. Under this principle, 'a man' and 'every woman' can form a Σ-sequence in a tree like the one shown in Figure 2.3.

Let us suppose that Q_j = a man and Q_i = every woman. Since every maximal projection (here S') dominating Q_j also dominates Q_i and vice versa, Q_j governs Q_i, thereby making it possible for Q_j and Q_i to scope over one another. General conditions of this nature are supposed to constrain movements at both the covert and overt levels.

Now the question that can be asked is: does this account necessitate a semantic component given what we have so far seen at different levels of form–meaning mappings? Well, if we go by May's account of LF, the answer is perhaps yes, given that certain constraints are stipulated. Besides a syntactic grounding in the design specification of grammar, LF has an interface with broader semantic–conceptual matters as

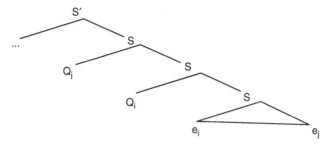

Figure 2.3 Σ-sequence of quantificational operators for quantificational scope

well. But to be clear, LF does not *represent* them, even if matters such as belief, inference and concepts might have access to LF, as May argues. LF is a syntactic level where semantic ambiguities are represented as derived from syntactic structures as if through a sort of 'constructional homonymy', to use May's words. Plus LF understood as such is not a semantic level of representation, although a pure semantic component may make reference to LF. This makes it possible for LF to be mapped onto further semantic specifications which might include contextually based interpretations. Actually, the issue can be looked at from another perspective. Let us see how. Uriageraka (2008) has stated that in the GB model of grammar, there is a mapping from D-structure through S-structure to LF, so conceptual information from D-structure is mapped onto intentional information at LF. Uriageraka adds that the reverse is not possible in natural language – which is why we cannot have the intentional representation ∃x ∀y (x knows y) pronounced as '*x* pfffix *y*' and ∀y ∃x (x knows y) as '*x* fffix *y*' in some imaginary human language. What this illuminates is that LF somehow mediates a mapping between two different kinds of meaning which have an asymmetric relationship, insofar as differences in LF representations having the same conceptual material cannot lead to different words. In fact, recent work in Minimalism (Chomsky 1995, 2000b) has made the Conceptual-Intentional (C-I) system an interface with LF so that LF can respond to, but does not represent, matters of belief, inference, concepts, etc. Hence we appear to have a semantic component mediated by LF without which natural language meaning is perhaps unrecoverable. It is LF that gets a semantic component to square up to an architectural specification in that LF representations can be further manipulated in such a way that semantic conditions and considerations rather than syntactic transformations independently determine the relative scope of quantifiers and other cases of similar types. Ultimately, this gives us another base in which mismatches of form–meaning mapping are rooted and which has gained an anchoring in linguistic theories.

This certainly does not exhaust all possibilities of the partial homology of form–meaning mapping. Linguistic structures are hierarchical in the sense that smaller structures are combined together to build larger structures at higher levels. And tree diagrams for linguistic structures reflect that quite well. It can be demonstrated that hierarchicality of linguistic structures is itself a local reflection of the partial homology of form–meaning mapping at a global but much deeper level. Let us have a few phrase structure rules to see how this obtains. For example, we can have the following simple phrase structure rules:

(33) S→ NP VP
     NP→ DET N
     VP→ V NP
     VP→ V
     (N = noun, DET = determiner)

Every rule in (33) specifies what a category can be rewritten as (indicated by the arrow '→'). Thus, for example, S can be rewritten as an NP followed by a VP. Now equipped with these phrase structure rules, we can move on to explicate how the hierarchicality of linguistic structures instantiated in tree graphs can be seen as a manifestation of a patchy correspondence underpinning a type of form–meaning mapping. Let us now build a tree only using these rules to illustrate the point made. Suppose we have a very simple sentence 'Jack loves the piano', the tree structure of which is provided in Figure 2.4.

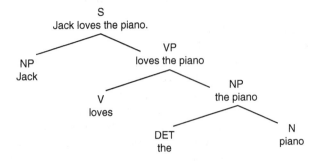

Figure 2.4   A tree structure for 'Jack loves the piano'

Here, one can see that the forms 'the' (DET) and 'piano' (N) combine to build 'the piano' (NP), and then 'loves' (V) combines with 'the piano' (NP) to build 'loves the piano' (VP). Finally, 'Jack' (NP) combines with 'loves the piano' (VP) leading to 'Jack loves the piano'. At each of the stages of combination the meanings of the forms combined form a larger complex of meaning. For instance, the meanings of 'the' (DET) and 'piano' (N) combine to form a larger complex of meaning manifest in 'the piano' (NP) and so do the meanings of 'loves' (V) and 'the piano' (NP) yielding the meaning of 'loves the piano' (VP), and so on. Therefore, the meaning of the sentence 'Jack loves the piano' is ultimately derived at the top node S. This process of the composition of meanings follows from the *Principle of Compositionality*, which consists in the requirement that the meaning of an expression be a function of the meanings of its parts. We have got a whole lot of congruity between form and meaning thus far. But the interesting thing to note is the fact that the meaning of the sentence 'Jack loves the piano' as a whole does not percolate down to any level below it in the sense that the meaning of 'Jack loves the piano' cannot be found and is not thus available at the level of the VP ('loves the piano') or at the level of the object NP ('the piano'), even though the meaning of 'Jack loves the piano' is derived from the meanings of these parts. Why is this so? To understand what is at stake, let us imagine that we actually have a flat tree structure and the meaning of 'Jack loves the piano' is derived at the top of the flat tree structure drawn up in Figure 2.5.

If the meaning of 'Jack loves the piano' were derived just out of the meanings of the parts ('Jack', 'loves', 'the', 'piano') strung out along the same horizontal line as shown in the flat tree structure in Figure 2.5, the meaning of the sentence 'Jack loves the piano' would permeate all levels above and below. And that would be a welcome scenario as long as we want to have a perfect congruity between form and meaning such that the meaning of a form pervades all levels of the form. This will give rise

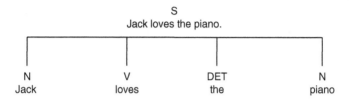

Figure 2.5 A flat tree structure for the derivation of meaning in 'Jack loves the piano'

to a situation in which it would not be hard to see how the meaning X of a form Y is present at every level at which Y can be (de)composed and the form Y of the meaning X is present at every level at which the meaning X can be (de)composed, as the flat tree shows us. So the long and the short of the story is that it is not exactly the juxtaposition of forms that leads to a given meaning; rather, it is the specific *relation* of forms in a certain configuration that leads to a given meaning. So this leads to the following generalizations:

(34) $R(F_1, ..., F_n) \rightarrow M_F$

(35) $F_1 + ... + F_n \rightarrow M_F$

What (34) states is that the meaning of a form F (M_F) emerges out of a specific (*n*-ary) relation **R** that holds on the forms $F_1, ..., F_n$ each of which has its own meaning, and this relation **R** is not equivalent to the relation of linear concatenation (symbolized by '+'), as (35) states. So what ultimately matters is the specific relation **R** that obtains among a set of forms and thus leads to a given meaning which has to somehow correspond to the form in a manner that depends on the exact nature of **R**. So it is (35) that could have been the ideal version of a perfect mapping between form and meaning. Nevertheless, it is (34) that gives us the right picture. In fact, the generalization stated in (34) is useful enough for virtually all kinds of constructions across languages. It can account for discontinuity in both linguistic phenomena and linguistic constructions. Agreement in languages is an example of discontinuity in linguistic phenomena. As discussed at the beginning of this section, sentences like 'These houses have glass windows', 'Those boys are nasty players' have agreement distributed all over the determiner and the noun on the one hand and over the noun phrase and the verb with its complement together on the other. That is why the string 'three men often comes to meet Sarah' is ungrammatical but 'John who has always followed three men often comes to meet Sarah' is fine. The thing responsible for this is discontinuous agreement. Going by what (34) states, we can say that in a sentence like 'John who has always followed three men often comes to meet Sarah', the noun phrase 'John' is in a *relation* (the relation is of agreement here) with the verb form 'come'. It is this relation that makes one understand that it is John rather than Sarah that often comes for a meeting. The same generalization holds true for languages (for example, many Bantu languages, Australian aboriginal languages) that allow for discontinuous constituents. An example from Warlpiri, an Australian aboriginal language, can be provided to show this:

(36) Maliki-rli ka-ju   wajilipi-nyi   wiri-ngki
     dog-ERG PRES-IMPF-1SGOBJ chase-NPAST big-ERG
     'A/the big dog is chasing me.'

                                (From Bittner and Hale 1995)

(ERG = ergative, IMPF = imperfective, OBJ = object, NPAST = non-past)

In (36) the constituents of the noun phrase 'a/the big dog' are not placed together, as can be seen from the placement of the adjective *wiri-ngki* ('big') right at the end of the sentence and far away from the head noun *Maliki-rli* ('dog') placed at the beginning. Certainly they are also in a special relation, as (34) states, and it is this relation that makes one realize that it is a/the big dog rather than a/the tiny mule that is engaged in the action of chasing. Overall, (34) can thus help capture many possibilities of the partial homology at the boundary between form and meaning.

Interestingly, discontinuity in language is not just restricted to such linguistic constructions and certain linguistic phenomena such as agreement. Discontinuity pervades natural language at many other levels manifested in many other linguistic phenomena as well. For example, the following sentences show what is at issue:

(37) What does Lilly believe that she saw__?

(38) What does John think whether to buy__?

(39) *Who/what did John ask where Mary laughed at__?

(40) *Which pen did you put a piece of paper in the pocket of a man who has always liked__?

(41) *Which food does Sid feel that philosophers who eat __ study the problems of quantum mechanics?

The sentences in (37)–(41) all involve the displacement of the relevant *Wh*-phrases at the beginning of the sentence, and these *Wh*-phrases are supposed to be interpreted in the gaps shown. Even if (37)–(38) are grammatical in English, (39)–(41) are not. This phenomenon, too, reveals form–meaning divergence. The relevant notion here is that of

semantic dependency between the verb adjacent to the gap and the
Wh-phrase, which is stretched out to hold across a large hierarchical distance. In the Generative framework it is claimed that the long dependency between the gap and the occurrence of the *Wh*-phrase is actually
summed over smaller dependencies/movements (through the top layer
of the embedded clause, the CP (complementizer phrase), in (37)–(38)),
while it is not so in (39) where the CP of the embedded clause already
contains a *Wh*-phrase ('where'). Hence the moral of the story is that
any dependency formed must be local in the hierarchical space of a
construction. But what about (40)–(41)? What actually prevents any
postulated dependency between the *Wh*-phrases and the relevant verbs
right adjacent to the gaps in (40)–(41)? According to Ross (1986), these
are cases of *intervention effects* in that the relevant semantic dependency
between the *Wh*-phrases and the verbs concerned cannot be established
when that very dependency belongs to and is part of a certain kind of
structure – in this case an adjunct clause attached to noun phrases ('a
man' in (40) and 'philosophers' in (41)). Constituents which are not
essential ingredients of verb phrases (subjects and non-complements)
are of such kind and thus *intervene* in any semantic dependency
between the *Wh*-phrases and the verbs, thereby creating what Ross
(1986) calls *islands*, which stall movement/displacement. The point that
we would like to drive home is that the manifestation of locality and
its constraints easily follows on from a patchy correspondence of form
and meaning at a larger scale. To see how this obtains, we can go about
exploring the consequences that arise from the cases in (37)–(41). It can
be observed that subjects, complements of verbs and adjunct phrases
(within verb phrases or subjects or complements) are all part of a vastly
complicated matrix of semantic dependencies. A semantic dependency
in terms of Dependency Grammar (Tesniére 1959) can be formulated in
a manner schematized below, by following Miller (1999):

(42) $X(Y_1 \ldots Y_n, *, Z_1 \ldots Z_m)$

(43) $X(*)$

Here, in (42)–(43) X is a syntactic category (a verb or a noun, for
example) and '*' stands for X flanked by dependents on both sides (as in
42) or by nothing on either side (as in 43). Such schemas can themselves
contain schemas of the same kind within themselves. Thus, if $X(Y_1 \ldots Y_n,$
$*, Z_1 \ldots Z_m) = S$, then we may also have $X((S_1 \ldots S_i)_1 \ldots (S_1 \ldots S_j)_n, *,$
$(S_1 \ldots S_k)_1 \ldots (S_1 \ldots S_l)_m)$. Under the present condition, it turns out that

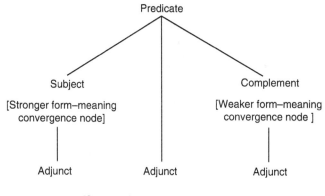

Figure 2.6 Weak and strong form–meaning convergence zones in dependency relations

certain dependents of verbs such as the complements of verbs maintain a weaker form–meaning correspondence leading to discontinuity in syntax, whereas other dependents of verbs such as subjects and adjunct phrases (which may in turn be dependents of nouns or other categories) regiment a stronger form–meaning correspondence that leads to a nullification of syntactic discontinuity in the hierarchical space of linguistic constructions. This can be mapped out as shown in Figure 2.6.

Figure 2.6 shows the lopsided character of form–meaning correspondences, as form–meaning convergence, as opposed to form–meaning divergence, occupies a vaster territory. And this asymmetric character is sufficient to deserve the credit for a partial homology of form–meaning mapping at a much larger scale. Needless to say, hierarchicality and locality derive from a much more fundamental aspect of natural language, that is, form–meaning partial homology. That way, this too comprises an aspect of language that a linguistic theory as a theory of language becomes a theory about. Most linguistic theories including Head-Driven Phrase Structure Grammar or Autolexical Syntax have incorporated this as part of the material determining their descriptive power in grappling with this aspect of natural language. For example, Head-Driven Phrase Structure Grammar, a sign-based grammatical theory, achieves success in accounting for many instances of form–meaning partial homology through the matching of features of signs called Attribute Value Matrices (AVMs) and their percolation across the hierarchical space of linguistic constructions for cases of weaker form–meaning convergence. Overall, this certainly does not obviate the need to look for other possibilities than just form–meaning partial homology and form–meaning full divergence.

2.1.3   Form–meaning full correspondence

So far we have seen how imposing certain constraints on form–meaning mappings can yield different aspects and characteristics of natural language that have defined and mapped out much of what linguistic theories have dealt with, debated, hypothesized about and in some respects agreed on. Given this situation, it would also be interesting to see what would ensue from further varying the grain of correspondence between form and meaning, especially by having them placed in the most constrained coupling. Hence we get form tightly coupled to meaning and vice versa. In fact, this position is in itself quite comprehensible since we want to have the greatest possible degree of congruity between form and meaning in such a manner that any change in form would be reflected in meaning and any change in meaning will have a mirroring in form. The *Principle of Compositionality* is itself such a thesis which was upheld by Gottlob Frege, who did not exactly call it the *Principle of Compositionality*. It was rather associated with what may be called *contextuality* which consists in the grounding of meanings in the contextual frame/setting – linguistic or otherwise (Janssen 2001). Later on this understanding came to be part and parcel of most work in formal semantics and beyond. Thus it constitutes the core hypothesis of Montague Grammar the foundations of which were erected on the *Principle of Compositionality*. Syntax and semantics in Montague Grammar are thought of as algebras which have a homomorphism with respect to one another. So all semantic rules are homomorphically mapped onto syntactic rules such that the meaning of an expression X is a function of the meanings of the expressions from which X is composed by means of syntactic rules. This can be expressed in the following way (Dowty 1979):

(44) $h(F_\gamma (<x_0, x_1, x_2, x_3, \ldots x_n>)) = G_\gamma (<h(x_0), h(x_1), h(x_2), h(x_3), \ldots h(x_n)>)$

Here, h is the homomorphism, and F_γ and G_γ are syntactic and semantic operations respectively which are closed under h. The underlying idea is to make interpretations of expressions ride on a closer coupling of form with meaning. Semantic structures can thus be built in a compositional manner as a function of the semantic structures of the expressions that are parts of the whole expression. So for example, the semantic

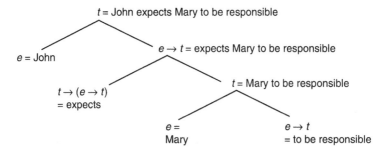

Figure 2.7 A type-logical tree for 'John expects Mary to be responsible'

structure of a sentence 'John expects Mary to be responsible' can be compositionally derived in the manner shown in Figure 2.7.

In Figure 2.7, e represents an entity denoting a noun/noun phrase and t is truth value which is for propositions expressed in clauses/sentences. The arrow represents the mapping/function from one semantic value to another. Thus, 'John' has the semantic value 'e'; a verb phrase of the form 'expects Mary to be responsible' (which is similar to an intransitive verb) has the semantic value '$e \rightarrow t$' mapping the semantic value of 'John' onto that of a proposition (a truth value t), and similarly, the verb 'expects' has a semantic value that maps a truth value onto the semantic value of a verb phrase. This way one can easily infer or deduce the form of semantic values of 'Mary', 'Mary to be responsible' and 'to be responsible'. One can check that both e's at the bottom of the tree are cancelled out to give rise to t at the mother node, and then the t's are cancelled out at the next level and so on, finally leading to a t at the top of the tree which is the semantic value of a proposition. This is what a compositional semantic derivation looks like, as per the formula in (44). However, one may immediately feel that given the characterization of compositionality ambiguity in natural language apparently poses a problem for the compositionality thesis. Thus a sentence like 'Alex saw the girl with his binoculars' has an ambiguity arising from the coexistence of two meanings: one of the meanings of the sentence is that Alex saw the girl using his binoculars (as a tool, perhaps), and the other is that Alex saw the girl who happened to carry his binoculars in her hands. It appears that the meaning of the sentence as a whole cannot be a function of the meanings of the parts. Even if this apparently troubles the compositionality thesis, the cause of concern disappears when one observes that the catch lies in the fact that the way the parts combine to derive the meanings is also important. The ambiguity is structurally grounded, and the two different meanings can be structurally distinguished. So we can have two structural counterparts giving rise to two different meanings: [$_S$ Alex [$_{VP}$ [$_{VP}$ saw the girl] [$_{PP}$ with his binoculars]]] versus [$_S$ Alex [$_{VP}$ saw [$_{NP}$ the girl with his binoculars]]]. In other words, the ambiguity depends on whether we attach the prepositional phrase (PP) 'with his binoculars' to the VP 'saw the girl' or to the NP 'the girl'.

Furthermore, there are still other cases of semantic fluidity that call for a bit of sensitive attention. The following cases can be marshalled to demonstrate the nature of the problem:

(45) a. Crystal believes that Superman is formidably strong.
 b. Paris is so beautiful that everybody wishes to visit the city.

(46) a. The three boys saw a big lion and suddenly it attacked them.
 b. He came to his senses as Jim realized that perhaps he fainted.

The pair of sentences in (45) is different in nature from that in (46). Let us first look at those in (45). If we replace 'Superman' with 'Clark Kent' in (45a), the truth value of the sentence changes in that Crystal's belief is about Superman's having formidable strength as far as his mental state is concerned. Crystal certainly does *not* believe that Clark Kent is formidably strong just because the reality warrants that Superman and Clark Kent are one and the same person. Likewise, the substitution of 'the capital of France' for 'Paris' will change the meaning in (45b), even though Paris is in fact the capital of France. What happens in these cases is that the *extension*, that is, the referent, remains the same, although the *intension* characterized by the meaning varies. This is not a new problem; it was recognized long back by Frege himself, then by William V. Quine and later by Montague. The problem for the *Principle of Compositionality* seems to involve the concern that the meanings of the sentences in (45) change even if the denotation of a certain part of the sentences is the same as that of something else replacing that part. However, the problem can be circumvented if the notion of meaning involves intensions as well in order that the meaning of an expression can be taken to be a function of the extensions and intensions of the expressions the expression is composed of and of how these expressions are combined. Above all, much hinges on what kind of a function the function is when we say the meaning of an expression is a function of the meanings of the parts of that expression. Montague also had a similar idea incorporated into his intensional logic. What about (46) then? Note that (46a) involves an anaphoric reference mediated by 'it' and 'them' in connection with 'a big lion' and 'the three boys' respectively, while (46b) has a cataphoric reference involving 'he' and 'Jim'. The problem is that taken in isolation the pronominals ('it', 'them' and 'he') do not mean anything (indeed, they might refer to many things in the universe!), and if so, it is not clear how they would contribute to the meaning of the whole sentences. The key to the solution again appears to be hidden in the association of the compositionality thesis with contextuality which has to be taken into account when one wonders how to associate a pronominal with its plausible referent/antecedent in a given sentence. The details of this need not bother us here as they can be dealt with in a satisfactory manner (see for details, Janssen 1997). Suffice it to say that the *Principle of Compositionality* ensures a smoother convergence between form and meaning and is perhaps a useful principle for much of natural language. And that is what has made it a part of semantic theories.

Despite the fact that the *Principle of Compositionality* holds true for many types of form–meaning transparency, it certainly does not make sense applied at a more fine-grained level of form. We can take phonology, for example. The aspect of form is manifest in phonology as well, and on the basis of this it can be shown that phonological forms need little grounding in the *Principle of Compositionality*. For example, the word 'book' has a phonological form /buk/, and this form has a meaning. But the meaning of /buk/ is not combined out of the meanings of /b/, /u/ and /k/, which taken separately have no meaning. This has also been called the *Duality of Patterning* (Hockett 1958), which states that forms can become meaningful when combined out of some meaningless discrete elements/symbols. So the *Principle of Compositionality* does not apply at this level of form; the type of form it applies to must be at a higher level of complexity. Syntax or morphology[1] (which is about the internal organization of words) fits the bill. From another perspective, there are other ways of seeing how form–meaning convergence obtains in a transparent manner. It can also be seen in the growth of a sentence structure, as shown by the following examples:

(47) A man that girls that boys that neighbours look at like love hates funky dresses.

(48) I know a man who waters plants that grow right in the middle of the garden that is located behind the house …

These are cases of embedding in natural language which fall under what linguists call *recursion* in that the same type of structure can be iterated infinitely, though one may argue over the status of what is implied by recursion in connection with infinite iteration (see e.g. Pullum and Scholz 2010; Luuk and Luuk 2011). What is important for us is that such growth of sentence structure is an epiphenomenon of the co-construction of form and meaning in the sense that each stage of structural growth of a sentence in a potentially infinite iteration of the relevant linguistic structure (whether phrases or clauses) is correlated with a meaning. So in a more general sense, incremental growth of form goes hand in hand with meaning. This insight has been a central theme of Dynamic Syntax (Kempson et al. 2001). A similar tendency can also be observed in Categorial Grammar (Moortgart 1997), which has been inspired by Montague Grammar in essence. Here syntactic structure is just a medium for the derivation of semantic structures. This can be illustrated with a suitable example (Figure 2.8). Let us look at the derivation of a sentence 'John believes Mary to be beautiful' which is similar in relevant structural aspects to the sentence 'John expects Mary to be responsible' that we used at the beginning of this section.

Here we have a set of primitive categories like N (noun), NP (noun phrase), S (sentence). Any other complex category is derived through a combination of these primitive categories by means of backward and/or

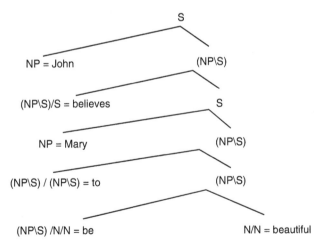

Figure 2.8 A tree structure for the derivation of 'John believes Mary to be beautiful' in Categorial Grammar

forward slashes which are equivalent to functions. The compositional rules via the cancellation of categories are similar to the ones applied in Figure 2.7 above (used at the beginning of this section in connection with Montague Grammar). Since the slashes are functions, they are sensitive to the order of application of functions. Thus Categorial Grammar also achieves similar results when juxtaposed with Montague Grammar.

In sum, form–meaning mapping in a highly constrained relation can also unpack insights into the depth of natural language, although one may be highly surprised to see it in natural languages which, unlike artificial languages, do not always maintain the highest possible standard of form–meaning transparency. Natural languages are usable because they have such variability at the boundary that bridges form and meaning in a more general sense, as we see in the present context. In addition, this is what makes the study of language so exciting. What is remarkably interesting is that it is the patchy correspondence of form and meaning that has occupied a larger space not only in this chapter but also in the landscape of linguistic theories. Does this suggest that there may be something outlandish about the partial homology of form–meaning mapping over which we linguists cudgel our brains every day? Perhaps the answer lies elsewhere. It is not actually the partial homology of form–meaning mapping that carries a tag of overwhelming strangeness which linguists swoon over. Rather, linguistic theories are designed to describe and explain certain aspects of language, but not others. That is why we do not perhaps have a unified theory of linguistics though theoretical physicists from the other side of the academic circle are trying to achieve that. But in other ways, the mapping of form and meaning encompasses virtually the entire skyscape of linguistic theory in general. Still there is something left unsaid and unexplored, for, even if merely form–meaning mapping may be enough to let us get off the ground, finally we also wish to see what is beneath and above the ground as well. This is what we turn to in the next chapter.

2.2 Summary

Stitching things together, we can now say that the questions that were raised at the beginning of this chapter appear to have become sharpened enough such that we are now in a position to have a glimpse into the answer(s). The correlation of form and meaning is perhaps the most intriguing aspect of natural language that makes natural language what it is. And it is this aspect that can entitle a theory of language to be what it is by virtue of the fact that a linguistic theory has to delve into it anyway. As we have seen, this aspect is vastly complex and is not a single-faceted entity. Rather, form can itself be compared to a theory and meaning to an empirical domain, and the way they correlate to one another unfolds the intricately rich fabric of their correspondences as one tries to see how the theory (that is, form) matches the structure of the empirical domain (that is, meaning). Just as there might be a huge variation in any approximation one aims at while testing a theory against the empirical facts, with many theories looking consistent with the same body of empirical facts and many domains of empirical facts looking compatible with the same theory, the same can also be true of form and meaning. And this is exactly what we have seen so far. In spite of all this, the relation of form and meaning is still unclear and shrouded in mystery. Is the relation mental or computational or what? Mind and computation are indissociably linked to and in a substantial sense underlie any notion of form–meaning mapping. What if the relation is mental? This is what we shall probe in the next chapter.

3
How Language Relates to the Mind

This chapter will discuss the relation of the human mind to language, as the title of the chapter indicates. Language is the essence of what we often associate with humanity. Language constitutes the inner domain of human life as it unifies human life with everything that language connects humans to – thought, concepts, expressions, significance, meaning and so on. However, there is an important sense in which language links to humanity by virtue of a projection through and within the human mind which is the innermost core human cognition revolves around. So in this sense, language is part of the underlying substrate of human cognition that defines not merely who we are but also who we would have been and would in turn be. The grounding of language, or rather of grammar in a kind of psychologism, emerged with the advent of Generative Grammar, as was briefly mentioned in Chapter 1. So far, on the other hand, we have seen how the duality of form and meaning imposes some conditions on the characterization of the system(s) of language that we aim at studying. Needless to say, these conditions are far from clear, not so much because of the complexity that mediates between form and meaning as because of how to make sense of the complexity which is to be ultimately relativized in terms of some well-defined criteria and principles. Whatever these criteria and principles are, they may be evoked to clarify and, if feasible, to explain the mediating relation between form and meaning. If language finds a projection through and within the human mind, we have to figure out where we fix the fit between what is projected – if it is language that is projected – and what projects – if the human mind projects.

The question is whether it is form or meaning or the relation between them that is projected through and within the human mind. It may be of substantial interest if we can find out, as part of our inquiry, whether linguistic form is actually projected in the mind, for any such under-standing of form as projected in the mind can help us understand the realization conditions that come to constitute something as tangible as linguistic form – however concretized. And then we can also figure out how something as intangible as meaning becomes keyed to linguistic form by looking into its instantiation in the human mind. This may ultimately leave us in a space where the grounding condition that articulates the mediating relation of form and meaning can be made explicit. In fact, if we go with the formulation of Chomsky (1980), we can see that he suggests that form, meaning and their relation are mentally represented:

> I am assuming grammatical competence to be a system of rules that generate and relate certain mental representations, including in particular representations of form and meaning, the exact character of which is to be discovered, though a fair amount is known about them. (p. 90)

Chomsky's (grammatical) competence is an aspect of what he calls I(internalized)-language in that the system of rules that (partially) con-stitutes the knowledge of a language is a cognitive structure by virtue of being represented in the mind. Such grammatical competence specifies 'the configuration and structure of the mind/brain and takes one ele-ment of it, the component L, to be an instantiation of a certain general system that is one part of the human biological endowment' (Chomsky 1985). One may note that there are a number of assumptions that undergird the description of grammatical competence. These need a bit of clarification. Let us see how we can go about it.

There is an independent cognitive system of the human mind dedicated to language, and grammatical competence or I-language (as opposed to E(externalized)-language consisting of a collection of descriptive state-ments of language and/or speech events, set of linguistic behaviours and responses) is an aspect or mode of the language faculty thus con-strued. What Chomsky calls 'knowledge of language' involves primarily knowledge of grammar, and apart from that, the conceptual system along with the system of pragmatic competence. Thus knowledge of grammar consists of the system of rules and principles, the conceptual system that interprets semantic structures and the system of pragmatic competence that mediates the use of the grammatical competence in communication. These are more or less disjoint systems in the language faculty though they have some amount of interaction as determined by the requirements of rules and principles. Thus the language faculty as an independent component of the human mind is configured and structured around a system of rules and principles which constitute the competence or I-language of a native speaker of a language. According to Chomsky, the mind goes through a number of states within the boundary conditions set by experience, and the initial state of the sequence of relevant states of the human mind is characterized by our genetic endowment for language, namely Universal Grammar (UG), which consists of some *principles* (these do not vary across languages) and *parameters* (they vary across languages in binary values). Plus the intermediate and steady states of the sequence of states are characterized by the represented grammar in the mind as it is acquired and then becomes stable. Thus UG is a partial characterization of the initial state of the mind, and the internalized grammar is a partial characterization of the steady state after the represented grammar in the mind stabilizes at the steady state.

The system of rules and principles constituting grammatical competence or I-language is abstracted from the steady state of the mind. This is one of the reasons why the internalized grammar is a *partial* rather than full characterization of the steady state of the mind. Another reason having to do with the abstractness, although to a lesser degree, of the grammatical competence or I-language is that the grammatical competence or I-language is an *instantiation* of UG much like an instantiation of a specific computer program. To be clearer, UG is not a grammar like the represented grammar of a language L in the mind is; rather, UG is a set of conditions (available at the initial state of the mind) on the possible range of grammars for possible human languages. Understood in these terms, the internalized grammar in the mind is a kind of program realized from the set of conditions on the possible range of grammars for possible human languages. If there exists a relation of instantiation between the internalized grammar in the mind and UG which is far more abstract than the internalized grammar in the mind, it appears that the direction of abstraction is from the internalized grammar in the mind towards UG, or conversely, the direction of realization is from UG towards the internalized grammar. Additionally, there is another level of abstraction with respect to the nature of the internalized grammar in the mind, given that the internalized grammar can be conceptualized by way of abstracting away from possible psychological mechanisms that realize the internalized grammar in question. All such psychological mechanisms belong to what Chomsky calls performance, which accounts for the use of language in real circumstances and may thus include false starts, speech errors, parsing difficulties and things of that sort. However, one should be a bit circumspect in making a sense of the abstraction from the internalized grammar in the mind towards UG and that from psychological mechanisms/parsing strategies to the internalized grammar in the mind. The whole thing can be schematized as shown in Figure 3.1.

The former kind of abstraction stems from the curling up of a set of conditions that unfold the specification and the determination of a particular grammar of a specific language out of a range of possibilities fixed by the general envelope of the structure of language, while the latter kind of abstraction has to do with idealization from noises, tampering messiness, etc., as is standard in the natural sciences. In short, the former kind of abstraction is organism-internal, and the latter is theory-internal or simply methodological.

There has been a lot of debate on the first kind of abstraction linking UG to the specification and the determination of a particular grammar of a specific language (see for recent discussions, Elman et al. 1996; Berwick et al. 2011; Crain 2012; Clark and Lappin 2011). We shall not touch upon this issue until Chapter 8, where it will be dealt with at length in connection with the notion of learnability after a detailed examination of the link between mind, language and computation is done. Rather, we shall concentrate on the second kind of abstraction involving the internalized grammar and the psychological mechanisms that realize it. Looked at from the conversely related perspective, the second kind of abstraction can be juxtaposed with the realization relation between the internalized grammar and psychological mechanisms that realize it. They are not the same thing, as we will see below. In fact, there is a lot of complication surrounding the realization relation

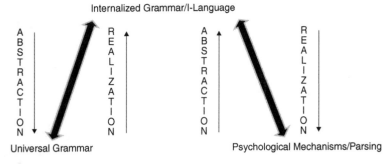

Internalized Grammar/I-Language

Universal Grammar   Psychological Mechanisms/Parsing

Figure 3.1   Two kinds of abstraction/realization of internalized grammar/ I-language

that obtains or may come to obtain between the internalized grammar as part of I-language and the relevant psychological mechanisms. And there is a lot more obfuscation underlying the abstraction that connects the internalized grammar with the psychological mechanisms which the internalized grammar is viewed to abstract away from. These two different issues deserve independent treatment and hence will be scrutinized separately. So let us see what the first opens up for us.

3.1   I-language realization in psychological mechanisms and psychological reality

One of the still hotly debated issues in current linguistic theory revolves around the relation between language, grammar and psychological mechanisms. Knowledge of language is grounded in the language faculty which is a system of cognitive structures in the mind. The language faculty grows in the mind by virtue of the principles of UG. Under this construal, children may not actually *learn* a language even in the sense in which UG specifies the envelope of the range of possible grammars out of which a specific grammar is realized as a function of UG within the conditions on the *content* of relevant linguistic experience which is supposed to be degenerate and minimal. Ultimately, UG causally leads to the growth of a specific grammar that comes to be represented in the mind of the speaker. So a person does not know a language, rather a grammar that generates the language. But what is the nature of the relation of knowing that holds between the person and the grammar concerned? As has been emphasized by Chomsky (1980, 1985), the relation is not exactly that of 'knowing' in the ordinary commonsensical use of the word 'know'. Rather, the person who possesses the knowledge of grammar in fact 'cognizes' the grammar represented in the mind. Hence the relation of 'cognizing' holds between the person having knowledge of grammar and the grammar represented. And this relation ensures that the knowledge of grammar represented is unconscious because native speakers of languages cannot introspect within their minds to access the contents of the representation of grammar.

Moreover, the knowledge of grammar represented is not an intentional object under the relation of 'cognizing'. What cognizing specifies is to be cashed out in terms of a notion of a *tacit* state of knowledge, or simply a mental representation, which is not *about* what is represented or known just as a line as a mathematical object may be deemed to be a representation without anything for it to represent in a substantive sense. That is, the grammar represented in the mind is not an object towards/about which one can have beliefs when one has knowledge of grammar. As a matter of fact, it is even suggested that the notion of a relation of cognizing between a speaker and the mental grammar is best rendered by being replaced by the notion of a state of the language faculty, for it is supposed that there is no substantive sense that attaches to the notion of how the mental grammar and its categories can be about something (see Chomsky 2000a; Antony and Hornstein 2003). Note that this issue does not turn on the question of whether we can frame a notion of intentionality that involves unconscious mental states which are about something. And even if such states are attributed to cognizing, general properties of how inferences are drawn and assimilated, or of how one can have thoughts about the mental grammar, do not hold in the case of cognizing. Nor does the property of interpretation, which involves inferences, having judgements or thoughts and understanding which are also intrinsically intentional, apply to cognizing. Surely there can be many things that are about something; for instance, maps are about locations, pictures of landscapes are about scenes and so on. These are not mental relations; plus there can of course be mental states which are unconscious but are about something (unannounced or unacknowledged beliefs, for example). But Chomsky (2000a) does not make much of the notion of intentionality, insofar as intentionality involves a mental state or an object which can be directed at or about something, not merely because he thinks only internal relations among internal elements (rules of grammar, principles, categories, etc.) of the language faculty can be made sense of, but also because internal representations which are objects represented in the brain much like mechanisms of insect navigation or of bird songs have no *real* interface with the world out there.[1] This is also because of the way the language faculty comes to be instantiated in the mind – the language faculty grows in the cognitive substrate of the human mind just as a human organ like the liver or kidney grows in the body. This aspect of the thesis about the language faculty has been a bone of contention for decades (Matthews 2006). For example, Collins (2004), in trying to dispel confusions centring on the language faculty disputes, has argued that the thesis about the language faculty has not exactly been an epistemological project in the sense that the language faculty generates grammars, but there is no question of whether these grammars are true or false of languages in question, and that a person having knowledge of grammar does not represent the grammar in the mind in a way that enters into the *causal* implementation of intentional generalizations (beliefs, thoughts, etc.) in computational states of the mind, contrary to what Fodor (2000) is believed to have assumed. This is inevitable because of the entire debate revolving around the question of whether the representation of grammar in the mind can or should be a part of the parsing mechanism. For Fodor the answer has been yes, and also for many others including Bresnan (1982), Jackendoff (2002) and Sag and Wasow (2011). In fact, much hinges on the issue of where exactly we can make the cut at the juncture between language/grammar and psychological mechanisms. This issue is formidably diffuse and intricately hard.

It may be noted that the realization of the system of grammatical competence in psychological mechanisms also bears on the linguistic methodology which consists in relying on linguistic judgements of native speakers for what is called the *descriptive adequacy* of grammars. Such a methodology meets the conditions of a description of the underlying grammars, insofar as this evaluates the descriptive adequacy of grammars on a principled basis. Descriptively adequate grammars have to be further evaluated by a linguistic theory in terms of whether they can explain language acquisition from impoverished linguistic experience, which is a matter of what is called *explanatory adequacy*. It looks like a situation in which grammars are theories that are put to the test for descriptive adequacy and explanatory adequacy, the former being important for specific grammars of particular languages and the latter for UG. And this is how the issue of making the relevant cut at the juncture of language/grammar and psychological mechanisms turns on the methodological criteria and practices in linguistic theory. Recently, Chomsky (2004, 2005, 2007) has gone beyond these two kinds of adequacy, proposing to reduce properties of linguistic structures to interface systems such as the Sensory-Motor System (SM)/the Articulatory–Perceptual (A-P) interface and the Conceptual–Intentional System (C-I), which are also components of the language faculty in the broader sense (the language faculty in the narrow sense includes only Merge, the fundamental operation that builds syntactic objects from Lexicon) (Hauser et al. 2002). All this can be delineated in more detail for the sake of shedding light on the thorny question of I-language realization in psychological mechanisms. In the Minimalist Program (Chomsky 1995), the architecture of the language faculty looks like that shown in Figure 3.2.

Lexical items are drawn from the Lexicon in selected arrays or sets called Numeration and then the binary operation Merge (external or internal)[2] applies to any two syntactic objects and outputs a combined syntactic object. Thus the structure built is Spelt-Out to the interfaces PF and LF which are again accessible to the SM/A-P system (responsible for linearization done at PF and articulation/perception) and the C-I system

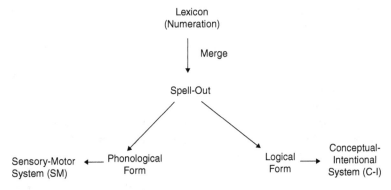

Figure 3.2 The architecture of the language faculty in the Minimalist Program (Chomsky 1995)

(mediating conceptual representations, discourse-related properties, beliefs, intentions, etc.) respectively. So in an intensional sense,[3] the language faculty generates pairs of the kind <SEM, PHON> and makes it accessible to PF and LF as the phonological component (PF) maps a derivation to PHON (phonological representation) and the semantic component (LF) to SEM (semantic representation). Any derivation has to meet the *legibility conditions* imposed by the interfaces, namely the SM/A-P system and the C-I system. For example, case is an *un*interpretable feature and what this means is that it cannot be interpreted to have meaning at LF. Hence this has to be eliminated; in the Minimalist architecture of grammar this is done by means of the internal Merge of noun phrases to a position (typically in the SPECIFIER[4] position of the tense phrase (TP) for external arguments and of the (light) verb phrase (vP) for internal arguments) that can eliminate this. Hence we cannot have a sentence like '*went out John to see his dad'. From this it can be easily inferred that the description of I-language has bent a bit towards the conditions of cognitive mechanisms/systems with the development of Generative Grammar, especially when the talk is about the *legibility conditions* imposed by the interfaces, and such description has in fact oscillated between an abstracted plane of reality and the level of psychological/parsing mechanisms.

Essentially, we ask questions about the psychological organization that makes the instantiation of I-language or what Ludlow (2011) calls *psy-language* viable. But this is not an easy question, as we will see below. There can be some possible avenues. Perhaps there is some unique but otherwise baffling property of our psychological organization by virtue of which I-language is instantiated in the language faculty, and this property seems to lie neither in the system of grammatical competence nor in the relevant mental organization but in the mediating relation connecting the two. Or perhaps there is some significant property of grammar by virtue of which it comes to be realized in the psychological substrate, and this property is plausibly cognitive. Do these possibilities make any substantive difference? Whatever the answer may turn out to be, this cannot be just a matter of stipulation. Indeed, this issue has been hooked to the question of what has been called the *psychological reality* of grammars. Given what has been discussed so far, this is not an innocuous term and carries substantial theory-internal motivations and methodological assumptions. The psychological reality of grammars would demand that derivational operations in the language faculty be reflected in the psychological/parsing operations in controlled psycho-linguistic or neurolinguistic experiments. But it cannot stop there as the methodological or meta-theoretical requirements the psychological reality of grammars invites may well extend beyond this. It has been used to see how far linguistic theory can be realist or merely instrumen-talist. Realist theories (as in physiology or neuroscience) carry ontologi-cal claims with respect to the domain of objects a theory is a theory of, whereas instrumentalist theories (as in mathematical physics) do not have to carry any such ontological import and possess explanatory and predictive power without clinging to any relevant ontological import (Seuren 2004). If so, it appears that the notion of the psychological real-ity of grammars requires a linguistic theory to pass the test of being true at the level of mental/psychological reality when the linguistic theory in question claims that the object of inquiry, that is, grammars of lan-guages, are mentally represented.

Chomsky (1980) has maintained that the notion of the psychological reality of grammars is misguided and misleading. The reason for this is that the notion of the psychological reality of grammars requires 'imputing existence' to the psychological apparatus which can already be described by means of descriptions of particular grammars and UG, for Chomsky thinks something else over and above linguistic evidence may not be required to buttress any linguistic hypothesis that explains a range of linguistic phenomena. We should not, as Chomsky argues, ask for psychological reality any more than physicists ask for physical reality for the objects to which physical theories and hypotheses apply. This point in many respects lines up with Soames (1984), who believes that the objects of linguistic theories are not mental states and compu-tational operations and processes which actually belong to the domain of psychological theories. So for him, linguistic theories are *conceptually distinct* and *empirically divergent* from psychological theories even though psychological theories can be illuminating for an understanding of the cognitive structures of language. Overall, this seems to indicate that the objects of which linguistic hypotheses are true cannot be the objects of which psychological hypotheses are true, at least not in the same way. However, Chomsky also thinks that psychological evidence is welcome, insofar as it comes unlabelled and for the linguistic system of rules and representations as a whole, not separately for the reality (whatever that turns out to be) and for the theory that posits rules and mental representations. Nevertheless, it is still unclear how the mental representation of the system of grammatical competence or the entire language faculty can have a grounding beyond the obvious and trivial fact that language is processed through and within the mind. Given the shifting between an abstracted plane of reality and the level of psychological/ parsing mechanisms, this problem has slipped into a seemingly inescapable quagmire, especially when one insists that the mentally represented grammar as an object is different from psychogrammar which characterizes aspects or features of a speaker's mind by virtue of which a speaker knows facts about the language he/she speaks, and that these facts are determined by the mentally represented grammar (George 1989).

Unfortunately, there has not been any illumination from the side of psycholinguistics which has tried to resolve the current problem by using the realist criteria of testing aimed at teasing out the truth by inspecting the ways in which the mentally represented grammar could be told apart from the psychogrammar. The attempt to figure out how derivational operations in the language faculty can be reflected in the psychological/ parsing operations did not pan out the way theoretical linguists expected (Fodor et al. 1974). What is at least clear is that the mentally represented grammar or I-language enters into parsing performance which is guided by the mentally represented grammar, as Pritchett (1992) argues. He shows that the following *garden-path* sentences, for example, can be perfectly resolved at each stage guided by the competence grammar.

(49) Without her donations to the charity failed to appear.

(50) After Todd drank the water proved to be poisoned.

(51) Susan convinced her friends were unreliable.

(52) The patient persuaded the doctor that he was having trouble with to leave.

All these sentences in (49)–(52) induce a garden-path kind of difficulty in processing. In (49) this difficulty arises in the position of the word 'failed', in (50) in the position of the word 'proved', in (51) in the position of 'were' and in (52) in the position of 'to leave'. All this is to suggest that the difficulty in processing is due to the difficulty in interpreting an already theta-marked constituent outside of the position in which it has been theta-marked, and that the resolution is constrained and guided by the principles of grammar that include the Theta Criterion, which is responsible for the assignment of theta roles to the arguments of a predicate. This explains why, for example, in (49) the noun phrase 'donations to the charity' has to be reanalysed as receiving the subject theta role (THEME) of the verb 'fail', which is wholly consistent with 'her' getting its theta role from 'without'. Thus the reanalysis does not violate rules of grammar, and the postulated parsing difficulty is itself explained on the basis of obstacles to the satisfaction of (global) rules and principles of grammar in a local manner.

Even if this points to the necessity of having a mentally represented grammar that guides and constrains parsing mechanisms in linguistic performance, this still does not tell us whether the mentally represented grammar coincides or is identified with the parser. In fact, the position that grammatical competence guides parsing mechanisms and/or strategies which realize that grammatical competence is rather uncontroversial. Chomsky (1980) has also urged that the study of I-language and the study of linguistic performance should support each other, for the former can project insights into the psychological/ parsing mechanisms realizing grammatical competence as much as the latter can illuminate the nature of the mental representation of I-language. But the crux of the problem revolves around the question of how to go about figuring out the ways in which linguistic performance or mechanisms thereof can lay bare the nature of the mental representation of I-language. Even today there do not appear to be conceptually coherent and methodologically sound criteria for fulfilling this goal. In this connection, it is worthwhile to note that Peacocke (1989) has offered a principle called the *Information Criterion*, which states what it takes for a grammar to be psychologically real. Peacocke's *Information Criterion* says the following:

Take any statement q of grammar which is derivable in G from $A_1 \ldots A_n$ by means of $T_1 \ldots T_j$: then the fact that q holds for the subject's language has an explanation at the level 1.5 by some mechanism or algorithm which draws upon the information that $p_1, \ldots,$ and the information that p_n, and does so by using the transition-types expressed by $T_1...T_j$. (p. 116)

There are a number of assumptions in the criterion that deserve some clarification here. Peacocke assumes that the *Information Criterion* holds true at the subpersonal level at an intermediate level between Marr's (1982) level 1 and level 2 which are a part of Marr's three-level schema that specifies for a cognitive domain (say, the visual system) the *computational level* (the level of what is to be computed and why), the *algorithmic level* (the level that specifies which algorithm will be used to compute a given function and how) and the *implementational level* (the level of realization of the algorithm in hardware which may be computer hardware or the human brain or something else physical). Additionally, Peacocke also thinks that facts about meaning and the structure of expressions can be explained by facts about the information that is drawn upon by mechanisms or algorithms in the mind of the language user, and this can be done by relativizing those facts to individuals. Therefore, for example, in the sentence 'John loves Mary' the verb phrase 'loves Mary' has the structure, or rather the structural description [$_{VP}$ [$_V$ loves] [$_{NP}$ Mary]], and a grammar containing such structural rules (such as a *phrase structure grammar*) is psychologically real as long as the verb phrase 'loves Mary' is assigned the structure [VP [V loves] [NP Mary]] on the basis of some mechanism or algorithm drawing upon the information that the verb is followed by the noun phrase in a verb phrase and the information that 'loves' is a verb while 'Mary' is the noun phrase. This is what the *Information Criterion* states when G is a grammar, $A_1... A_n$ are the relevant (tokens of) rules, and $T_1...T_j$ are transition types implicit in rewrite rules as in S→ NP VP, VP→ V NP.

Now the question is: does the *Information Criterion* pave the way for a realist grounding of the mentally represented grammar which is thought to be distinct from the psychological/parsing mechanisms realizing grammatical competence? Rather than clarify the matter, the *Information Criterion* in fact compounds the complications that we have come across so far. The problems with the *Information Criterion* can be presented here for consideration.

First, the psychological reality of a mentally represented grammar is placed to hold at a level in the language faculty that specifies the general character of an algorithm without a concomitant specification of any *particular* algorithm in any unique manner since particular algorithms are specified at the second level of Marr's three-level schema. This is based on the observation that for any task (or rather a function) to be executed, the same task properly specified can be computed by many algorithms using the same body of information, or conversely, the same algorithm can execute the task using many bodies of information. Thus, for instance, an algorithm for picking out the third word in a sequence of words in a string may draw upon a characterization of words in terms of spaces that separate words from the left direction or in terms of spaces that separate words from the right direction or in terms of a sequence of letters/characters with relevant linguistic features. The formulation of the *Information Criterion* carries the presupposition that the algorithm or mechanism (that draws upon the information that something called X is followed by something else Y and individuates X and Y separately) is different from the source of the information or from the information itself which presumably resides in or coincides with the mental representation of grammar. The question is what actually stops such information from being described algorithmically? For all our lack of understanding of mental algorithms, the domain of algorithms extends to cover rules like S→ NP VP, VP→ V NP that constitute the information base whatever mechanisms or algorithms end up ultimately drawing upon. This has indeed been the standard practice at least in Generative Grammar in which rules and constraints are algorithmically specified at whatever level we choose – whether at Marr's level 1 or at level 1.5 or at level 2 – when trying to define the abstraction function. This issue will be touched upon in the next section and dealt with in far greater depth in Chapter 4 when we turn to the relation between language and computation.

Second, there are no intrinsic constraints on the *Information Criterion* that prevent it from stretching out to apply to thermometers, calculators or casseroles or even taps. One may notice that the act of some mechanism or algorithm accessing and drawing upon some information by means of some transitional rules which are causally responsible for changes in the states of a system may obtain in devices like thermometers, calculators or casseroles or even taps and also in many more tools. And in such cases, it is flimsy and indeed clumsy to attribute individually grounded psychological reality to all these devices and tools, or even ask questions about psychological reality. The fact that the *Information Criterion* holds regardless of whether the domain to which it applies is modular or not and that the information states need not be linguistic makes the *Information Criterion* more easily amenable to any such extension, which at its best is nonsense.

So ultimately we are stuck where we were earlier. The supposition that there is a grammar mentally represented that makes the use of language possible when linguistic competence enters into linguistic performance does nothing to cleave the quandary. The vector of the problem has projected itself onto the domain of a relation that supposedly obtains between the realization of grammatical competence in psychological mechanisms and what Devitt (2006) calls *linguistic reality*. We have already been grappling with the conception of the psychological reality of grammar, and then the conception of linguistic reality, rather than detracting from any characterization of the psychological realization of grammar, adds something to it. This deserves some elaboration as it is tangential to the current discussion in ways that we shall soon see as we move through the maze. One of the reasons why the notion of linguistic reality, as propounded by Devitt in connection with his problems with the conception of psychological reality, is relevant here is that he has also made an attempt to eliminate the prevailing messiness associated with the relation between grammar and the mind. And as we proceed, we can discover that the relation between grammar and the mind is shadowed by complications, puzzles, paradoxes. But before things take off the ground, Devitt's problems with the conception of psychological reality can be fleshed out. He thinks that a theory of representation systems is different from a theory of the competence to use representations. At this point this sounds familiar, as we have already seen that Soames (1984) also believes that the objects of linguistic theories are *not* mental states and computational operations and processes. But there are some subtleties that have a different flavour. For Devitt, there must be a set of structure rules that govern language which is produced by the state of (grammatical) competence, and there is a set of processing rules that enter into the exercise of (grammatical) competence when (grammatical) competence produces linguistic expressions but the embodiment of these processing rules constitutes (grammatical) competence. So the set of structure rules is different from the set of processing rules, and this is more so because the set of structure rules must be *respected* by (grammatical) competence, or in other words, the set of structure rules *governs* language or the linguistic system which constitutes the linguistic reality. An example that Devitt has provided illustrates what he has in mind: bee dance with its own complex pattern of sequences of movements and directional positioning signifies the location of food. And thus, semiotically, this is a representational system that produces bee dances, but the set of structure rules that governs the representational system of bee dance is different from the set of processing rules that says how in reality bee dances are produced.

These are some of the things that Devitt espouses. Now we can articulate what all this means for the situation we are faced with.

When Devitt speaks of the embodiment of processing rules constituting (grammatical) competence, it appears that he risks commingling the Chomskyan notion of competence with performance. That is the charge made by Collins (2007) and Slezak (2009). But it soon becomes clearer that Devitt's notion of competence is broader than that of Chomsky, and thus aligns more easily with skills and abilities comprising the essence of know-how. That is the reason why the embodiment of processing rules can also be a part of competence in his sense, though he acknowledges that structure rules – which say, for example, anaphors must be bound in their local domain or auxiliary verbs in English have to be fronted to form interrogatives – can at best be implicit in the processing rules constituting (grammatical) competence. More surprisingly, Devitt insists that grammar, or for that matter, language does not tell us anything about the psychological states of grammatical competence or simply about whether structure rules are represented in the language faculty or not. First of all, one should consider the general distinction between *explicit encoding* and *implicit encoding* made by Pylyshyn (1991). *Explicit encoding* requires explicitly encoded rules and their representation in a system, as in a calculator, for instance, that explicitly encodes rules of addition, multiplication and division, while *implicit encoding* can be seen in the visual system that operates with some assumptions involving light reflection from the surface, mapping of physical discontinuities onto visual images, etc. which are constraints not exactly represented anywhere in the visual system in the sense that interpretations of the operations of the visual system must be in accord with these constraints. Now we can make sense of what Devitt might mean to say. For all his commitments to the stance that linguistic intuitions do not tell us anything about the represented rules of the language faculty, he seems to mean that the system of rules that forms grammatical competence in Chomsky's view is not *explicitly encoded or represented* in the mind; rather, such a system of rules can at best be *implicitly present* in the language faculty. Under this construal, the system of rules is never a part of the language faculty but in fact external to the mind.

If this is so, we now have a very sketchy glimpse into the nature of the system of rules, however construed. This is because the system of rules is now pushed outside of the mind but there are still rules which are used for processing. Thus psychologically grounded rules weakly coincide with the structure rules of the linguistic system external to the mind. Overall, does this advance our understanding of the psychological realization of I-language in any way? The matter cannot be resolved just through argumentation that merely consists in rigorously following a number of otherwise sound premises to deduce a conclusion. We need to see it all through a thorough examination of some linguistic phenomena in order to spell out the consequences that emanate from it. With some examples from a range of linguistic phenomena we can more plausibly see in what ways the connection between grammar and the mind hovers over a quagmire we have stepped into. Let us look at the examples below.

(53) John$_i$ always finds himself$_i$ in trouble.

(54) John$_i$ said that a picture of himself$_i$ is on sale.

In the sentence (53) above, 'John' and 'himself' co-refer each other, and thus the anaphor 'himself' is said to be bound by 'John'. If this is what holds in the sentence (53), the sentence (54) tells a different story. In (54) 'John' certainly binds 'himself' but one can observe that this holds across a clause, which is not allowed by the *binding principles* in Generative Grammar. So *binding principles* allow (53) but not (54), in that there is a concept of *locality* that obtains in the domain in which this binding applies. Thus, in (53) the local domain is the domain characterized by the tense phrase (TP) in the clause that contains both the binder ('John') and what is bound ('himself'), whereas in (54) the binder ('John') is in a different tense phrase from the one in which we find 'himself'. Note that cases of long-distance anaphor binding are also found in other languages like Finnish (the sentence (55)), Chinese (the sentence (56)), Japanese (the sentence (57)) etc.

(55) John$_i$ näki Fred$_j$ katsovan   itseään$_i$/$_j$
     John saw Fred-GEN watch-PTC-GEN self-POSS
                  'John saw Fred watch himself.' (Steenbergen 1991)

(56) Zhangsan$_i$ zhidao Lisi$_j$ renwei Wangwuk$_k$ zui xihuan$_i$/$_j$/$_k$
     Zhangsan know Lisi think Wangwu most like self
     'Zhangsan knows that Lisi thinks that Wangwuk likes self. '
                                           (Pollard and Xue 2001)

(57) Takasi$_i$-ga   Kenji$_j$-ga   zibun$_i$/$_j$-o suisenshita-to   omotta
     Takasi-NOM   Kenji-NOM   self-ACC recommended-COMP thought
     'Takasi thought that Kenji recommended self.'
                                           (Motomura 2001)
(NOM = nominative case, ACC = accusative case, GEN = genitive marker, COMP = complementizer, PTC = particle)

Setting aside the question of whether we can (re)formulate *binding principles* considering them to be principles or parameterized rules in all possible worlds, we can safely assume that rules postulated in Generative Grammar operate in accordance with principles. Whatever this actually turns out to be, we need not bother about it since our question lies elsewhere. But how do we know (or even 'cognize') all the facts about (53)–(54) described above? How does one know that there is some rule that makes the binding in (53)–(54) possible? Or are there different rules for (53) and (54) separately? Suppose that we formulate a rule that states that anaphors must be bound in a local domain that contains both the binder and what is bound. This rule is similar to one of the *binding principles* (Principle A). With this rule we come to discover that (53) is compatible with this, but (54) is not. But how does one know this rule? What is at least clear is that we know this through our interpretation of what the binder is and what is bound by the binder. Is there any other way we may know but not cognize (in the Chomskyan sense) that in (53) 'John' binds 'himself' in a local domain but does not do so in (54)? Perhaps there is not any. The only way is to take recourse to interpretation which is what tells us that (54) does not conform to the rule just proposed. But how do native English speakers cognize this rule? The answer to this question will take us through a number of horrendous puzzles and inconsistencies, as we will see. Let us see how. The relevant rule here cannot be formulated except with reference to how we interpret the binder and what it binds. In fact, that is what tells us that (54) does not conform to the rule. Also note that we want to have the rule as something mentally represented or cognized by native speakers. How is this possible? Once we see that the relevant rule at hand cannot be formulated without our interpretation of what binds what, it is nothing more than an inconsistency to insist that the relevant rule has to be mentally represented as such in the mind. To see how this breeds an inconsistency, we have to go deeper into it. Suppose for the sake of argument we allow for the possibility that the rule is mentally represented or cognized by native speakers, as well as accepting that we cannot know the rule except through interpretation. If this is the case, this leads to a paradox.

Here is how. The mentally represented rule is the one cognized by native speakers, and if it is so cognized, it stays at the level of some state of the mind/brain in virtue of being a *non-intentional* object of the mind's cognizing. That is, the rule cognized *cannot* be cognized by native speakers in an intentional manner; above all, that is what the word 'cognize' means when it is used by Chomsky (1980, 1985). If this is indeed the case, the rule identifying a mental representation ceases to be a rule, because all that the rule in question states is that 'John' binds 'himself' in a local domain, which obtains by virtue of a semantic dependency between 'John' and 'himself' but this semantic dependency cannot be figured out in a non-intentional way. The semantic dependency between 'John' and 'himself' plus the concomitant notion of locality cannot be figured out in a non-intentional way, for the very act of doing that is intentional and involves the individuation of the meanings of 'John' and 'himself'. To cling to mentally represented rules thus construed is impossible. Well, this may be possible if and only if we hold that at the non-intentional level the mind inside the cranium somehow does all this. Then this inexorably gets us into the homunculus fallacy, which will invite another homunculus mind inside the one we posit and ad infinitum. Therefore, the rule in question is not a rule – a contradiction! On the other hand, if the rule is indeed formulated through interpretation as this is what we have allowed for, then we end up with the conclusion that the rule is both intentional and non-intentional. This is another contradiction. We are now stuck in a paradox. It should be made clear that no appeal to the grammar-internal principle of the Theta Criterion will be of much help, primarily because the Theta Criterion consists in the assignment of theta-roles to the arguments of a predicate, which is a first-order fact. How the theta-roles of the arguments relate to each other – a second-order fact – goes beyond the domain of the Theta Criterion. Thus it is not surprising that binding (or rather variable binding) and co-reference are not reducible to the Theta Criterion. Had that been possible, we could have got rid of variable binding and co-reference altogether by having all matters of relational interpretations of a predicate's arguments reduced to first-order grammar-internal conditions. Certainly, we cannot pursue this course.

One may still try to escape this paradox by saying that the rule recognized as such is mentally represented or cognized by native speakers but *denying* that we know or even cognize the rule only through interpretation. Let us proceed with this possibility. If this is the case, then we get bogged down in another paradox. Now suppose that there is another rule – let us call it R2 different from the earlier rule, which may be called R1. Suppose that R2 is for (54) and R2 states that an anaphor may be bound by its binder across a local domain in an extended domain that includes the binder and what is bound. And then we say there is another rule R3 such that R3 = R1 ∪ R2 and so on R_n = R1 ∪ ... ∪ R_m when $n - m = 1$.[5] That is, the rules go on ad infinitum. Now we say that they are all mentally represented but immediately an objection comes forth. How come we can have potentially an infinite number of rules represented in the

mind since the two rules R1 and R2 are descriptively sufficient to cover
(53)–(54) and perhaps many such cases in English (and possibly in other
languages)? Now let us hold on for a moment. The notion of descriptive
adequacy of rules or something of that sort having to do with simplicity,
minimality, etc. exists only at the intentional level of our minds. Have
we not already *denied* that we know or even cognize rules only through
interpretation? Above all, the notion of descriptive simplicity (along
with our interpretation of 'John' and 'himself' as being co-referential,
and of how 'John' binds 'himself' in different ways in (53)–(54)), is *not*
transparent to the non-intentional level of the mind that cognizes rules.
The system of rules does not in itself 'know' what is simple or descriptively adequate. Other than that, any appeal to explanatory role will not
work since the rules do indeed explain the linguistic facts, and besides
that, this appeal to explanatory virtue is again intentionally grounded.
As we home in on the practice of theoretical linguists, we observe that
we formulate rules for sentences or sets of sentences and test their validity
against the linguistic judgements of native speakers (see for an interesting discussion, Schütze 1996). And in doing this, we make reference not
merely to E(xternal)-language(s) but also to our intentional way of doing
things as we form beliefs, hypotheses and theories about things. Rather,
this activity is itself intentional. Getting back to the possibility which
we allowed for in connection with the ensuing paradox, we come upon
another paradox. The potentially infinite set of rules $R_n = R1 \cup \ldots \cup R_m$ is
mentally represented but at the same time it cannot be (having an infinite number of rules mentally represented is vacuous as our finite brain
has no space for the representation of infinite rules). It is a contradiction! Additionally, there is no other way of eliminating this contradiction than by making reference to our interpretation that figures out not
only how binding obtains in different ways in (53)–(54) but also what is
adequate – descriptively or explanatorily or otherwise. But as soon as we
give in to this temptation, we fall into the trap of another contradiction
in that the set of mentally represented rules is now at the intentional
level but at the same time *not* at the intentional level, as we have cleaved
to the premise that rules are mentally represented or cognized by native
speakers. This is again a contradiction!

Similar inconsistencies or paradoxes also arise in other cases. Let us
look at the following examples:

(58) What has Max bought__?

(59) Who __has kissed her?

(60) I wonder who John wants to meet__.

(61) I know what he likes to eat__.

(62) What a beautiful place this is__!

(63) How come she hates pizza?

All the examples (58)–(63) involve a *Wh*-element. Some are questions and some are not, but all involve displacement or movement[6] such that the *Wh*-element is interpreted in a position different from the one in which it appears. This is indicated by the gap.[7] Current proposals suggest that such dependency between the gap and the *Wh*-element, or rather the postulated movement, is driven by certain features, namely an *un*interpretable *Wh*-feature and a Q-feature in the complementizer head in a complementizer phrase (CP) which enters, through AGREE (an operation in the Minimalist Program responsible for checking, valuation and elimination of features), into a checking relation with the *Wh*-element bearing an interpretable *Wh*-feature (see for detailed discussions, Chomsky 1995; Simpson 2000; Cable 2010). Essentially, the idea underlying *Wh*-movement along with other movements is that *un*interpretable features need to be erased, and this is only possible through an establishment of minor/smaller dependency links that add up to the (long) dependency that we see between the gap and the *Wh*-element. In other words, the dependency that we see between the gap and the *Wh*-element is summed up by smaller such dependencies all of which boil down to an operation of elimination of semantically vacuous features such as the categorical features of *Wh*-forms present in the position on the surface form of a sentence at which the *Wh*-element can be found (typically the phrase CP). It has a schema: $[_{CP} X^{WH} [_{TP} (X^{WH}) \ldots [_{vP} \ldots (X^{WH}) \ldots]]]$ – the *Wh*-element X^{WH} can be displaced either from within the TP (tense phrase) or from the vP (light verb phrase). Hence it is the semantically vacuous categorical features of *Wh*-forms which are causally responsible for any dependency that obtains between the gap and the *Wh*-element; it is as if a *Wh*-form–meaning mismatch is tolerated to eliminate other (possible) form–meaning mismatches involving categorical features of *Wh*-forms (present elsewhere) but with no semantically viable content. Hence, it appears that grammar economizes on or optimizes form–meaning mismatches. This is what is generally posited to be happening in, for example, (58) in which the dependency between 'what' and the gap at the end of the sentence is due to the necessity to remove a form–meaning mismatch – present at the place where 'what' appears – involving categorical features of *Wh*-forms with no semantically viable content. Now it can be seen that even if this is the general character of any rule involving *Wh*-elements, the exact (type of) rule will vary in some of the examples (58)–(63) appropriately based on the features of the positions (namely, the CPs) where the *Wh*-elements are found. So we will require rules R1 for (58)–(59), R2 for (60), R3 for (61), R4 for (62) and R5 for (63). (58)–(59) are plain interrogatives; (60) is also an interrogative without the status of a question; (61) is a free relative with the category of the moved *Wh*-element matching that of the complement the verb takes ('know' can take a noun phrase); (62) is a case of exclamation with the *Wh*-phrase displaced to the front, and (63) is an idiosyncratic interrogative with a complex *Wh*-adjunct 'how come', which is not displaced.

It is quite evident that the rules will differ in most of the cases here. But how do we know that these rules will differ? As the matter is about the mental representation involved, the rules will have to vary in mental representation such that the rules thus cognized will account for the systematicity in the patterns of *Wh*-movement. This is an intelligibly valid condition. But then how can such rules be a part of the cognized system of rules which is not an intentional object of a person's knowledge of grammar thus construed? Suppose that the rules R1 … R5 are, as demanded, mentally represented at a non-intentional level. Now if they are so represented in the mind, the rules must be represented or individuated in the mind in terms of the *exact nature* of the (semantic) dependency between the *Wh*-element and the gap where the *Wh*-element is supposed to be interpreted. Thus, for example, the exact nature of the (semantic) dependency between the *Wh*-element and the gap in examples like (58)–(59) involves a dependency between the displaced *Wh*-element and the gap which is the position of one of the arguments of the verb with the resulting interpretation of the sentences as questions. Similarly, the rule R2 also requires a dependency between the displaced *Wh*-element and the gap that hosts one of the arguments of the verb with the resulting structure of an interrogative owing to the verb 'wonder', which takes interrogative CPs; but the interpretation of the sentence is not that of a normal question. The rule R3 involves a dependency between the displaced *Wh*-element and the gap but with no accompanying interpretation of an interrogative, whereas both R4 and R5 have a commonality in the interpretation that incorporates an element of surprise or expectations exceeded or simply not matched. However, R4 and R5 differ in that the former is not an interrogative but involves the displacement of a *Wh*-element while the latter does not involve displacement (see Collins 1991), although both do not involve auxiliary inversion, which is typical of interrogatives. Recall that all the rules R1 ... R5 *essentially* exploit a single *Wh*-form–meaning mismatch with a view to eliminating other (possible) form–meaning mismatches involving categorical features of *Wh*-forms (present elsewhere) but with no semantically viable content.

Coming back to the point of the discussion, we must say that if R1 ... R5 are mentally represented at a non-intentional level, the rules must be represented *and* individuated in the mind in terms of the *exact nature* of the (semantic) dependency between the *Wh*-element and the gap. How is this possible? After all, all these interpretations of form and meaning are not injected inside the rules. It is equally preposterous to say that the entire mind working out interpretations is pushed inside the rules. Here is a possibility. We say that the mind as a whole is not injected into the rules; rather, the relevant interpretative generalizations come to be instantiated as part of the rules in connection with the maturational growth of UG as the instantiation of I-language comes to be grounded in the language faculty. And hence these interpretative generalizations become embodied in the appropriate form of the rules represented in the mind. There are two crippling problems with this possibility thus presented.

First, the Minimalist architecture of the language faculty places the C-I interface right at the periphery where the products of narrow syntax become available for conceptual and intentional elaboration and are thereby interpreted – and if so, there is no way this is possible. On the one hand, interpretative generalizations are embodied in rules which operate in virtue of Merge, AGREE and other global and local constraints, and on the other hand, operations such as Merge, AGREE and other global and local constraints operate with such rules within the confinement of narrow syntax without any access to and hence without any intermittent intrusion into the C-I system. This is inconsistent at best. However embodied in the rules interpretative generalizations are, such rules clearly obviate the necessity of postulating the C-I interface, the operation of which hovers all over and thus permeates every operation and constraint of grammar. This is certainly not the way the Minimalist architecture is assumed to operate. More seriously, this will undermine the very character of formally driven linguistic computation which is not supposed to be sensitive to matters of interpretation and supposedly abstracts away from psychological mechanisms the residue of which is now implicit in the system of rules which is also believed to abstract away from those psychological mechanisms (this issue deserves a far more detailed engagement and so will be taken up in Chapter 4, which discusses the relation of language to computation). In fact, under this conceptualization no rules with embodied interpretative generalizations can apply to the formation of new sentences. This is because the formation of new sentences will require the relevant rules to identify and individuate the relevant interpretative generalization (that applies to the displacement of *Wh*-elements) *online* in the mind rather than offline for each new case, for any sentence may have an arbitrarily long dependency between a *Wh*-element and the gap with many potential *Wh*-elements (consider, for example, a sentence like 'Who knows where John saw what?'), and any interpretative generalization however embodied in rules cannot at all determine the exact dependency between a specific *Wh*-element and the gap where it is interpreted. The *very act* of identifying, individuating and determining each new dependency between a specific *Wh*-element and the gap where it is interpreted is itself intentional, and thus pulls the mind into it. Worse than that is the fact that each such type of dependency reserved for each type of rule (say, R1) has to be differentiated from other types. If it were not so, R1 … R5 will all be indistinguishable from one another. But figuring out how they could differ cannot also be determined by interpretative generalizations, however embodied in rules.

Second, the other problem is also severe. Having at least one interpretative generalization for each rule will be extremely cumbersome for the system of rules, however represented in the mind. So for example, having just 20 interpretative generalizations for rules for all different kinds of *Wh*-movements in English will lead to 20! possible ways of permutations of the interpretative generalizations given the fact that we form sentences of mixed types as well (as in 'Either I wonder who John wants to meet or I know what he likes to eat or how come he has shaved himself?'). Many such permutations would be possible. Then consider what the figure would be for, say, 100 interpretative generalizations for rules; it would give us 100! possible permutations. The human brain does not have any space for all of these possibilities. There is no way we can restrict the operation of a rule to a single clause beforehand in order to allow it to work its way step by step through a number of clauses. It should be noted that as far as the nature of the system of rules at the non-intentional level of the mind is concerned, we cannot stipulate this from outside. To put it another way deliberately phrased in the intentional language, the non-intentional level of the mind does not simply 'care' what our stipulation is or would be or might have been. From another perspective too, interpretative generalizations for rules will be formidably unwieldy and hence intractable. One may also consider the interaction of the rules for *Wh*-movements with other rules for countless other constructions. Let us say we have $n = 10$ interpretative generalizations for rules for *Wh*-movements, and $m = 30$ other interpretative generalizations for other kinds of rules. In that case we can potentially have $2^{m \times n}$ possible ways of interaction, which is certainly a formidably large number ('×' indicates multiplication, and the base is 2 because there exist two values ('+' and '−') for each way of interaction). Once again, there is no obvious reason why the human mind should have such a horrendous number of interpretative generalizations embodied in rules. All that the mind can do is engage in interpretation online without there being anything like interpretative generalization embodied in rules which are represented in the mind non-intentionally. The same arguments also suffice for any possibility based on the evolution (cumulatively gradual or punctuated or saltational or otherwise) of the embodiment of interpretative generalizations in forms of rules.

In all, there does not appear to be any way the rules R1 ... R5 are mentally represented non-intentionally without at the same time the process of interpretation of the mind kicking in. It should be borne in mind that the mind's interpretation – whether conscious or unconscious – involves cognitive processes and is thus ultimately constituted by psychological processes and mechanisms of inferences, thoughts, beliefs, conceptualization and so on, regardless of whether they are reducible to something non-intentional or not. Enforcing a non-intentional kind of mental representation of rules to the exclusion of the mind's interpretation must get entangled in inconsistencies, contradictions and paradoxes of immeasurable magnitude. As soon as we push the cognitive process of interpretation out of the system of rules mentally represented in such a manner that the cognitive process of interpretation cannot be intentionally oriented toward the system of rules mentally represented, any distinction whatsoever between the rules R1 ... R5 will be obliterated, and there would not remain any principled ground for differentiating one rule from another because all the rules (except R5) commonly involve the displacement of *Wh*-elements the exact form of which involves an independent *type* of semantic dependency between the displaced *Wh*-element and the gap. This is both conceptually absurd and empirically incoherent. On the other hand, if we factor in the cognitive process of interpretation, there is no sense in which the rules R1 ... R5 can be mentally represented *nonintentionally* without any concomitant contradiction. Perhaps there is more we can say about such problems. Let us move ahead to see some more cases.

(64) The instructions are easy to follow__.

(65) This dog is being difficult to handle__.

(66) *It is being difficult to handle this dog.

(67) That he is aggressive is hard to swallow__.

(68) *It is hard to swallow that he is aggressive.

(69) John certainly is__and Mary may well be__easy to irritate.

(70) This book is hard to put down__ without finishing__.

The examples in (64)–(70) are all cases of what is called *tough*-movement. It is so called because of some idiosyncratic properties associated with such constructions, as was observed by Chomsky (1977) in sentences such as 'John is easy/tough to please__'. The essential properties are: (i) The noun phrase ('John', for example) is interpreted in the gap indicated but this has the properties of displacement of both an argument (a case of what is called *A-movement*) and a non-argument (a case of what is called *A-bar movement*, also mentioned in Chapter 2). Since 'John' is interpreted as the object of 'please', it is an argument of 'please' displaced to the front; but this is problematic because it would license a long dependency which will violate the *locality* of movement/displacement (a version of what is called the *Subjacency Principle*) – which favours smaller dependencies between the gap and the displaced item, as was discussed in Chapter 2. Because of this it was proposed that there must be a movement of a null operator from the object position of the embedded verb ('please', for example) to the complementizer phrase (CP) of the embedded clause (...[$_{CP}$ Op$_i$ [$_{TP/IP}$ to V t$_i$]]). (ii) From a different perspective, this invites another dilemma because the matrix subject ('John') has to be co-indexed with the *trace* of the object (t$_i$), and thus they can be bound – which violates Principle C of *binding principles* (which requires referential expressions to be free) since the trace is like a *Wh*-trace because of the operator movement and thus has the features of a referential expression (R-expression) (the trace is non-anaphoric and non-pronominal).

Though many of the assumptions of the Government and Binding (GB) framework have since been abandoned, these peculiar properties underscore most of the current approaches to *tough*-movement which roughly oscillate between the direct-insertion-of-the-subject account (which may also postulate a complex non-lexicalized predicate in the form 'easy/tough to V') and a movement account (see Partee 1977;

Nanni 1980; Mulder and den Dikken 1992; Rezac 2006). To see how the entire ensemble of peculiarities of *tough*-movement is sandwiched between these two possibilities, we can focus on examples (66) and (68). These are marshalled to provide evidence against any account of movement of the object to the matrix subject position since (65) and (67) are fine as the corresponding versions of *tough*-constructions of (66) and (68) respectively. Additionally, there are cases where the movement of the object to the matrix subject position cannot account for scope effects of certain quantifiers as in (71)–(72) below.

(71) Nothing is hard for Melvin to lift.

(72) It is hard for Melvin to lift nothing.

As was pointed out by Postal (1974), the sentence (71) has a wide scope reading of the quantifier 'nothing', whereas (72) has a narrow scope reading of the same quantifier. (71) has a paraphrase like 'it is not the case that there is some x such that x is hard for Melvin to lift (everything may be easy for Melvin to lift)' but (71) has a paraphrase like 'there is some x such that it is hard for Melvin not to lift x' (Melvin cannot sit around and it is hard for him to do something else since maybe he has been advised to lift nothing). Similarly, (70) also needs to be accounted for in a manner that treats the parasitic gap (after 'finishing') differently from the gap posited for the operator or from the object of the embedded verb, in that a movement right from the parasitic gap through the intermediate gap to the subject position is unwarranted under this construal. Nevertheless, it is quite clear that displacement of the object of the embedded verb to the matrix subject position is possible in many cases as in (64) and (69). Also, many binding properties demand this. So, for example, the sentence below would violate Principle A of *binding principles* if the matrix subject is not posited to have been displaced.

(73) Pictures of himself$_i$ are hard for John$_i$ to see__.

(74) It is hard for John$_i$ to see pictures of himself$_i$.

The sentence (74) shows how such violation can be circumvented if the noun phrase 'pictures of himself' is interpreted back to its place at LF (an operation of *reconstruction*).

Whatever the advantages and disadvantages of both approaches, the purpose here is not to investigate them. Certainly, both these approaches may well have disjoint effects across the vast swathe of *tough*-movement constructions across languages. What bothers us is the contention that there may be rules for cases like (64)–(74) that are mentally represented non-intentionally. Going along with the variation in the empirical data, we may now suppose that there are in fact two rules R1 and R2 – R1 is for cases with the possibility of displacement/movement, and R2 is for cases involving the surface insertion of the matrix subject. Both rules are mentally represented as part of a system of rules at a non-intentional level of the mind, or rather cognized by native speakers of English. But again how do we know that these are the rules that are mentally represented in the minds of native speakers of English? The answer seems to be straightforward. We have sufficient linguistic evidence that warrants that this must be so; otherwise it would not have been possible for native speakers to generate such sentences with such clear regularity. Above all, that is what explains the competence of native speakers who find substantive differences between the sentences advanced in support of the movement account and those put forward for an account of the surface insertion of the matrix subject. This is well understood. Let us go with this scenario, given this condition. Now if the two rules R1 and R2 for (64)–(74) are mentally represented as part of one's grammatical competence, they will turn out to be indistinguishable from each other, and then by virtue of that, there would be no way for native speakers to discern substantive differences between the sentences advanced in support of the movement account and those put forward for an account of the surface insertion of the matrix subject. How can this be possible? Let us ponder over it for a while. What is it that differentiates R1 from R2? Or rather, what is it about R1 or R2 that makes one distinct from the other? Clearly, no formal syntactic features or features used in syntax will be able to draw the required distinction.[8]

We may try. Let us say in the case of R1 that a bundle of formal features of the noun phrase in question may or may not be present to be pronounced in the object position of the embedded verb, whereas in the case of R2 the bundle of formal features of the noun phrase must be absent in the object position of the embedded verb. If this is the case, this would not prevent anyone from forming sentences like '*There is/ are easy to follow the instructions' or '*There is/are easy to follow__' or even '*There is being difficult to handle__' and many such idiosyncratic and outlandish formations. Now suppose we add another stipulation to save the whole idea. We now say that when (in the case of R1) a bundle of formal features of the noun phrase is not present to be pronounced in the object position of the embedded verb, any bundle of formal features with the appropriate selectional restrictions satisfied must be present in the subject position of the matrix clause, and when a bundle of formal features of the noun phrase is present to be pronounced in the object position of the embedded verb, the subject position of the matrix clause will have 'it'. We also add that when (in the case of R2) the bundle of formal features of the noun phrase is absent in the object position of the embedded verb, the matrix subject may possess any other relevant bundle of formal features with the appropriate selectional restrictions satisfied. Both stipulations are question-begging.

First, what forms the basis of the justification that when (whether in R1 or R2) a bundle of formal features of the noun phrase is not present to be pronounced in the object position of the embedded verb, the matrix subject may possess any bundle of formal features with the appropriate selectional restrictions satisfied? But how on earth would it be possible for the rule to figure out, just with the help of formal features, the appropriateness of the selectional restrictions to be satisfied? Second, the other problem is worse than the first. This stipulation will culminate in the obliteration of a distinction between R1 and R2 because both of them now satisfy and state the same condition – that is, a bundle of formal features of the noun phrase has to be absent in the object position and the subject position of the matrix clause can have any bundle of formal features with the appropriate selectional restrictions satisfied. So we end up with the same problem the stipulation was supposed to solve.

Note that with the additional stipulation the problem with '*There is/ are easy to follow the instructions' looks as if it is solved, but actually it is not. It can be easily checked that the difference between R1 and R2 is *not* between the fact that an expletive 'it' is inserted in a *tough*-predicate frame like '___easy/tough to V Object' and another fact that any appropriate subject should be inserted in a *tough*-predicate frame like '___ easy/tough to V'. If indeed the difference between R1 and R2 boils down to just this, R1 and R2 cannot account for any of the empirical facts in (64)–(74). For example, the rule R1 cannot account for the ungrammaticality of (66) and (68) when juxtaposed with (65) and (67), for all the modified version of R1 says is that there will be an insertion of 'it' in a constructional frame like '___easy/tough to V Object', which cannot explain why (66) and (68), when compared with (65) and (67), are ungrammatical. Similarly, the rule R1 cannot also say why 'The instructions are easy to follow' and 'It is easy to follow the instructions' have a similarity in meaning. On the other hand, the rule R2 cannot especially account for the facts in the pairs (71)–(72) and (73)–(74). It cannot also say why '*To handle this dog is being difficult' is ungrammatical even if it conforms to R2. Therefore, R1 and R2 cannot be formulated with the help of just formal syntactic features, and if so formulated, R1 and R2 will be incapable of accounting for *tough*-predicate constructions across the entire range of the phenomenon in question. Even a unified rule combining aspects of both R1 and R2 will face the same difficulty for the empirical reasons just considered.

The lesson to be driven home is that there appears to be no way the two rules R1 and R2 can be distinguished in the mental representations involved when incorporated as part of the grammatical competence at a non-intentional level, contrary to empirical facts which suggest otherwise. This will also lead to the conclusion that the mentally represented rules as part of the grammatical competence do not have anything to do with what is observed in empirical facts. This conclusion goes against and hence is fiendishly incompatible with the foundations of Generative Grammar. At least, it cannot be something Chomsky (1980, 2007) has so far subscribed to. The other horn of the dilemma is that if we pull the mental process of interpretation into the ambit of the mental representation that constitutes the rules, the rules concerned cease to be cognized by native speakers and hence are not represented in the mind. Again, this is a contradiction – a contradiction entangled in a recalcitrant paradox that cannot be eradicated by means of any stipulations.

To sum up, there does not seem to be any determinate way that rules, when looked at as part of the grammatical competence at a non-intentional level, can be mentally represented. Either they are just not there, or if present, do not comport at all with empirical facts and generalizations. Even if grammatical competence or I-language is posited to be distinct from the psychogrammar or psychological/parsing mechanisms that realize the grammar, any gap, however palpable it may be, between the internalized grammar in the mind and psychological mechanisms that realize it entraps us in vicious cycles of paradoxes and inconsistencies that cannot be solved internally. Consequently, any such relation, however construed, between the internalized grammar and psychological mechanisms that realize it becomes destabilized. The obverse of this is that Devitt's (2006) structure rules or anything of that sort cannot perhaps exist in a reified form when it transpires that in no sense can the mind's interpretation be severed from any linguistic rules whatsoever. Thus, it seems that structure rules cannot govern an independent linguistic reality other than what structure rules, or rather linguistic rules themselves, constitute. That is, there is perhaps no distinction between what governs and what is governed when we say structure rules govern an *independent* linguistic reality. But the entanglements that the relation of realization (obtaining between the internalized grammar and psychological mechanisms that realize it) encompasses certainly do not exhaust the gamut of all possible ways language can be related to the mind. We now turn to the relation of abstraction between language and the mind.

3.2   The abstraction of I-language from psychological mechanisms

Now we shall look into the abstraction that connects the internalized grammar to the psychological mechanisms which the internalized grammar is viewed to abstract away from. Abstraction by way of idealization is useful in (natural) sciences because it helps the scientist to build his/her model of reality, segregating it from noises and unwarranted turbulence in real situations. This is what drove Chomsky (1965) to articulate his theory of I-language that abstracts away not merely from performance factors derived from psychological/parsing mechanisms but also from variations of form and meaning in a speech community which, however, form an object of study for sociolinguists. Ironically, this is what propelled Hymes (1972) to propose the notion of 'communicative competence' which unites both Chomsky's notion of grammatical competence and natural language speakers' knowledge of pragmatic strategies in the niche of contextual settings, norms and speech functions and so on. Chomsky (1980, 1985) has used the analogy of a computer program that abstracts away from hardware operations when characterizing grammatical competence that too abstracts away from how it is realized. A representative quotation from Chomsky (1995) can be provided below.

> A particular language L is an instantiation of the initial state of the cognitive system of the language faculty with options specified. We take L to be a generative procedure that constructs pairs (π, λ) that are interpreted at the articulatory-perceptual (A-P) and conceptual-intentional (C-I) interfaces, respectively, as 'instructions' to the performance systems (p. 219).

These lines quite clearly indicate what kind of abstraction Chomsky requires I-language to have. For Chomsky, a language, or rather I-language, is a generative procedure that generates derivations each of which has the form of a sequence of symbolic elements $(\alpha_1, \alpha_2, \alpha_3, ..., \alpha_n)$ when α_n is a pair (π, λ). This is what is also called a function defined in *intension* rather than in extension. That is, I-language is a generative procedure that defines a function generating sequences of the form $(\alpha_1, \alpha_2, \alpha_3, ..., \alpha_n)$ with α_n being a pair (π, λ) such that π is a PF (Phonological Form) representation and λ is an LF (Logical Form) representation. It is only in this sense in which I-language is supposed to abstract away from psychological/parsing mechanisms that the generative procedure I-language is taken to need only specify a function in intension that maps onto pairs of the kind (π, λ), but how the function in the real world is realized is a different issue altogether. The fundamental operation which is a part of narrow syntax is Merge for constructing syntactic objects of enormous complexity from smaller syntactic objects. Thus, the outputs of Merge can be a part of any α_i in the sequence $(\alpha_1, \alpha_2, \alpha_3, ..., \alpha_n)$. Overall, the idea that a function defined in intension need not specify anything about its implementation in an algorithm or about realization in hardware is a version of what is called *functionalism*. The specific brand of functionalism in the current context is associated with *mentalism* – that is, there are abstract mental objects and operations that can be characterized independent of how they are instantiated in reality. Hence the rules and principles of the generative procedure (which I-language is taken to be) determine properties of sentences in terms of their phonological and semantic structures just like principles of arithmetic determine properties of number. From this perspective, the notion of the determination of properties of sentences by the generative procedure of I-language can be conceived of within the boundaries of what the language faculty allows for. That is, the language faculty constrains what may be taken to be the determination of properties of sentences by the generative procedure of I-language. Given this characterization, it appears that the relation of abstraction between the internalized grammar in the mind and the relevant psychological mechanisms is transparent to the language faculty.

The tantalizing question of how a function that may well define infinite structures formed by recursion can be realized in the mind is a moot point not yet resolved, given that the grammar represented in the mind is finite, but the language generated by the grammar may well be infinite. For example, Neeleman and van de Koot (2010) argue that the internalized grammar may best be characterized at the top level, namely the computational level of Marr's three-level schema. But from this it does not follow that the internalized grammar cannot be characterized at the second level, that is, at the algorithmic level. Nothing that Neeleman and van de Koot have discussed precludes this possibility. This possibility will be explored in greater detail in Chapter 4 in connection with an exploration of the relation between language and computation. However, it is still not clear how and in what ways a stance on grammatical competence that does not prefer to reduce the system of grammatical competence to the performance mechanisms differs from another stance that allows for the exercise of the system of grammatical competence in language processing. Chomsky (1980) does allow for the latter possibility and in doing so, does leave open a scope for ways in which other cognitive systems might interface with the system of grammatical competence. This can be observed in Chomsky (2005, 2007) as well. What is noticeably recurrent in current developments of Generative Grammar is that every operation beyond *external* Merge (*external* Merge simply builds syntactic objects from outside whereas *internal* Merge (or Move) merges syntactic objects from inside the syntactic object already constructed) has to be motivated by requirements posed by the interface systems, namely the A-P interface linked to PF and the C-I interface linked to LF. One may wonder whether this move does not actually risk pushing the system of grammatical competence into the domain of cognitive systems that mediate processing of language in real time. This possibility has indeed been entertained (Golumbia 2010). However, it is perhaps a mistake to entertain such a supposition. The only way the motivation of any operation beyond *external* Merge by means of requirements posed by the interface systems is cashed out is in terms of *interpretability* of features. Chomsky (1995) has contended that categorical features of verbs and nouns (such as verbal features of verbs, and nominal and person–number–gender features (φ-features) of nouns) are interpretable at the C-I interface but case features of verbs and nouns, person–number–gender features (φ-features) of verbs are not. Though the notion of interpretability that drives *internal* Merge has been reconceptualized in different ways (see for details, Pesetsky and Torrego 2004), the underlying logic remains the same – any feature that is *un*interpretable needs to be eliminated to fulfil the requirements of the interface systems which thus need to be served at every stage of syntactic operations.

However, it can be easily shown that this notion of interpretability barely captures anything cognitive systems that mediate language processing are engaged in. One of the reasons is that feature *un*interpretability can be arbitrarily defined for any operation beyond *external* Merge in a whimsical and patently wishful manner. For example, if we have functional categories such as T(tense), C(complementizer), F(focus), V(verb), A(aspect) and so on, we can easily say any syntactic item that undergoes *internal* Merge in a certain case will have an *un*interpretable feature of one of those functional categories, assuming of course that this depends on the exact target phrase for displacement/movement headed by any of these categories (for instance, a noun phrase can have an *un*interpretable A(aspect)-feature if the target is an aspectual phrase). Thus, if we have, say, 30 such categories, the number of possibilities of combinations of interpretable and *un*interpretable features amounts to 2^{30}. This is indeed a concern given the kind of work found in Cinque (1999). This simply suggests that we can at least wishfully satisfy our desire of defining interpretable and uninterpretable features in billions of ways as long as we need to capture the 'why' of syntactic operations in diverse ranges of linguistic constructions. Whether the issue of inter-pretability versus *un*interpretability is really something that concerns the mentally represented grammar or I-language may ultimately have nothing to do with the operations and structures of cognitive systems that engage in language processing. It has indeed been criticized by Van Valin (2003) on the grounds that many of the *un*interpretable fea-tures such as person–number–gender features (φ-features) of verbs, like categorical features, are actually interpretable features in that they are capable of contributing to semantic interpretation in some languages such as Lakhota (which displays no movement) and Mam (which apparently has movement). Therefore, we cannot help but contend that there does not perhaps exist any coherent notion of interpretability/ *un*interpretability that can be cashed out in terms of the requirements constituted by the operations and structures of cognitive systems, since the very notion of what is interpretable in the language faculty and in what ways will always plunge the entire system into contradictions, paradoxes and puzzles of unimaginable proportion, as we have already observed. On the other hand, if languages have interpretable features with concomitant movement, or conversely, *un*interpretable features without movement, to follow the lines of reasoning of Van Valin (2003), the notion of interpretability/*un*interpretability turns out to be a non-issue. Maybe it is a kind of straw man that is exploited by theoretical linguists in order to argue for impetuously crafted accounts. More importantly, the discussion pursued in section 3.1 gives us no justification for maintaining that cognitive processes of interpretation are transparent within the bounds of the language faculty in a coherent and consistent manner.

The point of the discussion in the earlier paragraph is to uncover the fact that the system of grammatical competence does *indeed* abstract away from psychological/parsing mechanisms and perhaps does so completely. Moreover, the system of grammatical competence does *not* appear to meet conditions posed by the cognitive systems that engage in language processing, and more significantly, it is cut off and hence insulated from the cognitive systems. If this is so, the generative procedure of I-language cannot make any contact with and reference to conditions posed by the interfacing cognitive systems that engage in language processing. The reflex of this implication may help us formulate in a better manner the problem of how to state in the specification of the finite grammar in the mind sufficient conditions for generating infinite languages. To be clearer, an abstraction different in kind can be found in Cognitive Grammar (Lakoff 1987; Langacker 1987, 1999) in which the system of grammar is considered to be a symbolic system of (syntactic–phonological) units that are mapped onto representations of conceptualizations. And such conceptualizations are grounded in the sensory–motor and perceptual processes. This leads to the view that conceptualizations are fundamentally and formally derived from aspects of perception, memory and categorization. Under such a view, rules and principles of the symbolic system of grammar are conceptual schemas which have a sufficiently general character in the rest of cognition. Hence the system of conceptualized schemas lies at an abstract level different from the one at which such schemas may be used in real time. Thus this constitutes a view of *domain-general* abstraction of what is conceptualized *from* what really is – a rough analogue of the competence–performance distinction. At this juncture, we may take note of Gross's (2005) caution, especially when he prefers to distinguish what is conceptualized in the mind from what really is/exists, while he argues that neither of these two should necessarily accord with one's reflective conception of the object concerned. So if we are concerned about the object called language, what is conceptualized or represented in the mind (the grammar or the symbolic system mentally represented) differs from what really is/exists (the language we utter and comprehend), but whether this may align with one's (pre)reflective conception of language is a question that we cannot decide by means of our *reflectively* formulated stipulations as well. This ultimately gets us moving in a self-terminating circularity. In order to see how one's (pre)reflective conception of language seeps into the model of what is conceptualized or represented in the mind only to vitiate it at the core, let us look at how the generative procedure of I-language works.

The generative procedure of I-language starts with an array of lexical choices and maps it to the pair (π, λ). The task of the array is to display what the lexical items are and how many times each of them is selected.

The concept of an array of lexical choices has been telescoped into what Chomsky (1995) has called Numeration, which is a set of lexical items indexed and is characterized as a set of pairs (LI, i) when LI is a lexical item and i is an index. Thus the sequence $(\alpha_1, \alpha_2, \alpha_3, ..., \alpha_n)$ will actually look like (<N, ϕ>, <N, D_1>, ..., < ϕ, D_n>) when D_n is a pair (π, λ). What this means is that N (Numeration) will start with a selection of lexical items and decrement the index of the lexical items until it becomes zero; derivations $D_1...D_n$ will operate on the lexical items selected to build syntactic objects which can further be taken for the construction of larger structures. This will continue until we reach < ϕ, D_n> when N will be empty, and from the pair (π, λ) the PF representation π will be Spelt-Out to PF and the LF representation λ to LF. Essentially, the mapping is thus from N to pairs of the form (π, λ) with a compatibility between π and λ expressed by N. With this in the backdrop, let us see how we can derive some constructions of nested and crossed dependencies. But before we do that, we can have an idea of what nested and crossed dependencies are. Recall the discussion in section 2.1.3 where the notion of *recursion* in a linguistic construction that builds upon itself was introduced. We encountered the following sentences repeated here as (75) and (76).

(75) A man that girls that boys that neighbours look at like love hates funky dresses.

(76) I know a man who waters plants that grow right in the middle of the garden that is located behind the house ...

Sentence (75) exhibits nested dependency in that if one draws a line connecting the phrases in each dependency link, all these lines will be nested within one another, as shown in Figure 3.3.

But sentence (76) displays adjacent dependency because of the linear progression of dependencies shown in Figure 3.4.

Sentences (77) and (78) are also similar to (75) as they have a similar kind of nested dependency.

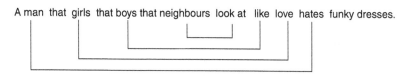

Figure 3.3   Nested dependency

Figure 3.4 Adjacent dependency

(77) The huge tree the old man everybody loves takes care of overlooks our house.

(78) This is the piano that I wonder which piece of music to play__on__.

Nested dependencies have been observed to be easier to process than sentences of crossed dependency which are rarer across languages (Christiansen and MacDonald 2009). The following sentence from Dutch is an example of crossed dependency (the numbers indicate the dependency between a noun phrase and a verb phrase).

(79) de mannen hebben$_1$ Hans$_2$ Jeanine$_3$ de paarden helpen$_1$ leren$_2$. voeren$_3$
the man   have   Hans Jeanine the horses helped teach feed
'The men helped Hans teach Jeanine to feed the horses.'

(Christiansen and MacDonald 2009)

Now we can check how a mapping from N to pairs of the form (π, λ) can derive sentences of the kind (75)–(79). Suppose that the sentence to be generated is (77). Lexical items with the relevant features and other relevant functional heads like T, C, light verb head v, etc. will be picked up. One may now observe that there is nothing that can prevent an *infinite* number of LIs from being chosen *infinite* times such that the procedure that underlies N will never stop. And hence the sentence (77) will never be derived! It should be noted that the rationale behind the selection of sentences of the type (75)–(79) is that the relevant problem sentences of nested and crossed dependency give rise to can also be phrased otherwise, although the problem pointed out is general enough, perhaps across the entire range of linguistic constructions. Since sentences like (75)–(79) all come under the type NP^n VP^n, we can also say that there is nothing that can prevent an infinite number of nouns (that will add up to an *infinite* number of NPs), or equivalently, an *infinite* number of verbs (that will add up to an infinite number of VPs) from being chosen in N such that the procedure underlying N never stops. Why so? Recall that the system of grammatical competence is not an intentional object of knowing and believing. Nor can the system be positioned at the intentional level of the mind as we do not access I-language intentionally. Apart from that, I-language is at an abstract level that idealizes away from performance mechanisms and hence is beyond space and time as we are reminded that the operations of the language faculty do not occur in real time (Chomsky 1995). If so, then what can really stop the procedure underlying N from indefinitely continuing the task of 'choosing' lexical items? As things stand, there is in fact none. The problem also remains in the derivation-by-*phase* model of Minimalism having small local domains of derivational operations called *phases* (Chomsky 2001). The reason is that N (Numeration) – as it is related to lexical choice that precedes the operation Select, which selects lexical items from N – is pre-derivational, inasmuch as the mapping is from N to pairs of the form (π, λ), and hence this ensues from what is chosen and how. The warning that something would not count as a derivation unless all indices are reduced to zero does not apply here, since if the task involving lexical choice can never be complete, the task of reducing indices to zero does not arise at all. The warning is confined to the *selection* from N, not to N itself. On the contrary, if this warning is reinforced on lexical choice itself, no sentence can ever be derived because any arbitrary number of lexical choices the indices of which are reduced to zero thereby reduces to nonentity, and as a consequence, the language faculty cannot generate any sentence at all! At this stage there cannot be any way of resolving the problem by merely partitioning N into smaller subsets, namely sub-Numerations or sub-arrays, because it would be easy to state the same problem at any level of the division of N, or we can have an infinite number of sub-arrays. Additionally, there is no scope for any stipulation that N must be finite since we are dealing with a model of competence rather than with a model of performance.

Similar to earlier puzzles and paradoxes, the ensuing paradox in the present context is that if one gives a description of grammatical competence at a non-intentional level of the mind beyond space and time, one cannot in any way clamp down any stipulation that N must be finite without being inconsistent. On the other hand, if one adverts to *intentional* cognitive processes to constrain lexical choice, the model of competence in the language faculty which is, by fiat, specified at a non-intentional level of the mind beyond space and time becomes intentional! A contradiction again! And we hope that there is no homunculus inside the language faculty that makes the lexical choice possible. Worse than that, it is easy to state that the problem of determining whether a procedure underlying N ever stops is a version of the *halting problem* – which says that there exists no algorithm that, given a machine M and an input *x*, can decide whether or not M halts on the input *x* (Goldreich 2008). Similarly, we can say that there is no algorithm that, given the generative procedure of the language faculty and N (or a set of sub-Numerations/sub-arrays), can decide whether or not the generative procedure of the language faculty halts on N (or on a set of sub-Numerations/sub-arrays). And the proof of this would follow quite straightforwardly by assuming there exists no algorithm that decides whether or not the generative procedure of the language faculty halts on *itself* as an input. Thus the proof will be similar to the one provided by Alan Turing himself for the *halting problem*. The consequences of this insight will be explored more deeply in Chapter 4.

The upshot of the whole thing is that the paradoxes and inconsistencies surround the generative procedure of the language faculty looked at from an abstract level, that is, the grammar represented in the mind. We do not trespass on the extension of language which, for Chomsky, is a derivative property and hence uninteresting. Plus we can continue to circumvent the problem of stepping into the arena of E-languages and talk about the generative procedure of the faculty of language. The paradoxes and inconsistencies revolving around the generative procedure of the faculty of language thus remain unresolved and unaffected whatever the take on E-languages is. We shall conclude by looking at some further puzzles and paradoxes. To show how they emerge, we will look at the phenomenon of raising/control. The phenomenon of raising/control has been one of the hottest topics in natural language syntax in the tradition of Generative Grammar. The difference between raising and control is indicative of the kind of form–meaning divergence discussed in Chapter 2. It is one of the most remarkable properties of natural languages rather than artificial languages like Pascal or C. Hence the difference between raising and control serves as a useful diagnostic for detecting displacement in natural language. Here are some cases.

(80) John seems to be worried about his wedding.

(81) Ray is likely to retire soon.

(82) Steve believed the guy to have justified his case.

(83) She wants Bill to wait for her.

(84) The professor proved him to be wrong.

(85) John tried to flee to France to pursue his passion for art.

(86) Mary loves playing baseball.

(87) We hope strongly enough to overcome the obstacles in all possible ways.

(88) They convinced the doctor to release him from the hospital.

(89) We have asked him to step down.

The examples (80)–(84) are cases of raising whereas (85)–(89) are examples of control. The most significant and essential criterion that helps make out the relevant difference is that in all cases of raising, an argument (whether the external or the internal argument) of the embedded predicate is not seen where it is theta-marked (or interpreted) but appears elsewhere in the matrix clause (either in the subject position or in the object position). Thus, (80)–(81) are cases of subject raising in that the subject 'John'/'Ray' is interpreted in the theta position of the embedded predicate '__be worried about his wedding'/ '__retire soon' but in fact appears in the matrix clause. (82)–(84) are cases of object raising as the object has been displaced from where it should be interpreted. Hence in (82) it is not the guy who Steve believed; rather, the object of Steve's belief is the proposition that the guy (has) justified his case. Similar considerations hold for (83)–(84). On the other hand, (85)–(89) exemplify typical features of control since the relevant argument of the embedded predicate is interpreted where they should be but this interpretation via theta-marking of the relevant argument is distributed across all the embedded predicates along with the matrix predicate. It looks as if there is a kind of sharing of the same argument by many predicates across clause boundaries. Because of this property of control, a null argument PRO is used and indexed with the (noun) phrase that is overtly present. Thus, in (85) 'John' is an external argument of 'try', 'flee' and 'pursue'; in (86) 'Mary' is the external argument of both 'love' and 'play', and in (87) 'we' is an external argument of 'hope' and 'overcome'. The examples (88)–(89) illustrate object control, as 'the doctor' in (88) is also the external argument of 'release', and 'him' in (89) is also an external argument of 'step down'.

There has been a lot of debate on whether or not control involves movement/displacement just like raising (Culicover and Jackendoff 2003; Boeckx and Hornstein 2004; Landau 2008; Ndayiragije 2012). Essentially, it appears that the debate centres on the question of which option out of the operations AGREE and (internal) Merge is conceptually viable and more empirically accurate. Whichever turns out to be ultimately correct, our focus is different. What is essential is that displacement in whatever way triggers form–meaning divergence whereas any non-movement mechanism is not expected to do so. AGREE in the Minimalist conception of the language faculty is an operation that is crucial for the valuation and subsequent deletion of *un*interpretable features; hence AGREE is also causally responsible for *internal* Merge. Though the domains of the two operations may largely overlap, they may perhaps be disjoint in many cases as AGREE is also posited to be required for agreement/concord in natural language, irrespective of whether or not this involves, through *internal* Merge, displacement. The interesting point to note is that control is also, at least in part, a case of form–meaning divergence due to the sharing of an argument among many predicates, while raising is certainly a case of form–meaning divergence to the fullest extent. Natural languages afford to have many possible ways in which form and meaning can converge or even diverge. The entire Generative apparatus has been developed with this in mind, and in fact, it is form–meaning divergence that is, more uniquely than anything else, responsible for the technology the Generative apparatus possesses. Therefore, it has been maintained that the externalization of the outputs of syntax through PF stands in an asymmetric relation to the operation of transfer of what is shipped off to LF. That is, displacement (or form–meaning divergence) in natural language is thought to be necessary because of the requirements of the A-P interface that cannot read all copies of a form that undergoes movement, whereas on the semantic side the C-I interface needs the features of all copies of the form undergoing movement (Chomsky 2007). This is exactly the reason why the derivation-by-phase model looks like a mechanism that ships out the incremental outputs of syntax to PF in a sequence of phases, with LF remaining uniformly constant because form–meaning divergence is now reducible to PF differences. This is another way of stating how the language faculty meets the conditions posed by the interfaces. Figure 3.5 shows the phase-theoretic model in bare outline.

If this is indeed the case, this presents us with further puzzles and paradoxes. If the copies of a form undergoing movement are to be deleted except the one to be available at PF (because there has to be one copy of the item that was inserted in Numeration), the language faculty has to 'know' which one. How do we make sure that the language faculty 'knows' what the relevant copy is? There has been independent work on *chain* (the sequence of all copies) formation and *chain* reduction for the linearization of the outputs of syntax at PF that targets the highest copy (see for details, Nunes 2004). However, this cannot determine

Lexicon

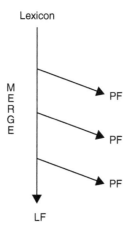

Figure 3.5 The phase-theoretic model of the Minimalist architecture of the language faculty

which copy is the relevant one and which one is not in the possible range of variations of form–meaning coupling. To see what the problem is, let us have a general schema for raising/control examples. Suppose we assume that in both raising and control we need a (noun) phrase, say X, the features of which are displaced to the matrix clause, regardless of whether any intermediate X is a PRO or not. This is an assumption that remains neutral with respect to a preference between a movement-based account and an AGREE-based account.

(90) $[_{CP\ matrix} \cdots [_{TP\ matrix} \cdots FF\text{-}X_i \cdots [_{TP1} \cdots FF\text{-}X_i \cdots [_{TPn} \cdots FF\text{-}X_i \cdots]]]]$

The schema (90) underlines what is common in both raising and control. Now even if PF uniformly erases all other Xs except the topmost one, what remains important for LF is that all the Xs in cases of control are theta-marked whereas only the last X is theta-marked in the case of raising. But this barely scratches the surface. Let us consider the following examples as well.

(91) John proposed to Mary to help each other.

(92) Ann and I have decided to marry ourselves to one another.

(93) Ann and I have decided to marry one another to ourselves.

The example (91) is a case of split control as 'John' and 'Mary' together bind the reciprocal 'each other' (Landou 2008), whereas (92)–(93) are cases which show that the theta-roles of the object of 'marry' are still present and cannot be nullified by any relation that obtains between the controller and the controlee even if it may be argued that the noun phrase 'Ann and I' has been displaced to the front absorbing the theta-roles of the predicate 'marry' (Uriagereka 2012). More specifically, (92)–(93) pose problems for a binding to obtain between 'Ann and I' with both the reflexive 'ourselves' and the reciprocal 'one another', and that too in an interchangeable manner. What these examples show is that we need to have an account of how the relevant anaphors in (91)–(93) are bound, regardless of whether the controller is displaced or not. As shown above, this goes beyond just a statement of the Theta Criterion, in accordance with which the relevant external and internal theta-roles are assigned to (noun) phrases. Aside from this, there are other properties of control/raising that reveal the intricacies that we are concerned about. The pertinent examples (95)–(96) are taken from Postal (2004).

(94) (a) There are likely to be some volunteers in the hall.
     (b) *There hope to be to be some volunteers in the hall.

(95) (a) They believe close tabs to have been kept/*placed/*maintained on her movements.
     (b) *They convinced close tabs to be kept/placed/maintained on her movements.

(96) (a) Something$_1$ is the matter with my transmission, but that sort of thing/*it$_1$ is not the matter with his.
     (b) *Something/Lots of things can be the matter with your transmission without being the matter with mine.
     (c) Something/Lots of things/Nothing seem(s) to be the matter with your transmission.

The examples (94)–(95) show that cases of control are not amenable to expletive insertion and also incompatible with idiomatic chunks, as in (94b)–(95b), while examples of raising are not (94a)–(95a). Interestingly, the examples in (96) show that control (in 96b) is resistant to what Postal (2004) calls *anti-pronominal contexts*, which bar pronouns; but raising freely allows for it (96c). Postal (2004) argues that raising leaves a null weak definite pronoun in the gap from where the relevant item is displaced but control may not because some pronominal (PRO) as a controlee may already be present in the embedded predicate. If this is so, it is not clear whether control involves movement/displacement in the sense discussed above.

But the question we wanted to ask is different. How does the language faculty meet the conditions of the interfaces (the A-P and C-I interfaces) while it has a rule or a set of rules for control/raising represented? The paradox that emanates from both these demands is that if the language faculty meets the conditions of the interfaces (A-P and C-I interfaces), a rule or a set of rules for control/raising cannot be represented, or conversely, if a rule or a set of rules for control/raising is represented in the language faculty, the language faculty cannot at the same time meet the conditions of the interfaces (A-P and C-I interfaces). Let us see why this is so.

First, suppose that the language faculty meets the conditions of the interfaces (the A-P and C-I interfaces) as described. All that the language faculty has to make sure is that a legible PF representation goes to PF so that the legible PF representation can be 'read' by the A-P interface, and also that a legible LF representation goes to LF so that the legible LF representation is 'readable' at the C-I interface. This is ensured by what is called *Full Interpretation*. Note that the language faculty, under this scenario, satisfies the conditions that the interfaces present just as every CPU (central processing unit) manufactured meets the conditions posed by the hardware settings which obtain in the real context of integration in the motherboard in a desktop computer or a laptop. The language faculty thus does not interact with the interfaces in real time; it merely fulfils the conditions they pose in any outputs it generates. If so, no rule(s) for control/raising whatsoever can be represented in the language faculty in that any rule(s) for control/raising has(have) to factor in and continuously make reference to interpretations of arguments and their relation to one another across clause boundaries, and of idioms and non-arguments (expletives), and this requirement is banned because the language faculty does not interact with the interfaces in real time, nor is it an object of any intentional mode (believing, for example). Besides, there is no way the language faculty can store any micro-rules for such interpretations in specific cases of linguistic phenomena. This is implausible not merely because the order of magnitude of a collection of such micro-rules will exceed what human brains are capable of representing (also demonstrated in section 3.1), but also because we shall need, for any relevant set of interpretative micro-rules, another set of rules and so on ad infinitum. Further, one cannot even say that they are all genetically acquired by humans, simply because the human genome cannot encode specific interpretative rules for control/raising just as it cannot encode specific rules for walking on the moon or over a mountainous region even though biped walking in humans is genetically encoded. Likewise, we can say that a CPU manufactured for small devices cannot encode any specific rules/principles for interactions of different operations within a tablet or a pad or a netbook, even though it is designed in such a manner that it fulfils the conditions of integration in any of those digital devices.

Second, the second part of the paradox derives from the conditional: if a rule or a set of rules for control/raising is represented in the language faculty, the language faculty cannot at the same time meet the conditions of the interfaces (A-P and C-I interfaces). Imagine that a rule or a set of rules for control/raising is represented in the language faculty as desired. If the rules are so represented, they need to interact with the C-I interface, and such interaction requires active engagement with the C-I interface like any set of rules, if there is any, for mapping one set of visual representations onto another requires an active engagement with the visual system as a whole within which inputs and the outputs of such mapping are represented. But the language faculty, as it is conceived in the Minimalist framework, cannot do this precisely because the generative procedure of the language faculty exists beyond space and time and hence merely specifies legible PF and LF representations but does not engage in any online interpretation of such representations with the interfaces. The phase-theoretic model in fact exhibits this more clearly in the operations that occur in each phase. There are three phases, namely the DP (determiner phrase), vP (light verb phrase) and CP (complementizer phrase) each of which performs some syntactic operations locally and then sends off the PF and LF representations to PF and LF respectively; whatever moves over to the next phase to get involved in the operations of the next phase does so by shifting to the *edge* (usually the SPECIFIER of a phrase) of that phase first. Thus the series of three phases can be conceived of as a sequence of cycles of operations that map N (or rather sub-Ns) to the pairs <PF, LF> cyclically. There is no backtracking or global interpenetration of cycles, which would botch up the cyclicity of syntactic operations. Therefore, in no sense can the language faculty access the C-I interface across the entire phasal space CP–vP–DP, *even* in the logically incompatible space of the generative procedure of the language faculty and the actively operational mind juxtaposed. In all, without inviting a self-defeating contradiction, the language faculty cannot simultaneously meet the conditions of the interfaces and have rules for control/raising mentally represented.

3.3 Summary

In sum, the relation of abstraction of I-language from, and the relation of realization of the language faculty in, psychological/parsing mechanisms are fraught with innumerable inconsistencies, puzzles and paradoxes that seem to eat into the entire bedrock of Generative Grammar along with the Minimalist version of the language faculty. But contrary to this, we as language users succeed in language acquisition, representation and expression of linguistic thoughts, and also in language use because the language faculty, whatever it turns out to be, makes this viable. At this stage, what if we say that it is computation that is the missing link which can perhaps resolve the puzzles and paradoxes? It is a hope that many linguists possess. We shall look into this possibility too as we turn to Chapter 4.

4
How Language Relates to Computation

Language has a way of folding itself in representations of form and meaning which can be sequenced, stored, compared, altered and thus manipulated. And it is computation that may well underlie and hence underpin such operations. For the simple reason that linguistic representations have to be combined and also altered to build larger and larger structures, we need an operation that does this job, that is, an operation that manipulates representations of form and meaning in different sorts of ways the contributions of which are relevant to the construction of linguistic structures. It is this role that computation takes up. It is computation that assumes utmost significance when we require operations on representations of form and meaning to build linguistic structures in consonance with all constraints that apply to relations of linguistic form and meaning. However, it needs to be emphasized that such operations may obtain either in digital computers that we use in our everyday life or in human brains. And a lot, in fact, depends on where we believe linguistic operations can obtain, as any choice that we exert ourselves to make concerning this matter has wider ramifications for the way language really works. One obvious way of having computational operations apply to representations of form and meaning is to build tools for the processing of natural language(s) in computers. That is what we do in the field of computational linguistics which lies on the border between linguistics and computer science. But there is a lot more to talk about another way computational operations can manipulate representations of form and meaning, that is, if we believe that computational operations on representations of form and meaning hold right in the theatre of the human mind. And this brings with it a constellation of assumptions centred on the relationship between language and the human mind. Additionally, this also carries a bit of ontological baggage that clouds more than it lays bare what it tells us about the domain which language is supposed to be true of.

We have seen in Chapter 3 that the relationship between language and the mind is impregnated with certain puzzles and inconsistencies intrinsic to the very relationship, however construed. Thus, if we hold that computational operations on representations of form and meaning obtain in human brains, this way of understanding the system of rules and constraints that guide the construction of linguistic structures not merely extends the domain of computation from inert systems to natural living systems, but also purports to ground language, or rather the system of linguistic representations, rules and constraints, in mental operations which alone are not sufficient to specify the form of relations between linguistic representations and sets of rules and constraints. The supposition that mental operations – whatever they turn out to be in reality – are such as to perform their specific functions on linguistic representations of form and meaning thus does not appear to say everything of significance and explanatory value that we can say about cognitive operations. We fall into such a situation that we feel we need to say something more substantial than the trivial statement that cognitive operations operate on linguistic representations. So we come up with the aphorism that cognitive operations on linguistic representations are computations. Even if this does not certainly exhaust the compass of all that is cognitive, this is supposed to capture a lot about how the mind works. Hence this has formed the bedrock of what is often called the *computational theory of mind* (Fodor 1975; Pylyshyn 1984; Chalmers 2012). It needs to be emphasized that this is not simply a computational metaphor – simply saying that the human mind is like a computer. Rather, the *computational theory of mind* goes further than this and states that mental operations are mappings from designated inputs to outputs according to some well-defined rules by means of symbolic manipulation of digital vehicles in the form of linguistic strings. My purpose here is not to go into criticism of this view as there is already a growing amount of criticism levelled against it (see for details, Putnam 1988; Searle 1992; Penrose 1994; Bishop 2009). Rather, my purpose in this chapter is to see in what ways a relation between language and computation obtains at a more fundamental level and how such a relation with all its concomitant ramifications liaises with our current linguistic theory. What is necessary and what is not about this relation will fall out of the discussion as it unfolds.

Suffice it to say, formal operations on linguistic representations define the core of what is significant about linguistic rules and constraints which are considered to be part of an abstract (axiomatic) system. The following lines from Chomsky (1980) enunciate what is at stake: '... that rules of syntax and phonology, at least, are organized in terms of "autonomous" principles of mental computation and do not reflect in any simple way the properties of the phonetic or semantic "substance" or contingencies of language use' (p. 246).

This largely sums up the stance on the relation between language and the system of linguistic rules. Thus (mental) computation involves rules and associated linguistic representations. Be that as it may, the overall scenario is still oversimplified and underspecified. The reason is quite clear. If computation means something more than what is conveyed by (mental) operations, the notion of computation carries over all sorts of complexities associated with it into the realm of mental grammar. And the way it is used and in fact scaffolds much of the technical machinery in theoretical/formal linguistics needs to be elucidated. Hopelessly, this has never been thoroughly discussed, much less precisely demarcated; the link between rules and their associated linguistic representations, and (mental) computation has remained vague. Mainstream theoretical linguistics has perpetuated this vagueness at the expense of what is often seen as formal elegance and empirical adequacy. This is problematic for various reasons. On the one hand, if conceptual or methodological parsimony – that is, the postulation of fewer concepts or methodological principles to explain quite a great number of facts – is all that we require, then the notion of computation for cognitive operations on linguistic representations can be jettisoned all the way out of the window, if all the term 'computation' serves to do is decorate the battery of linguistic terminology with a widely popular label from the computational and information sciences. On the other hand, if the concept of computation is really something that simplifies a lot of theoretical descriptions and thus possesses great explanatory value, then it is worth retaining as a fundamental notion of linguistic theory. However, actual linguistic practice has got into it both ways in that the notion of computation has been used in a profusely indulgent manner, and at the same time, many aspects of computation as observed in computing devices are also brought forward for explanatory purposes. What this indicates is that a glib use of the notion of computation is juxtaposed with an appeal to its explanatory import. However, one may still wonder why this should be flawed, since the very notion of computation, or rather computability, is still an ill-defined notion, and that is why the *Church–Turing Thesis* (which equates computability in the physical world with computability in Turing machines), even if otherwise falsifiable, may not be or is not proved. If this is what is desirable or what we aim at gaining, why not use this vague but otherwise useful notion of computation with all its explanatory import? If so, we shall have to push ahead with the consequences that follow from an adoption of an otherwise useful notion of computation with all its explanatory import, precisely because computation brings with it all its subtle complexities as well as perplexities. This is what this chapter will explore in a deeper possible manner.

4.1   Linguistic representation and levels of representation

The notion of linguistic representation in connection with (linguistic) computation is crucial in linguistic theory. As we will soon see, it is the notion of linguistic representation that will help us understand the status of (linguistic) computation in linguistic theory. This is because (linguistic) computation cannot perform its functions in a vacuum; it operates on well-defined representations in accordance with well-defined rules. Linguistic representations of form and meaning are thus central to linguistic theory. Not surprisingly, we see that there are different levels of representation grounded in the architectural organization of grammar. And these levels of representation are organized in terms of differences in principles that govern such levels. Thus the Government and Binding model of Generative Grammar (Chomsky 1981) had four different levels of representation: D-Structure, S-Structure, Logical Form (LF) and Phonological Form (PF), whereas the current model of the Minimalist Program (Chomsky 1995) has just two: LF and PF. The motivation for any differences in levels of representation lies in discrepancies in terms of what the postulated levels contain and what they are fed into. For example, in the current Minimalist model of Generative Grammar, LF as a level of representation mediates mappings to semantic representations, while PF constructs mappings to phonetic representations. But there is another important distinction that should not be ignored. A set of levels of representation forms what is called a *plane*, which is organized in terms of its ontological distinctiveness that can be traced to a difference in the specific alphabet and principles (Anderson 2006). Thus, according to him, D-Structure and S-Structure (two different levels of representation) in the Government and Binding model belong to the same plane, whereas LF and PF are both different levels of representation and different planes. Similar distinctions have also been drawn up by Cann et al. (2012), though the terms they have used are a bit different; they have made a distinction between levels of representation which are ontologically distinct, and levels of structure which are distinct in terms of their formal principles and operations that contribute to empirically grounded generalizations. If we go by this characterization by Cann et al., D-Structure and S-Structure (together), LF and PF are levels of representation, but D-Structure and S-Structure are independent levels of structure.

However, this terminology is a bit confusing. Are not levels of representation also levels of structure in a sense? Each level of representation – D/S-Structure, LF and PF – is also structurally distinct and thus a different organization of structure. D/S-Structure is certainly a kind of organization of structure, LF represents aspects of semantic structure expressed syntactically, and PF represents phonological structure on a phonetic basis. Whatever the case may be, the underlying idea that comes out is clear enough. That is, the *ontological* distinction of linguistic representations and the *structural* distinction of linguistic representations are two completely different things; the former is motivated by (unique) differences in alphabets and specific principles, while the latter is based on differences in the nature of formal operations that apply to linguistic structures and can have empirical consequences. In this sense, the *structural* distinction of linguistic representations may, of course, feed the *ontological* distinction of linguistic representations; for example, in the Government and Binding framework the Theta Criterion applies at D-Structure but not at S-Structure and Case assignment is done at S-Structure but not at D-Structure. All this is grounded in the requirement for D-Structure to contribute to semantic representations and for S-Structure to phonological representations. These two distinctions are crucial for an explication of the notion of linguistic computation and should not thus be confused. But before we proceed to do that, a number of points need to be clarified. The difference between the *ontological* distinction of linguistic representations and the *structural* distinction of linguistic representations is substantial, insofar as it is responsible for splits in linguistic theories. For some theoretical frameworks the *ontological* distinction of linguistic representations is fundamental, and for others, it is the *structural* distinction of linguistic representations that is more fundamental. For instance, Lexical Functional Grammar (Bresnan 2001) has taken the *ontological* distinction of linguistic representations seriously because it has split form into C(constituent)-Structure and F(functional)-Structure, the former being syntactic and the latter being semantically grounded. Jackendoff's Parallel Architecture (2002) has also pursued the same path in keeping syntax different from both semantics and phonology, and vice versa, although there are connecting interfaces among them. Head-Driven Phrase Structure Grammar (Pollard and Sag 1994) and Cognitive Grammar (Lakoff 1987; Langacker 1987, 1999) have, on the other hand, conflated both distinctions into a single unified level or system of representation. In Head-Driven Phrase Structure Grammar, it is attribute-value matrices (AVMs) that incorporate a unified representation of syntax, semantics and morphology of linguistic structures, but Cognitive Grammar treats all structures (lexical, morphological, syntactic) as symbolic items having form and meaning fused together. But Generative Grammar has always considered the *structural* distinction of linguistic representations to be more fundamental, although it would perhaps be wrong to say that it has taken the *ontological* distinction of linguistic representations blithely. In fact, Generative Grammar has always vacillated between these two relevant distinctions (Anderson 2006). The *structural* distinction of linguistic representations has been significant to the extent that structural transformations alter the representation of structure at one level giving rise to another level that contains the altered representation of the structural output. And the *ontological* distinction of linguistic representations has been of considerable substance too, in that some unique principles with unique alphabets operate in ontologically different domains or modules of language. Thus phonology has phonemes, syllables, tone, etc. and principles like the *Maximum Onset Principle* (that prefers onsets to coda in syllables), *Obligatory Contour Principle* (that bans adjacent positioning of identical features in phonological representations at a pre-derivational stage), etc., while syntax has words, phrases, clauses and a number of syntactic principles (for instance, the *Extended Projection Principle* for obligatoriness of subjects). It appears that the Minimalist model of the language faculty has also enshrined the *ontological* distinction of linguistic representations as a fundamental distinction by having narrow syntax (involving Merge operations) segregated from both LF and PF. If this is the case, the current Generative model of grammar has fallen more in line with Lexical Functional Grammar and Parallel Architecture only in this regard.

The discussion so far shows that the difference between the *ontological* distinction of linguistic representations and the structural distinction of linguistic representations has played a pivotal role in guiding the development of linguistic theories and formalisms some of which have taken the difference seriously, and some others (such as Head-Driven Phrase Structure Grammar and Cognitive Grammar) have unified the differences into an integrated system, perhaps by respecting the Saussurean legacy of the integrity of signs, as pointed out by Jackendoff

(2002). However, this difference between the two *kinds* of distinction offers a way of understanding the general distinction usually drawn between (linguistic) representation and derivation, which separates representational theories such as Head-Driven Phrase Structure Grammar, Lexical Functional Grammar and also (in a sense) Cognitive Grammar from derivational theories like mainstream Generative Grammar and Optimality Theory (Prince and Smolensky 1993). What is common among the representational theories is that they have all bypassed the *structural* distinction of linguistic representations some way or other, or even cashed out the *ontological* distinction of linguistic representations in terms of the *structural* distinction of linguistic representations, while this distinction figures prominently in both mainstream Generative Grammar and Optimality Theory. Therefore, we can have equations like the following:

(97) Ontological Distinction$^+$ → Linguistic Representation
      Structural Distinction ↔ Linguistic Derivation

The sign '+' on top of '*Ontological* Distinction$^+$' indicates that the *ontological* distinction of linguistic representations is latent, especially for theories like Head-Driven Phrase Structure Grammar and Cognitive Grammar. It may also be noted that this equation in (97) has a unidirectional implication such that one cannot just deduce the *ontological* distinction of linguistic representations from mere linguistic representation; this is valid for a theory like Autolexical Syntax, which is representational but does not, by virtue of that, maintain a *ontological* distinction of linguistic representations in strict terms (see e.g. Sadock 2012). But, by contrast, one has to necessarily deduce the *structural* distinction of linguistic representations from mere linguistic derivation and vice versa (whether in mainstream Generative Grammar or in Optimality Theory), regardless of whether or not there exist different structural levels incorporated as part of the architecture of grammar for underlying and derived representations. The Minimalist model holds on to this bidirectional implication by means of a sequence of operations involving case checking through the deletion of *un*interpretable features and the internal Merging of parts of externally Merged items, all of which are done after the selection of lexical items from Numeration to derive linguistic structures that are ready for Spell-Out. Hence linguistic representations are *structurally* different at *every stage* of the application of the operation of Merge – whether external or internal.

4.2 What is (linguistic) computation?

Now equipped with the significant difference between the *ontological* distinction of linguistic representations and the *structural* distinction of linguistic representations, we can come down to the task of delineating what linguistic computation is and how it functions. But before we turn to this issue, it behoves us to hone our understanding of what computation is. Computation is one of the most confounded and unclear notions employed in cognitive science (Piccinini and Scarantino 2011; Fresco 2011). So when a question on whether something is computational or not is asked, much hinges on the fact that the right concept of computation is applied to the phenomenon that is to be scrutinized to see whether it falls under computation. Similar considerations apply to the case here, as we focus on language and wonder what can be linguistic computation. For all the vagueness surrounding the notion of (linguistic) computation, it appears that (linguistic) computation fits well with the classical sense of computation in which inputs are mapped to outputs according to some well-defined rules by means of symbolic manipulation of digital vehicles in the form of linguistic strings. This notion of computation is the narrowest in the hierarchy of notions of digital computation (Piccinini and Scarantino 2011). Much of formal linguistics has employed this notion of linguistic computation implicitly or explicitly, mainly because the representational vehicles of language are discrete in form. Still a question remains. Can we take linguistic computation as a *generic* computation that encompasses both digital and analogue computation? Even if this is a bit difficult to answer, the answer is more likely to be no. It is somewhat clearer that the digital notion of computation has been predominant all throughout the field of cognitive science in general and theoretical linguistics in particular; hence the analogue sense of computation does not apply to linguistic computation since in analogue computation computational processes are driven and determined by the *intrinsic* representational content of the vehicles that are analogue in nature, whereas digital computation involves mappings of inputs onto outputs that are executed without any regard to the content-determining properties of the representational digital vehicles (O'Brien and Opie 2011). The quotation from Chomsky (1980) at the beginning of this chapter '... "autonomous" principles of mental computation do not reflect in any simple way the properties of the phonetic or semantic "substance" or contingencies of language use' also makes it quite perspicuous that linguistic computation does not plausibly cover the analogue sense of computation. Therefore, linguistic computation cannot be considered to be a type of *generic* computation that encompasses both digital and analogue computation.

In this connection, we can introduce a more formal notion of computation grounded in proper functions proposed by Stabler (1987) for whom a system computes a function, say, F

if and only if,

a. there is an interpretation function, In, which maps a set of finite sequences of physical 'input' states of the system onto the domain of F, and an interpretation function, Out, which maps a set of finite sequences of physical 'output' states onto the range of F, such that

b. physical laws guarantee that (in certain circumstances C) if the system goes successively through the states of an input sequence *i*, it will go successively through the states of the corresponding output sequence *f* where Out(*f*) = F(In(*i*)) (p. 6)

Essentially, in the formal notion of computation any function F that is computed is relativized to a physical system, and the inputs which this function maps onto outputs are derived from an interpretation function just as the outputs are. Now suppose the function F maps x to y: $F(x) = y$. Here, x and y are sequences of physical states the computational relevance of which is derived through the interpretation functions *In* and *Out*. Another crucial notion is that only finite sequences of states of physical systems are taken to be inputs and outputs for any mapping executed by the infinite function F. That is, any function computed is an infinite function while any physical system is finite in nature, and this leads to a profound incompatibility. Stabler argues that this incompatibility can be circumvented by saying that the computationally relevant inputs and outputs must be finite sequences of physical states that realize an infinite function such that a physical system can *potentially* compute the infinite function if physical laws are compatible with this. This is a baffling issue and deserves an elaborate discussion. This will be done in the next section.

What is important for us is that the essential elements of the notion of computation can be extrapolated to what we make sense of in dealing with the concept of linguistic computation. When we talk about computation, we require (i) a function that is computed, (ii) a system which computes the function and also (iii) an effective procedure (also called an *algorithm*). This comes out clearly from the *Church–Turing Thesis*, which states that anything that can be computed with an effective procedure in the physical world can be computed in Turing machines. Now the question is: what is the physical system in the case of linguistic computation? Is it the human brain/mind? The computational thesis regarding the nature of human cognition has always maintained that it is the human mind or the brain that computes. The rationale seems to be understandable when the argument pronounces that the human brain is ultimately a physical object. Nevertheless, there is another independent sense in which the physical system for linguistic computation can be conceived of. If we follow Chomsky (1995, 2001) on this matter, it is the language faculty in the brain/mind that computes because the language faculty is considered to be akin to a physical organ within the confinements of our brain. The language faculty instantiated in the brain/mind has a computational procedure that engages in all kinds of linguistic computation. The next essential ingredient of computation is a function, or rather a computable function. In linguistic theory the domain of such functions may well correspond to the domain of formal operations that apply to structures to make *structural* distinctions of linguistic representations, if we go by what has been schematized in (97). In other words, the functions that can fall under linguistic computation are those which subscribe to linguistic derivation.

Now a question crops up because computable functions appear to be excluded from representational linguistic theories. Hence, if this is the case, can there be any reasonable sense in which we can speak of computable functions in the context of representational theories of language such as Head-Driven Phrase Structure Grammar or Lexical Functional Grammar, as the conclusion above appears to factor out representational theories? As far as this goes, it needs to be seen whether we can reliably talk about computable functions that operate on linguistic representations in representational linguistic theories. Most of these theories are as clear as possible on this matter, so far as we judge. Certainly, Head-Driven Phrase Structure Grammar or Lexical Functional Grammar has linguistic functions for the construction of linguistic structures (functions that map one structure onto another) just as cognitively grounded theories like Cognitive Grammar and Parallel Architecture have. For example, Head-Driven Phrase Structure Grammar has a function that maps two AVMs onto another unified AVM – a process of *subsumption* through which, say, phrases from words or from other phrases are constructed. Thus a feature structure of a noun phrase, say, 'snakes' containing category information (a noun) and agreement information (third person plural) can be unified with the feature structure of a verb phrase 'wriggle' containing category information (a verb) along with the relevant agreement information of the subject argument (third person plural) to give rise to a feature structure that specifies its sentential category along with all other (pieces of) information subsumed from the feature structures of 'snakes' and 'wriggle'. Similarly, the function that maps c-structures onto f-structures is also of such a type. In fact, it has been emphasized that representational operations in theories like Head-Driven Phrase Structure Grammar or Lexical Functional Grammar are constrained by computability considerations which require that there be effective procedures or algorithms for executing the functions corresponding to such operations (Shieber 1992). This also becomes clearer when Shieber (1992) highlights logical consistency and completeness as well as denotational consistency and completeness – which ensure consistency and soundness of the formulas in a logical system – as fundamental criteria for logical systems to serve as grammar formalisms, and this applies *in toto* to representational linguistic theories that embed formalisms (for instance, Head-Driven Phrase Structure Grammar or Lexical Functional Grammar). This makes sense when we understand representational linguistic theories such as Head-Driven Phrase Structure Grammar or Lexical Functional Grammar also as grammar formalisms that are specified in a *declarative* format so that any valid procedural interpretation can be imposed on them. It is this property that makes these grammar formalisms viable for their implementation in an architecture of language processing in the mind/brain or for computational processing for practical engineering applications. However, one should be a little cautious in treating the functions used in such grammar formalisms as computable functions, simply because not all functions are computable functions though all computable functions are obviously functions. Though the discussion in this paragraph has so far suggested that functions used in representational linguistic theories are computable, that is, there exist algorithms that can compute them, and, indeed, this is so, given a huge amount of computational implementation of grammar formalisms of Head-Driven Phrase Structure Grammar or Lexical Functional Grammar. Still we should take the relationship between a grammar formalism and the associated linguistic theory with a grain of salt. As Shieber (1987) has elsewhere mused over this relationship and then issued a warning, we may take it that the nature of computability of functions in such frameworks is underdetermined by formal constraints, for this may also be constrained by substantive constraints emanating from natural language phenomena, which is not explicit in the formalisms. In spite of this, it is at least clear that such functions are not postulated to be computed in the physical brain. All representational linguistic theories, being declarative in form, are neutral on this issue, as has been stressed throughout. Overall, as far as the formalisms of representational theories go, we can say, with a high degree of certainty, that the functions of such formalisms are *at least* computable functions. But it is doubtful that we can say the same thing about Cognitive Grammar or even about Parallel Architecture. Even if they have functions mapping structures onto structures, it stands to reason that such functions are also meant to be computed by the physical brain or by the language faculty (see for details, Jackendoff 2002; Culicover and Jackendoff 2005). Hence we leave this matter open.

All computable functions are indissociably associated with the notion of effective procedures or algorithms. Algorithms are central to the concept of computable functions, for computable functions are precisely those that can be computed by algorithms. This brings us closer to the exploration into the appropriate concept of algorithms intrinsic to the notion of linguistic computation. We can explore this in the context of the notion of linguistic computation employed in the Minimalist framework, which explicitly talks about linguistic computation, computational procedures, etc. However, the notion of algorithms in representational theories of language that effect functions for *unification* operations becomes more evident in what follows. In fact, the characterization of algorithms appropriate for linguistic computation can, with ease, be extended to representational linguistic theories. Recall from Chapter 3 that the computational procedure in the Minimalist model of the language faculty maps N to pairs (π, λ). It is the operation Merge that executes this mapping. And these operations must have an algorithmic character to be called computations; otherwise it does not make any sense to have operations which are posited to be computational in form and character. As was discussed in Chapter 3, Merge is a binary operation involving two syntactic objects, say α and β. Now the operation Merge will merge α and β to create γ {α, β} when γ is the label of the new object. An example can be given to illustrate this. Let us take the sentence below (also used in Chapter 2):

(98) John believes Mary to be beautiful.

The way the words of the sentence in (98) have been combined to build the sentence in (98) is shown in Figure 4.1 with the help of a tree as standard in Generative linguistics.

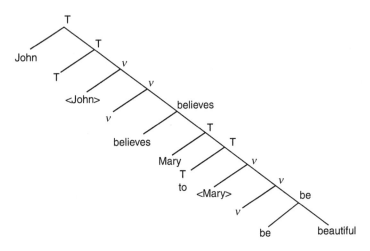

Figure 4.1 A tree structure for 'John believes Mary to be beautiful'

Here, the operation Merge builds the tree through an iteration of the application of the operation (with v denoting the (little) verb head and T the tense head[1]). 'Mary' and 'John' are placed in brackets to show that they have been internally Merged higher. 'Mary' and 'John' have been internally Merged in the sense that they are Merged into a structure higher than the structure Merge has so far built, of which 'Mary' and 'John' (independently) are already a part. The rest has come about through movement/displacement (external Merge). Now it needs to be seen whether this operation can be stated as an algorithm. In fact, it is easy to see that the operation Merge can be stated algorithmically. Here is how. First, Merge can be stated in the form of a binary function that operates on S, the set of syntactic objects. So it will look like: Merge $(S \times S) = S$. Second, the operation Merge in this form can be stated, by following Foster (1992), as a sequence of transitions between states of a machine – say, a Turing machine – each of which consists of a collection of label–value pairs. This can be shown below.

(99) $[SO_1: LI_1 \; SO_2: LI_2 \; L:\mathscr{L}] \rightarrow [SO: LI_1, LI_2 \; L: \mathscr{L}] \rightarrow [SO: \{LI_1, LI_2\} \; L: \mathscr{L}] \rightarrow [SO: \mathscr{L} \{LI_1, LI_2\}]$

(99) represents a sequence of states. Here, SO_i is a syntactic object, LI is a lexical item (including functional categories like tense T or verb v) and L is a label (of an SO). In (99), the left-hand side of the colon represents

a label and the right-hand side of the colon denotes the value of that label. Each structure enclosed within braces [ ] with such label–value pairs constitutes a state followed by the next state – the arrows represent the relevant transitions between such states. One can see that the values of SO_1 and SO_2 have been grouped in the second state. This gives us a handle on the representation of objects created by Merge as a pair, if required. However, the next state gives us a set that contains the values of SO_1 and SO_2, thereby having the flexibility that one can choose either of the states (the second or the third), as and when needed. Now, one can verify that each snapshot of a state from the sequence in (99) reflects a structural distinction of linguistic representations as Merge executes its operations. This is how the discussion in section 4.1 connects and leads to this understanding of algorithms intrinsic to linguistic computation. Interested readers can also check that (99) can be easily adapted for the purpose of the specification of algorithms for *unification* operations in representational theories of language. This also gets us out of the obligation to impose any (in)determinacy on the syntactic objects generated by Merge.

4.3 Infinite language from finite grammar in finite systems

So far we have devoted our energy to understanding how linguistic computation can be conceptualized by focusing on its fundamental ingredients, namely a computable function, an algorithm that executes that function and a system in which the algorithm is implemented. But there is more to it than meets the eye. Recall that Marr's (1982) three-level schema organized in terms of the computational level, the algorithmic level and the implementational level is an approach to the study of complex systems the analysis of which can be done by varying perspectives at various levels of detail or explanation. Taken in this sense, what matters at the computational level may be explained independent of any reference to the algorithmic level or/and the implementational level, and likewise, what is analysed at the algorithmic level may well be independent of any description either at the computational or at the implementational level (for a different view on levels of description, see Dodwell 2000). This is what helps us realize that a computable function can be characterized independent of the algorithm that computes it or even the system which implements the function. The same goes for an algorithm that executes a function by abstracting away from the physical system in which the algorithm is ultimately realized. However, there exists considerable vagueness wrapped around what the three levels – the computational, the algorithmic and the implementational levels – can be taken to mean in a model of a cognitive system, and this has spurred Foster (1992) to develop a more liberal notion of algorithms that does justice to various senses in which the three levels of Marr's schema are construed. Thus Foster's notion of algorithm, being handy enough, has been employed to see how the core operation of the Minimalist architecture of the language faculty can be assigned computational scaffolding, which is what it is claimed to possess. For Foster, an algorithm is a sequence of states or state transitions that can be pitched at any level ranging from a more detailed level at the bottom (the implementational level) to a more abbreviated, more abstracted level above (the computational level), and all this depends on the *abstraction function* that we define. That is, it is the abstraction function that we may define at a more abstract level of the mind which helps us say that a person has/entertains a certain thought which has a certain form, by having the function applied to a more detailed level of processing in the brain.

Turning our attention to the case of language, we need to figure out the connection of grammar to the notion of finiteness because all mentally represented grammars are ultimately finite, as Chomsky (1980, 1995) takes pains to emphasize. We may pause for a while and think over the rationale behind this. It is worth taking note of the fact that our brains are finite physical systems, and if there is a mentally represented grammar inside the boundaries of the cranium, the represented grammar has no other way than being finite. Even if grammars are finite formal systems, the languages they generate can be infinite. As it has already been demonstrated that the operations of grammar in the Minimalist framework have an algorithmic nature and algorithms are finite in form, it becomes clearer that a mentally represented grammar, in virtue of possessing an algorithmic character, has to be finite in this sense too. Above all, any effective procedure for executing (computable) functions has to have a finite and explicit representation, in the absence of which no computation will be possible because the machine will never halt. But one needs to be cautious in this regard, in that the finiteness of an algorithm does not guarantee the finiteness of the corresponding program – a program may run forever in a loop without ever stopping, but an algorithm has a definite length and end. In terms of the relation of programs to the characterization of algorithms, algorithms can be instantiated in programs and may thus abstract away from programs. Given Foster's notion of algorithms, algorithms too may be looked at as programs, if considered from a lower level of description. Now the seemingly innocuous but forbiddingly uncomfortable question is whether grammars can also be seen as programs. In so far as algorithms can also be looked at as programs from a certain level of description along with an abstraction function so defined, the answer appears to be yes. But on the other hand, it seems odd that a grammar mentally represented *may* be non-finite, if we assume that mentally represented grammars can also be programs.

All this does not stop right here. The more perplexing question of how to relate a finitely represented (mental) grammar to infinite languages creeps into any system of descriptions of natural language. And it is such a deep mystery that it has puzzled many people across the entire gamut of cognitive sciences. Not surprisingly, Chomsky (1980) has repeatedly resisted any claim that aims to demonstrate that natural languages are *recursive* or *recursively enumerable* despite several works that have shown that transformational grammars are equivalent to Turing machines in weak generative capacity (see for details, Peters and Ritchie 1973; Bach and Marsh 1987). What this means needs a bit of clarification.

First, when Chomsky resists the claim that natural languages are recursive or recursively enumerable, he must be thinking of some effective procedure, that is, an algorithm that executes the task of deciding about the membership of strings generated by a grammar. The concept of recursive or recursively enumerable is particularly based on the notion of the membership of strings generated by a grammar. If a set is a recursive set, this means that both membership and non-membership of its members can be decided by some algorithm whereas if a set is recursively enumerable, that means that the membership of its members can be decided or determined though nothing can be said about the non-members. All this can be executed on a machine by means of an effective procedure, that is, an algorithm. The class of languages recognized by Turing machines is generally called recursively enumerable languages, while context-free or context-sensitive languages are often called recursive languages which can be recognized by Turing machines too, but in such a case they are halting Turing machines. That is, the main difference between recursive sets and recursively enumerable sets lies in the unique nature of Turing machines which may or may not halt. The property of recursive enumerability is thus a special property of Turing machines. What Peters and Ritchie (1973) wanted to do was verify the generative power of generative grammars in order to see how this would chime with the learnability of generative grammars. It turned out that generative grammars (in the *Aspects* model) were more powerful than expected; this insight indicated that this would lead to difficulties for learners to learn generative grammars. Most importantly, the demonstration that generative grammars generate recursively enumerable languages means that the operations of generative grammars including transformations are analogously equivalent to operations in Turing machines and that generative grammars just like Turing machines generate recursively enumerable sets from a base component which is in the form of a context-sensitive base language or a regular set (as in Bach and Marsh 1987). Chomsky has been sceptical of any extrapolation that takes a tour from this step to the assertion that natural languages are recursive or recursively enumerable. The reason now seems to be clearer. Generative grammars may well be recursively enumerable for some reasons having to do with the specific operations intrinsic to formal devices in generative grammars; but this is far removed from anything that establishes that the class of natural languages must be recursive or recursively enumerable. This is mainly because of many complicating factors associated with semanticity, language use, beliefs, inferences, concepts, etc. which interface with the syntactic aspect of linguistic knowledge.

Second, there is another reason why Chomsky has tended to distance himself from the supposition that natural languages are recursive or recursively enumerable. Chomsky has always placed the empirical adequacy of grammars (in terms of both *descriptive adequacy* and *explanatory adequacy*) on the pedestal, as the following passage from Chomsky (1965: 62) shows:

> Thus one can construct hierarchies of grammatical theories in terms of weak and strong generative capacity, but it is important to bear in mind that these hierarchies do not necessarily correspond to what is probably the empirically most significant dimension of increasing power of linguistic theory.

Chomsky thinks so because if we demand that a linguistic theory, which happens to be an empirically adequate theory, should also be the least powerful theory, it may turn out that this theory is the most powerful theory in terms of both weak and strong generative capacity. Weak generative capacity has something to do with the generation of the list of strings generable by a grammar, whereas strong generative capacity is associated with notions of structural descriptions of linguistic structures in terms of constituent structures, derivations, intuitive notions of semanticity, etc. (but see Miller (1999) for a different take on the notion of strong generative capacity). Thus an empirically adequate linguistic theory can match Turing machines in terms of both weak and strong generative capacity. Berwick and Weinberg (1984) have also reiterated this point; it is misleading, as they believe, to 'put the mathematical cart' before the horse that embodies a deeper consideration of empirical significance of a linguistic theory. Another plausible rationale behind this belief is that the exact mathematical and/or computational property of natural language (whether natural language is context-free or context-sensitive or recursively enumerable) is not still known and this question is still barely understood (see for details, Mondal 2010).

Now we can move back from this digression into a different issue and concentrate on the worries pertaining to the generation of infinite languages by finite grammars in the mind/brain. It is worth emphasizing again that Chomsky does not ascribe anything of substantial insight to any observation about the class of languages generated by a grammar, since it is grammars that are of serious interest and of real empirical significance. But why then so much fuss over grammars, rather than over the languages generated, that may have the capacity of Turing machines? It takes a little bit of reflection to see that the concern has certainly not been merely with the languages generated. Rather, the worry about the excessive power of the generative procedure of generative grammars seems to relate more directly to the capabilities of Turing machines which have an infinitely long tape, can compute anything that is intuitively computable (qua the *Church–Turing Thesis*) and may not halt at all. This is what has worried many linguists and cognitive scientists. The measure of the generative capacity of generative grammars has been in terms of the outputs of the machine concerned, that is, in terms of the output set which may be recursive or/and recursively enumerable. Clearly, whatever the output set turns out to be, it does not ultimately matter much (as Chomsky thinks) so long as it does not say anything about the nature and form of the (mechanical) procedure itself. However, this does matter when a statement about the output can be easily translated into a statement about the mechanical procedure or about the form of the machine that produces it. It is a kind of reverse engineering from the nature of the outputs to the form of the machine that produces that set of outputs in question. Perhaps Chomsky does not appear to believe in this kind of reverse engineering.

On the one hand, if the generative procedure of generative grammars is equivalent in capacities to Turing machines, by virtue of the equivalence of grammars to machines (Hopcroft and Ullman 1979), this says something about the very form of grammar, not about the languages generated. The broader connection appears to be conspicuous now. If grammars are equivalent to machines, the grammar mentally represented can also invite the problem of infinity in spite of the finiteness of mental/neural capacities and resources. But how is this matter related to whether natural languages are recursive or recursively enumerable? On the one hand, Turing machines having infinite capacities allow for infinite languages, which is one of the reasons why one may worry about the exact computational property of the class of natural languages. But on the other hand, the question of whether natural languages are recursive or not bears on the question of how to restrict the class of grammars that generate recursively enumerable languages, recursive languages being a subclass of recursively enumerable languages. However, this does not mean that recursive languages cannot be infinite languages; rather, attempts to restrict the class of grammars that generate recursively enumerable languages so that it generates recursive languages are aimed at restricting the generative power of the class of grammars, or of the machine. Thus the problem of generation of infinite languages does not go away merely by postulating that natural languages form a recursive set.

In fact, the deeper ontological incommensurability between infinite languages and a finite grammar instantiated in finite mental/neural systems was what motivated Langendoen and Postal (1984) to propose that natural languages are vaster than even recursively enumerable languages, and they do not form a set in a general sense. Rather, natural language sentences form *mega*collections – collections of sets that do not exhibit properties of sets as such. By virtue of this, they demonstrate, through the *NL (Natural Language) Non-Constructivity Theorem*, that there is no Turing-machine-style constructive procedure for generating either syntactic rules or semantic rules at LF if the *NL (Natural Language) Non-Constructivity Theorem* holds for the class of natural languages. That is, the grammars for the class of natural languages are more powerful than even Turing machines, and hence the class of natural languages cannot be generated by any Turing machine. Nor can there be Turing-machine procedures for linguistic rules that operate on linguistic representations to produce sentences. As Langendoen and Postal argue, the supposition that there exist Turing-machine computable procedures for the abstract axiomatic system underlying natural language is actually flawed under a closer analysis and is thus doomed to crumble. Does this then mean that linguistic operations on linguistic representations as part of rule systems are not computations? For all we know, the answer to this question will take us through an enormously messy territory, and as we proceed further, this question, rather than the answer, will become sharper. However, recall that Chomsky has also resisted the claim that the class of natural languages is recursively enumerable, and by virtue of this, generative grammars appear to be unaffected by the ramifications of what Langendoen and Postal have demonstrated. But this is not the case. Langendoen and Postal and later on Postal (2004) have dexterously argued that the *NL (Natural Language) Non-Constructivity Theorem* brings into sharper focus the striking ontological incommensurability between vast collections of natural languages and the finite grammar that is represented in the mind. How can this deeper ontological incommensurability be avoided, let alone eliminated, if no Turing-style constructive procedures for mentally represented linguistic rules plausibly exist and if the mentally represented grammar cannot generate mental representations of vast collections of natural language sentences?

The problem can only be appreciated if it is understood, as Langendoen and Postal claim, as a problem of incompleteness of the formal system from which natural language sentences are generable. Thus they liken their theorem to the *Incompleteness Theorem* of the mathematical logician Kurt Gödel, who proved with the *Incompleteness Theorem* that any self-consistent axiomatic system that has axioms about, and thus describes, the arithmetic of natural numbers contains some undecidable propositions such that the notion of arithmetic truth cannot be defined within the formal system because of vicious paradoxes emanating from contradictions. This has an analogy with what is called the Liar's Paradox,[2] which can be demonstrated in the following way. If one says 'This assertion is false', one invites a seemingly innocuous but otherwise deeply puzzling paradox. Here is the way. If the assertion is true, it is false; on the other hand, if the assertion is false, it is true. In a sense, it follows from the *NL (Natural Language) Non-Constructivity Theorem* that if there is no algorithm or generative procedure for the generation of all natural language sentences, there cannot in principle exist any generative system – psychologically grounded or otherwise – that generates *all* natural language sentences, and had there been such a system, it would generate only a subpart of the entire *mega*collection of natural language sentences. And if so, this appears to establish that any such generative procedure or algorithm cannot exist for natural languages. The connection to Gödel's *Incompleteness Theorem* begins to be clearer now. Just as Gödel's *Incompleteness Theorem* states that there are true propositions about the arithmetic of natural numbers that cannot be proved to be true within the formal system that is otherwise complete and self-consistent, the *NL (Natural Language) Non-Constructivity Theorem* asserts that there are natural language sentences that are members of the collection of natural language sentences and cannot, nevertheless, be generated by a generative procedure or an algorithm.

However, McCawley (1987) took issue with Langendoen and Postal's use of the word 'generate' in the statement of the *NL (Natural Language) Non-Constructivity Theorem* because the theorem, according to him, uses the word 'generate' in its commonsensical, trivial or 'vulgarized' sense meaning 'yield as the output of a computational procedure determined by the grammar' (original quotation by McCawley). It is misleading, he argued, to use the word 'constructive' to mean 'proof-theoretic' or 'generative' or 'Turing-machine' since, for him, they mean completely different things. It is certainly the case that the word 'generate' has been used in Generative Grammar in the sense of specification of only grammatical but not ungrammatical sentences by a system of rules. However, it is not equally clear why this sense of the word 'generate' cannot apply to recursive enumerability (although Chomsky is sceptical of this, as discussed above; but see Kornai 2008). Furthermore, the notion of a proof-theoretic procedure implies the involvement of a deductive method of arriving at a theorem from a set of axioms by means of a sequence of derivational steps and a number of inference rules, and may well apply to the production of grammatical sentences from a set of well-defined linguistic rules and constraints by means of a sequence of derivational steps along with a number of inference rules (see for details, Peacocke 1989; Putnam 1961). For our purpose, even if we accede to the objection that the word 'constructive' in Langendoen and Postal is a bit vague, there is no denying that the problem of constructing infinite languages from finite grammars represented in the mind or instantiated in brains is, in a more general sense, still elusive.

There could be several ways of avoiding this incompatibility between a finite system and the construction or generation of an infinite number of linguistic expressions. One of the ways is already suggested in Stabler (1987), who proposes that only finite sequences of inputs and outputs are mapped by computable functions at any given time such that such sequences *can* range over infinite sets. Translated into terms that fit the current scenario, this means that the generative procedure of natural language operates with computable functions that map only finite sequences of linguistic objects or expressions at any stage of computation. In this sense, it seems plausible that phases in the current phase-based architecture of grammar achieve exactly this goal, although this view was developed with a different purpose in mind and computational efficiency figures high in this matter (the notion of computational efficiency vis-à-vis computational complexity will be dealt with in the next section). This is because of the fact that phases apportion the entire computational space into sub-domains within which the generative procedure of natural language is supposed to operate, thereby paralleling sequences of inputs and outputs that are mapped. The reason why the computational space needs to be cut down into smaller sub-spaces is to do with the finite resources (space and time in a Turing machine) that are available at any stage of computation. Since computable functions are grounded in number-theoretic functions, it is the infinite range of number-theoretic functions that motivates the partitioning the domain and range of computable functions into sequences of inputs and outputs. It is easy to see that number-theoretic functions may well produce sets that are denumerably infinite. For simplicity, consider the recursive function that outputs the successor of a natural number by adding 1: $f(n) = n + 1$ when n is the natural number the successor of which is derived by this function. This function can also be stated in Peano axioms. But what is important is that this function generates a set of natural numbers which is denumerably infinite, and for this reason, we may need to apply the suggestion that the domain and range of the function could be partitioned into sequences in order for the function to be computed on a finite physical system having resource limitations.

We now apply the same logic to the generative procedure of the language faculty that is assumed to operate with computable functions mapping only finite sequences of linguistic objects or expressions. Implicit in this is the assumption that linguistic expressions or constructions are analogous, or rather equivalent to natural numbers. Let us suppose that this is indeed the case. With this, we can now go ahead to figure out how we can obtain the same result for natural language sentences by trying to partition into sequences the domain and range of computable functions that operate on natural language sentences. We can try this out with the operation binary Merge, which, as we have seen, is the computable function that builds syntactic objects. Merge always operates from the bottom of a sentence; so a sentence like 'John loves a car' will be Merged this way: (John + (loves + (a + car))), the plus sign indicating the operation of Merge (functional categories like little *v* and T have not been taken into account here, though this will not affect the result). Now suppose we have an infinite sentence that goes like:

(100) (John + (loves + (a + car + ...+...+...)))

or like

(101) (John + ... + ... + ... + (loves + (a + car)))

(100) can be sentence like 'John loves a car that he bought from a shop that is located on the left side of the river that meanders from a place that is known for apples ...' And (101) can go on as 'John who is a good teacher in our town which is located in the central region of the state of Limousin which celebrates a festival ... loves a car'. (100) involves what is called *right-embedding* (because the embedding is on the right side) and (101) contains *left-embedding* (because the relevant embedding is concentrated on the left side of the sentence). Now suppose that we partition the domain and range of Merge into sequences of relative clauses for each of the cases in (100) and (101) such that in each case Merge operates just on a single relative clause and then moves on to the next relative clause in the sequence. Thus we may think that Merge will range over potentially infinite sentences of natural language. A closer inspection of this scenario reveals that this is not possible for natural languages. In the case of (100), the operations of Merge cannot start in the first place because the *potential* sentence is infinitely long; if Merge can never start, the question of whether it can operate on finite sequences of linguistic objects or expressions is utterly meaningless and hence vacuous. In the case of (101), on the other hand, Merge can continue running as far as the left side of the string '(loves + (a + car)', but then it may loop forever or stop because we do not know where the infinitely long relative clause that modifies 'John' ends. Also, paradoxically, an infinitely long sentence (especially in (101)) is not a sentence at all! Hence in these cases Merge or any computational procedure will continue forever or simply cease to operate on a string or a sequence of strings which is not a sentence by virtue of its infinite length – which does not then make Merge or any computational procedure, for that matter, a computable function for linguistic expressions, regardless of whether Merge is cashed out in terms of an algorithm or a program.

So far we have considered sentences of only two types of embedding; now we may also look at a sentence that exhibits *centre-embedding*. The following sentence (which was also used in Chapter 3) repeated below with slight modifications as (102) is an example of *centre-embedding*.

(102) The huge tree the old man everybody loves nurtures overlooks our house.

This sentence is of the pattern NP^n VP^n: NP repeated n times followed by VP repeated the same number of times. Now suppose that the number n

reaches countable infinity such that NP and VP are repeated *n* times exactly in the pattern shown above. Merge can again start operating from the bottom, but this will operate not exactly on (102) but rather on (103) because internal Merge or displacement gives us the surface form in (102).

(103) The huge tree (that$_1$) the old man (that$_2$) everybody ... loves (**that$_2$**) nurtures (**that$_1$**) overlooks our house.

The relative pronoun 'that' has been indexed at different locations and placed within parentheses to indicate the places where the gaps exist ('that' has been marked in bold in the gaps). Now Merge outputs (our + house) in the first phase (DP phase), then (overlooks + (our + house)) in the next phase (*v*P phase). Coming to the next verb phrase, Merge puts together 'nurtures' and 'that' to produce (nurtures + that). We get (loves + that) in a similar manner after this stage. But then the operation Merge will face the same situation as before, as it cannot operate any further and hence will stop because the end point of the infinitely centre-embedded verb phrase can never be reached by Merge.

Perhaps more inexorably crippling is the problem of absence of any possible equivalence of linguistic expressions to natural numbers in this context. What cannot pass unnoticed is the remarkable claim that Merge is equivalent to the successor function in mathematics (Chomsky 2008). If so, the operations of the successor function are parallel to those of Merge. Chomsky says:

> Suppose that a language has the simplest possible lexicon: just one LI, call it 'one'. Application of Merge to the LI yields {one}, call it 'two'. Application of Merge to {one} yields {{one}}, call it 'three'. Etc. In effect, Merge applied in this manner yields the successor function. It is straightforward to define addition in terms of Merge (X,Y), and in familiar ways, the rest of arithmetic. (Chomsky 2008: 6)

These lines are indicative of the kind of mathematical analogy that is at issue here. The successor function in mathematics is used to define natural numbers. The function is of the form: $S(x) = x \cup \{x\}$ – which basically says that every natural number can be derived from its predecessor(s) such that no two natural numbers can share the same successor and no natural number can have 0 as a successor. S is the successor function that yields the successor number when the predecessor number is *x*. Thus we start with 0 = { } and have *S*(0) = {0}= 1, then *S*(1) = {0, 1} = 2 and then *S*(2) = {0, 1, 2} = 3 and so on. Note that in each case a number is equivalent to the set of its predecessors; so {0, 1} = 2 and {0, 1, 2} = 3. What Chomsky means is that the function *S* can be replaced with Merge in a mathematically equivalent manner. If so, we can now model Merge on the successor function *S*. Starting with 0 = { }, as usual, we get Merge (0) = {0}= 1, Merge (1) = {0, 1} = 2 and then Merge (2) = {0, 1, 2} = 3 and so on. We can now generalize Merge from a unary function to an *n*-ary function restricting *n* to 2, because we want Merge to be a binary operation (Hinzen 2009). This gives us the following:

(104) Merge (0, 1) = {0, 1}
  Merge (2, {0, 1}) = {2, {0, 1}}
  Merge (3, {2, {0, 1}}) = {3, {2, {0, 1}}}
  Merge (*n*, {3, {2, {0, 1}}}) = {*n*, {3, {2, {0, 1}}}}

This is another version of the same successor function but in a binary format. Now let us try applying this to the cases in (101) and (103) (since Merge cannot get off the ground in (100), we leave it out of consideration for the case in hand). For (101), the relevant structure (before Merge falls into the trap of infinity) will look like:

(105) Merge (a, car) = {a, car}
  Merge (loves, {a, car}) = {loves, {a, car}}

And the relevant structure that Merge yields for (103) is the following:

(106) Merge (our, house) = {our, house}
  Merge (overlooks, {our, house}) = {overlooks, {our, house}}
  Merge (nurtures, that) = {nurtures, that}
  Merge (loves, that) = {loves, that}

Note that we have ignored the part in which self-embedding of one of the members from a set can serve as the categorical label for the set (as in '{loves, {loves, {a, car}}}', for example). Besides that, in (106) if Merge can ever traverse, though in a counter-intuitively metaphorical sense, the infinitely long structure, the whole noun phrase 'The huge tree the old man everybody ... loves nurtures' is supposed to be Merged to {overlooks, {our, house}}, which has not been shown in (106) precisely because of its very impossibility. Nonetheless this will serve our purpose at hand. First, note that each of the members of any set – whether embedded or not – in (104) is a natural number (certainly except zero), and each *n* (when *n* is a natural number) can be expressed as the successor number which is a member of the very set that contains the set of its predecessors itself as another member. This is another version of the equivalence of a natural number to the set of its predecessors. Now it is easy to see that this is not true of natural language in (105)–(106). Even though it holds that each of the members of any set – whether embedded or not – in (105)–(106) is a lexical item (we can introduce a null element *e* to assume the role of zero, but we can ignore it here), there is no coherent sense in which 'loves' is a successor lexical item of which the set {a, car} in {loves, {a, car}} is the set of its predecessors, or similarly, 'overlooks' is a successor lexical item of which the set {our, house} in {overlooks, {our, house}} is the set of its predecessors, for it is profoundly absurd to say that 'loves' is equivalent to {a, car} or 'overlooks' is equivalent to {our, house}. Second, the restriction that no two natural numbers can share the same successor holds true for natural numbers (this means that this restriction can be violated if and only if two natural numbers sharing a successor are the same number), but this makes no sense whatsoever in the case of natural language. Thus we cannot say, for example, 'loves' as a successor is shared only by the predecessor 'car' even if we license the preposterous presupposition that 'loves' is a successor of 'car'; certainly there are lots of nouns that can co-occur with 'loves' if we attribute the meaning of combinatorial co-occurrence to the relation of 'a predecessor of' or to that of 'a successor of' in the case of natural languages.

In other ways too, there does not seem to be any relevant linguistic sense that can be ascribed to these relations. What if we interpret it in the sense that makes reference to the length of linguistic strings such that the notion of a sequence of strings is all that matters? Let us pursue this option too. It is quite clear that the notion of the length of linguistic strings is neutral with respect to the direction in which the length of a certain string is measured. Thus a sentence string like 'John loves a car' has the length 4, which can be calculated from either direction – right or left. If so, what is a successor of some predecessor from one direction can certainly be shared by some other predecessor from another direction; thus, for example, if 'a' is a successor of 'car', 'a' can also be the successor of 'loves'. That we cannot eliminate this problem by enforcing the strict stipulation that Merge has to work its way out only in a bottom-up fashion, as is standardly assumed, comes to be evident from the case in (100), which exhibits *right-embedding* that augments the length of the string in a direction opposite to that of Merge. Additionally, if we also introduce self-embedding of one of the members from a set that can serve as the categorical label for the set (which follows from the definition of Merge in Chomsky (1995)), there is no way 'loves' can be the successor of 'loves' in {loves, {loves, {a, car}}} even in terms of the notion of the length of strings. The other problem here is that this kind of self-embedding is a top-down process, and hence the direction-neutrality of the length of strings springs into existence. Therefore, all this ultimately leads to the conclusion that there cannot be any successor of linguistic expression lengths because a linguistic expression length may have a successor which may well be shared by other expression lengths too (we can say 'Peter owns a blue-coloured bike that is beautiful' with as much ease as we may require to say 'John loves a car that is beautiful', if 'that is beautiful' is considered to be the successor shared by both expression lengths 'Peter owns a blue-coloured bike' and 'John loves a car'), thereby violating the number-theoretic restriction that states that no two natural numbers can share the same successor. Similar lines of reasoning can also be found in Pullum and Scholz (2010).

So far we have explored ways of reconciling indefinite computation with the finiteness of finite systems by having the domain and range of computational procedures portioned into sequences so that they can range over infinite sets. And we have seen that there does not seem to be anything substantial that lends credibility to this possibility. Now we can explore another totally different way of bypassing the incommensurability of indefinite computation with the finiteness of finite systems. We can say that the infinite set of linguistic expressions is *implicit* or latently *represented* in the finite mental grammar in a finite physical system of the neurobiological substrate. That is, we retain the status of the infinite complexity of the set of linguistic expressions as it is, and at the same time, we also accept the finiteness of the systems that are to execute computable functions generating an infinite set of linguistic expressions. The postulation that computable functions like Merge generating the infinite set of linguistic expressions are actually an idealization but are, as a matter of fact, instantiated in finite brains appears to be plausible, given that there are all sorts of computing devices that are finite but implement computable functions which range over infinite sets (digital computers, calculators or measuring devices, for example). This possibility finds its expression in Watumull (2012), who believes that Merge generates sets of linguistic expressions just as axioms generate theorems, and on that ground, we have to look no further than the finite system of computable functions to reach into infinity. Such arguments often have recourse to the principle of *mathematical induction* which holds on a set that is denumerably infinite because the principle of mathematical induction helps extrapolate from a finite procedure to a denumerably infinite set. So the infinite set of linguistic expressions is said to be inductively derived from the finite procedure or a *function defined-in-intension* effected by the finite brain.

This sounds reasonable for many functions that are especially implemented in machines. The addition function can be one good example. Or one can take the function that generates the Fibonacci sequence ($f(n) = n - 1 + n - 2$) which is surprisingly found to be represented in many natural objects (in artichoke, for example). However, this leads to nonsense when applied to linguistic expressions. Consider some of the cases of mathematical induction on the set of natural numbers.

(107) $1 + 2 + 3 + ...n = \dfrac{n(n + 1)}{2}$

(108) $1 + 3 = 4$
$1 + 3 + 5 = 9$
$1 + 3 + 5 + 7 = 16$
$1 + 3 + 5 + 7 + 9 = 25$
$\cdots$

(107) shows that the sum of n natural numbers in a series can be derived by a function different from addition, and (108) is a way of getting n^2 from the sum of n odd natural numbers. The principle of mathematical induction holds on both sets of natural numbers in (107) and (108) generated by the functions defined on the respective sets. Thus if, by virtue of the principle of mathematical induction, some proposition P holds for n, it also holds for $n + 1$. Now the question is whether we can imagine anything analogous to this for any set of natural language expressions or even for expression lengths. Any of the three ways of incrementing the sequence of linguistic strings, namely *right-embedding*, *left-embedding* and *centre-embedding*, may be considered in this regard. Let us consider the simple example that was expanded from (100) above: 'John loves a car that he bought from a shop that is located on the left side of the river that meanders from a place that is known for apples...'. Here, each relevant expansion is in the form of a relative clause (Rcl) which can serve as a newly concatenated linguistic object in the sequence of strings. This gives us the following schema:

(109) John loves a car + Rcl^n

The expression in Rcl^n indicates that the number of concatenated relative clauses in a sequence after the string 'John loves a car' can be countably infinite. Does this sequence of strings show anything that is even remotely analogous or equivalent to the sequences of natural numbers in (107)–(108)? What can be interesting mathematical properties of sequences of linguistic expressions in this context so that we can test the principle of mathematical induction on the relevant set? One may well say that a recursive definition in terms of phrase structure rules will do the job. But this is not so. Consider, for example, the following rule schema for (109):

(110) NP$\rightarrow$ (Det) N
　　　 TVP$\rightarrow$ V NP
　　　 S$\rightarrow$ NP TVP + Rcl^n

　　　　　　　　　　　　　　(Here, TVP = transitive verb phrase)

We are well aware of the fact that such context-free rules overgenerate and often produce deviant or odd or even ungrammatical sentences ('John kisses awareness that drinks cans of beer...' or 'Himself kisses John who kicks himself...'). We need layers of context-sensitive information to factor out many such sentences. Hence we cannot have an equivalence like 'John loves a car that he bought from a shop that is located on the left side of the river that meanders from a place that is known for apples...' = S$\rightarrow$ NP TVP + Rcl^n. Note also that the set of numbers is closed under the basic arithmetical operations – addition, subtraction, division and multiplication. That is, the inputs and outputs of any (combination) of these operations are ultimately members of the set of numbers. There is no sense in which we can even fancy applying analogous operations to sequences of strings. The only relevant operation applicable is concatenation, as is well known in formal language theory. It is only in the intuitive sense of concatenation that the principle of mathematical induction appears to be pertinent to natural language expressions. But again, it is not clear how to make sense of an application of the principle of mathematical induction even on the basis of the intuitive sense of concatenation, which consists in the principle that a linguistic expression X – which is a *concatenation* of two linguistic expressions Y and Z – can itself be an input to the operation of concatenation, and that all such linguistic expressions are closed under the operation of concatenation.

Similarly, it is also worth ascertaining whether the compositional function posited under the umbrella of the *Compositionality Thesis* can be of any help in relation to the employment of the principle of mathematical induction for natural language expressions. Thus one may argue that the compositional function for linguistic expressions can be inductively generalized from a finite set to an infinite set of linguistic expressions. It is indeed the case that the *Compositionality Thesis* is a guiding principle for the structure-building operations in natural language; but this does not qualify as a sufficient criterion nonetheless to elevate the *Compositionality Thesis* to a level appropriate for the principle of mathematical induction to hold. Note that the principle of mathematical induction states that if some proposition P holds for n, it also holds for $n + 1$, by way of that induction. It is clear that this holds true for simpler cases like 'John drives his car very fast' which can be composed like this: $[_S$ John $[_{VP}$ $[_{VP}$ drives $[_{NP}$ his car]] $[_{AdvP}$ very fast]]] and also extended as: $[_S$ John $[_{VP}$ $[_{VP}$ $[_{VP}$ drives his car] $[_{AdvP}$ very fast]] $[_{VP}$ ignoring $[_{NP}$ traffic signals]]]] and so on. But when we look at cases like 'Terry kicked the bucket yesterday', 'Bill beats around/about the bush during his lectures', 'I have always taken this fact for granted', etc., the matter becomes hazier. As a consequence, any specification of the compositional function cannot be made without further stipulations in order to save the whole idea of applying the principle of mathematical induction.

Even if we stipulate that certain idiomatic expressions are not composed internally but apply as a whole, this does not explain why we can use 'around' and 'about' interchangeably in 'Bill beats around/about the bush during his lectures'. Nor can we account for the variable-like nature of the noun phrase required for the object in 'I have always taken this fact for granted'. Either the compositional function needs to be specified in broader terms to accommodate these cases, or the compositional function has to be relaxed for semi-regular or irregular patterns in natural languages. Either option verges on risking the generality of the principle of mathematical induction, which is not understood to steer clear of particularly idiosyncratic numbers when applied to a numerical series. Thus no substance can be ascribed to the claim that the infinite set of linguistic expressions can be inductively generalized under closure of the compositional function however conceptualized.

Thus far we have explored ways of escaping from the problem of the ontological incommensurability between an infinite extension of linguistic expressions and a finite mental grammar. The problem has been couched in terms that relate to the postulation of a computable function for generating an infinite extension of natural language expressions. It has been shown that the notion of a computational procedure of the language faculty as part of the mental grammar is vacuous, for the grounds on which such a procedure for natural language has been motivated do not lead us anywhere. If there is any stronger reason to believe that there cannot exist any generative procedure within the language faculty, it is the *halting problem* that demarcates the limits of computability. In Chapter 3, it was stated that the problem of determining whether a procedure underlying N ever stops could be shown to be a version of the *halting problem*, according to which there exists no algorithm that, given a machine M and an input x, can decide whether or not M halts on the input x. Extrapolating this to the case of the language faculty we can state that there is no algorithm that, given the generative procedure of the language faculty and N (or a set of sub-Numerations/sub-arrays), can decide whether or not the generative procedure of the language faculty halts on N (or on a set of sub-Numerations/sub-arrays). And the proof of this would follow quite straightforwardly by assuming there exists no algorithm that decides whether or not the generative procedure of the language faculty halts on *itself* as an input (Turing 1936). When we state that there is no algorithm that, given the generative procedure of the language faculty and N (or a set of sub-Numerations/sub-arrays), can decide whether or not the generative procedure of the language faculty halts on N (or on a set of sub-Numerations/sub-arrays), we shall have to invoke the problem of self-reference to prove a version of the *halting problem* for the generative procedure of the language faculty. Suppose that the generative procedure of the language faculty specifies a function h such that if any program specified by the generative procedure of the language faculty halts on N, h outputs 1; if not, then h outputs 0. Now let lexical items inserted in N be strings and H be a program that encodes h; H takes programs specified by the generative procedure of the language faculty and strings as inputs, and outputs exactly what h outputs. And let us also construct another program P specified by the generative procedure of the language faculty which can be defined as follows: P runs in infinite loops, if H outputs 1 and P ends if H outputs 0. Once can easily see the contradiction that emerges when P along with its program text is input to H. It goes like this: if H outputs 1 by taking P as an input, then P runs in infinite loops and if P runs in infinite loops, H must have output 0, and on the other hand, if H outputs 0 by taking P as an input, then P must have halted and if P ends, H has output 1. We end up with contradictions in both directions. Therefore, we arrive at the conclusion that there is no algorithm or program that, given the generative procedure of the language faculty and N (or a set of sub-Numerations/sub-arrays), can decide whether or not the generative procedure of the language faculty or any program specified by it halts on N (or on a set of sub-Numerations/sub-arrays).[3]

We now affirm that the *halting problem* for the generative procedure of the language faculty may give rise to non-computability. But, as Hehner (2010) argues, the inference about non-computability deduced from the demonstration that the *halting function* is inconsistent is stretching the point too far from a mere demonstration of a kind of inconsistency of specifications of programs. Simply framed, the *halting problem*, for Hehner, does not prove non-computability; rather, it proves an inconsistency in the specification of the halting function. If so, he thinks that it makes no sense to propose a *halting program*, given that the *halting function* itself is inconsistent. This argument does not in fact go through in the present context for two reasons.

First, Hehner believes that termination is not essential for a non-interacting computation because specifying a termination without a temporal bound is useless on the grounds that we may never be able to observe when the program violates the specification. This means that programs are to be construed as partial functions, not as total functions, given that partial functions map only a subset of elements from a set in the domain onto the range. The implications for the generative procedure of the language faculty are then quite clear. It follows that the generative procedure of the language faculty *must* specify partial functions and *may* be uncommitted with respect to any time bound for computation. It appears to be true of the generative procedure of the language faculty in the Minimalist architecture, for any mapping from N or any subpart of N out of the entire lexicon is a partial function, and the generative procedure of the language faculty is outside the spatio-temporal bounds (a point which is also stressed by Seuren (2004)). However, it is worth emphasizing that the proof of the *halting problem* for the generative procedure of the language faculty presented here has not relied upon the presupposition that the computability assumption is the cause of inconsistency. Rather, it is the postulation of a generative procedure of the language faculty per se that leads to the *halting problem*. Questions about (non-)computability that may well ensue from the *halting problem* are an epiphenomenon in the current context. Note that the *halting problem* with the generative procedure of the language faculty may have the computation on linguistic representations stall, given that a mapping from N to pairs of the form (π, λ) is made viable through the operation Merge. Even if the generative procedure of the language faculty halts on N, there is no guarantee that the mapping from N to pairs of the form (π, λ) made viable through Merge can be kick-started, especially when no lexical item or a null lexical item is inserted in N.[4] Thus, regardless of anything else that the *halting problem* with the generative procedure of the language faculty may reveal, uncertainty generated by the *halting function* surrounding the generative procedure of the language faculty *does* cast doubt on any computability assumption about the generative procedure of the language faculty. As a matter of fact, this uncertainty may illuminate nothing whatsoever about the computability of the generative procedure of the language faculty. Therefore, the postulation of any computability assumption about the generative procedure of the language faculty is the effect, rather than a cause, of inconsistency manifest in the *halting problem* with the generative procedure of the language faculty.

Second, Hehner's argument has perhaps missed the role of recursive definitions that play an important role in the contradiction laid bare by the *halting problem*. This has been pointed out by Huizing et al. (2010). And if so, Hehner's argument leaves the conclusion about non-computability unaffected. Nonetheless Hehner's argument has a bearing on semantic transparency vis-à-vis (non-)computability assumptions, and by virtue of that, this carries over to the present case about the language faculty. But any notion of semantic transparency or a lack thereof latent in the formulation of the *halting problem* with the generative procedure of the language faculty is muddled because of interpretative effects of semanticity hovering over the computational system of the language faculty on the one hand, and the architectural requirement for an independent level of mapping of syntactic representations generated by the computational system onto the semantic representations on the other. Such muddling has been unmasked in Chapter 3, and we shall see more of it in the next chapters. Overall, we can say with a greater degree of certainty that we can propose the halting program for the generative procedure of the language faculty, primarily because the inconsistency itself does not *necessarily* have to incorporate the *halting function* to begin with. This is what we shall turn to now.

A mapping from N to pairs of the form (π, λ) is sequentially subsequent to the operations that obtain within N. Thus anything that imposes inherent constraints and limiting conditions on N blocks, by way of these very constraints and limiting conditions, the mapping from N to pairs of the form (π, λ). The *halting problem* of the generative procedure of the language faculty for N (or on a set of sub-Numerations/sub-arrays) is of such type. The *halting problem* is an abstract limiting condition on computation in computability theory. It can appear in various different versions, though the underlying idea is the same. It would be really interesting if the fundamental results of the *halting problem* can be demonstrated for the generative procedure of the language faculty in a more concrete form. In fact, there is a more concrete version of the *halting problem* that can translate all the formal essentials of the abstract notion of *halting* into a more transparently immaculate format. This more concrete version of the *halting problem* is called the *busy-beaver problem*, which was shown to be equivalent to the *halting problem* by Rado (1962). But before we proceed, let us have a clearer idea of the *halting problem* with respect to the operations of the Turing machine.

A Turing machine works with the alphabet of symbols {0, 1} and has an infinite two-way tape with square boxes for symbol processing. The read/write head of the machine reads, prints or deletes symbols on each of the squares of the tape and on the basis of this, moves one square right or left only to go into a new state out of a finite number of states. The *halting problem* for Turing machines is essentially a problem of indeterminacy and undecidability. That is, there is no way an algorithm can be derived from the Turing machine that tells us whether the Turing machine will halt on an input or not. In a more general sense, this applies for any arbitrary input with the universal Turing machine. It is because of the *halting problem* that Turing machines generate *recursively enumerable sets*, the definition of which involves Turing machines not deciding on non-members of a set. Looked at from this perspective, the connection between *recursively enumerable sets* and Turing machines begins to be clearer: if Turing machines may not halt at all on an input, the question of the existence of an algorithm that decides for sure if a Turing machine will halt on an input that is not a member of a set of natural numbers is unsolvable. Equipped with this understanding, we may now explicate the *busy-beaver problem* in its basic form.

The *busy-beaver problem* is a problem of determining the maximum number of 1s that can be left by a Turing machine, or rather by a class of Turing machines on a tape which is all blank. Another way of seeing this is in terms of the maximum number of steps that a Turing machine performs while writing 1s on the squares of the tape before it halts. That is, there can be a *busy-beaver function* that can map a Turing machine onto the set of natural numbers. The function grows formidably in proportion to the number of states of the machine concerned. It has been observed that the function that maps a Turing machine onto the maximum number of steps that a Turing machine performs before it halts is larger than the one that maps onto the maximum number of 1s that can be left by a Turing machine. The *busy-beaver function* grows so fast that it exceeds any computable function. Hence it is a hallmark of non-computability. With just seven states the maximum of number of 1s that are left by a Turing machine or the maximum number of steps performed becomes fiendishly large and barges into the non-computable.

For the sake of simplicity let us just consider the maximum number of 1s that can be left by a Turing machine as part of a *busy-beaver function* $\Sigma(n)$. The following results on the growth of $\Sigma(n)$ are relevant.

(111) $\Sigma(1) = 1; \Sigma(2) = 4; \Sigma(3) = 6; \Sigma(4) = 13; \Sigma(5) = \geq 4098;$
        $\Sigma(6) = \geq 1.29 \times 10^{865}$

This can be shown in tables by adopting the relatively simpler notation in Cooper (2013). The numbers 1 and 0 on top of a table are the two symbols of a Turing machine and the figure on the left of each box in a table indicates the state number. Any configuration of a Turing machine is in the form: (symbol written, Left/Right, new state), as can be seen in Figure 4.2.

A one-state Turing machine produces only one 1. Now we can look at the table that specifies the operations of a two-state Turing machine that produces four 1s (Figure 4.3).

The sequence of operations of the two-state Turing machine can be written as shown in Figure 4.4.

(112) $\Sigma(2) = 4$

	0
0	1 R 2

Figure 4.2 Table of operations of a one-state Turing machine

	0	1
1	1 R 2	1 L 2
2	1 L 1	1 R 3

Figure 4.3 Table of operations of a two-state Turing machine

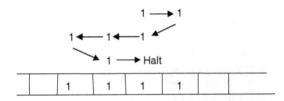

Figure 4.4 Movements of the read/write head of a two-state Turing machine

In Figure 4.4 arrows of the → type indicate a right movement and the other type ← indicates a left movement. What the sequence drawn up in Figure 4.4 denotes is that the Turing machine first erases 0 and writes 1 following 1R2, then moves right, enters state 2 and writes 1 by following 1L1, then moves left and retains 1 following 1L2 and enters state 2, then moves left and writes 1 by following 1L1 and enters state 1, then moves left again and writes 1 following 1R2, and then ultimately moves right and halts (going by 1R2) because there is no third state of the machine. It is clear from (112) that the total number of 1s left by the Turing machine is 4 and the sum total of all binary digits (in Figure 4.4) is 6, which is the number of total steps performed. Note that we arrive at this only by assuming that the infinite two-way tape is all blank in all of its squares before the Turing machine starts and that it starts in state 1. The status of the tape after the computation is shown right below the schematic representation of the transitions (one can get this result by drawing vertical lines from each 1 and/or from the stack of 1s). Let us now have a look at a three-state Turing machine (Figure 4.5).

The sequence of operations of the three-state Turing machine has been drawn up as shown in Figure 4.6.

(113) Σ(3) = 6

	0	1
1	1 R 2	1 L 3
2	1 L 1	1 R 2
3	1 L 2	1 R 4

Figure 4.5 Table of operations of a three-state Turing machine

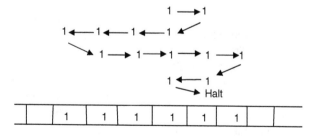

Figure 4.6 Movements of the read/write head of a three-state Turing machine

There are six 1s on the tape left, as shown in Figure 4.6 and (113). And the transitions of this three-state machine can be specified in a manner similar to the way described for a two-state Turing machine.

Now it is easy to state the *busy-beaver function* on the generative procedure of the language faculty in such a manner that the task of determining the maximum number of 1s that can be left by a Turing machine (or a class of Turing machines) on a tape can be modelled on the process of increasing the index of a lexical item inserted in N by 1 when the indices are all 0, to begin with. Each lexical item inserted in N increments the index by one. Just like the *busy-beaver function*, the function specified by the generative procedure of the language faculty that inserts lexical items in N will grow so fast that it will exceed any computable function. This function is thus to grow in proportion to the number of states of the machine concerned. Significantly, these states of the machine having the generative procedure of the language faculty can be defined by the principles as well as parameters for particular languages (Watumull 2012), who has actually gone so far as to apply the Turing machine model itself to the generative procedure of the language faculty.

The take-home message for the nature of the putative computational system of the language faculty is quite clear. Structural distinction telescoped through the notion of linguistic derivation, as discussed in section 4.1, ceases to be meaningful for the language faculty if and only if the posited computation may not even take off the ground, or if there exists an uncertainty about linguistic computation taking off the ground. Without linguistic computation taking off the ground, no derivation can exist. Thus the structural distinction of linguistic representations that comes as a consequence of linguistic derivation may also not emerge. Structural distinction of linguistic representations is central to the framework of Generative Grammar, insofar as structural distinction motivates different levels of representation in the architecture of the language faculty. But bereft of the notion of computation that gives rise to the structural distinction of linguistic representations, the putative computational system of the language faculty becomes empty of any real consequence. From a more focused perspective, if the generative procedure of the language faculty specifies functions that are undecidable because no algorithm can decide for sure whether the generative procedure of the language faculty will ever stop on N or not, the generative procedure of the language faculty or the putative computational system of the language faculty is *intrinsically* crash-prone, regardless of whatever the nature of the performance system for language. In this sense, approaches such as Frampton and Gutmann's (2002) make no sense whatsoever, since on their view feature sharing across a number of heads rides on selectional features/properties of all heads introduced, thereby eliminating a great deal of computational complexity generated by derivational possibilities on the one hand, and many potential crashes of derivations at a later stage on the other. Implicit in Frampton and Gutmann's approach is the requirement that an operation called *Select* has to pick up heads (both functional and lexical) along with their complements from a certain lexical base; if so, the *halting function* can be imposed right on *Select* itself, and the rest of the reasoning about undecidability follows and hence remains intact even in this version of the story of linguistic computation. Besides, the generative procedure of the language faculty is *intrinsically* crash-prone, regardless of whether crashes of derivations are prevented at the initial stage or at some later stage (especially at the C-I and A-P interfaces). And in fact, even if feature sharing (in virtue of a coalescence of nominal agreement features on different heads) on the basis of selectional properties of heads may obviate possibilities of derivational crashes, this does not in any sense do away with the *halting problem* with *Select* or any other function specified by the generative procedure of the language faculty owing to the *inherent* character of computation itself that is attributed to the system of the language faculty.

There is another subtle issue that needs to be clarified at this point. The *halting problem* with the generative procedure of the language faculty need not prove anything about language processing in real time mediated by the performance system of language processing. That we have false starts, parsing difficulties and scores of many other things we experience in our ordinary use of language is not *caused* by the *halting problem* with the generative procedure of the language faculty any more than operating system crashes and other software application crashes in digital computers that we use are triggered by the *halting problem* with the Turing machine. Thus, when saying that no derivation may run without linguistic computation taking off the ground, we mean to *exactly* say that the *halting problem* with the generative procedure of the language faculty casts doubt on the possibility of existence of any mechanical procedure that can ensure that the generative procedure of the language faculty halts and executes the mapping from N to pairs of the form (π, λ). And in the absence of any such mechanical procedure, the generative procedure of the language faculty ceases to have any explanatory value or empirical significance, for there will be no mechanical way of telling a halting generative procedure of the language faculty apart from a non-halting one. The deterministic character of the generative procedure of the language faculty having been lost, the putative computational system of the language faculty turns into an inelegant, imperfect and non-optimal solution to the demands of the interface systems. In more concrete terms, in the absence of any mechanical way of telling a halting generative procedure of the language faculty apart from a non-halting one, Merge operations may or may not start off with N, and even if they do, we are never sure that the operations will continue running or terminate somewhere ultimately building grammatical constructions. As a consequence, the outputs of the language faculty do not *necessarily* (but rather *contingently*) answer to the conditions imposed by the interface systems, contrary to what Collins (2004) may get us to believe. Nor can the language faculty be viewed as a set of *sui generis* conditions that the normal operation of a human brain has to meet, simply because any such conditions do not have a determinate character, and in virtue of this, the relevant aspect of the complex system of the language faculty which is specified by those conditions may well be visible in human brains even *without* these conditions. We can also see how this affects the line of reasoning that will be employed for an examination of the exact nature and form of computational complexity in the putative computational system of the language faculty. This is what we shall deal with now.

4.4   Linguistic computation and computational complexity

We can now take stock of what we have done so far by inspecting what we started with. We have probed the issue of whether linguistic computation is realized in or abstracts away from psychological mechanisms and have finally observed that the matter is more muddled than is imagined. Then the problem of how infinite languages derive from finite bio-cognitive systems is thrashed out with further perplexities emerging from the way the putative computational system of the language faculty is assumed to be designed. At this point, it appears that the theory of computational complexity in theoretical computer science might be of use in helping disentangle the knots, on the grounds that the theory of computational complexity can unravel the nature of complexity of linguistic computations which are assumed to run the putative computational system of the language faculty. This is significant not only for an understanding of the form of complexity of linguistic computations, but also for an investigation of the very character or property of computations which are construed as linguistic. This has the potential to tease out the truth as we examine the ways in which the theory of computational complexity may and may not apply to linguistic computation. In sum, if linguistic computation owes its very character to what is characterized as computational, formal operations as part of linguistic computation *must* be subject to the restrictions clamped down by computational complexity.

We can now have an idea of what computational complexity means. Computational complexity is a measure of resource limitations (mainly space and time) in computation which may well be modelled by some version of a Turing machine having an infinite tape with boxes for symbol processing. A task for such a machine can be difficult or easy as a function of the space and/or time that is required for the computation. Usually, this depends on the length of the input; thus computational complexity functions are defined as functions of the input length: $O(f(|\text{Input}|))$ – here O means 'on the order of'. Different complexity classes exist for different tasks with varying levels of difficulty. For example, some decision problems can be solved by a machine in time (or space s) t as a polynomial function of the input length. Such decision problems fall under the class P (Polynomial Time) when the machines in question are deterministic Turing machines the transitions of which are *fully* determined by the input and the state-symbol configurations. However, there are other decision problems which can also be solved in polynomial time but are computed by non-deterministic Turning machines the computational paths of which are *not* fully determined by the input and symbol-state configurations; as a consequence, non-deterministic Turing machines may follow various possible computational paths conforming to instructions, given a configuration (Frixione 2001). Such decision problems fall under the complexity class NP (Non-deterministic Polynomial Time). Hence it becomes clear that every non-deterministic Turing machine can also, in principle, behave like a deterministic Turing machine in each of these computational paths. So it appears that P ⊆ NP; but whether P = NP is still a mysterious problem in theoretical computer science. For our purpose, we can see that the theory of computational complexity says that finding a solution to a problem is more difficult than verifying the correctness of a solution, which is the essence of the puzzle surrounding P versus NP (Goldreich 2008). This will be useful in characterizing the computational complexity of linguistic computations.

In fact, one can trace the complexity of linguistic computations right from the point where N is built. N, being an unordered set of pairs containing lexical items and indices, conceals vestiges of enormous computational complexity, since the form of N itself leads to computations arising from a formidably non-deterministic branching out of operations. Consider, for example, an N of, say, 10 lexical items. If we try out all possible sequences of derivation from such an N, we can have 10! possible derivations many of which may not make grammatical, or rather convergent, derivations. But the order of complexity is so high that it exceeds any exponential function – a point raised by Johnson and Lappin (1997). This is more so because of the application of economy constraints to derivations from N, economy constraints being constraints that select a subset of derivations out of a large set on the basis of the fulfilment of criteria imposed by economy constraints (for example, minimality conditions favouring and sanctioning derivations with a short movement/displacement over those with a long movement/displacement). For economy constraints to apply to a set of derivations from N, all the derivations from N must have to be scanned at least to the point where derivations are to crash, as Johnson and Lappin rightly argue. And if this is the case, computations must traverse the enormous factorial space of all these paths – which will make any such linguistic computation intractable. Furthermore, if there are preferences with regard to overt versus covert movements (any overt movement is assumed to be prior to the point (Spell-Out) at which derivations are shipped off to PF and LF), the non-determinism snowballs further, thereby increasing computational complexity to a greater extent.

However, it can be noted that the current phase-theoretic architecture of Minimalism has done away with covert movement construed in architectural terms, and on this account the amount of non-determinism appears to have been scaled down. Additionally, the phase-based machinery allows for local linguistic computations so that all local computations restricted to each phasal domain (CP, vP, DP) can pave the way for computations in the next phase till the point the CP phase is reached. This is supposed to considerably tame computational complexity. However, this is not quite true, as we shall soon see. Consider, for example, an N such that N = {T, C, v, man, the, girls, give, did, when, flowers}, which has the cardinality of 10 (because of 10 items in N). And now let us first see how we express a mapping from N to pairs of the form (π, λ) in the non-phase-theoretic architecture of Minimalism. Case and φ-features need to be checked and deleted through the matching of Probe (the item containing *un*interpretable φ-features and/or the EPP (Extended Projection Principle) feature, which is responsible for the surface appearance of subjects in natural languages) and Goal (the item containing the *un*interpretable case feature) which come into a relation called Agree, which deletes the *un*interpretable features of both and usually gets the Probe to assign a case to a Goal. So far so good. Assuming, for simplicity, that we have four main features, namely case feature, φ-features, EPP feature and the Q feature (responsible for *Wh*-movement; see Cable (2010) for significant details on the Q feature), gives us four different featural dimensions which can have two distinct choices each, because each (type of) feature is binary/digital in terms of the absence/presence of the relevant feature. Generally, T, v, C and Determiner Phrases (DPs) have φ-features;[5] both T and C can have the EPP feature; DPs have case features, and finally, C and *Wh*-elements have Q features.

Now we have 4 types of items (T, v, C and DPs) for φ-features, 2 types of items (T and C) for the EPP feature, 1 type of item (DPs) for the case feature and 2 types of items (C and *Wh*-elements) for the Q feature. Given that we have an N = {T, C, v, man, the, girls, give, did, when, flowers} of cardinality 10, an algorithm that executes the mapping from N to pairs of the form (π, λ) will run in a computational time of *at most* $_2 4^n \times {}_2 2^n \times 2^n \times {}_2 2^n = {}_2 4^6 \times {}_2 2^2 \times 2^3 \times {}_2 2^2 = 16,777,216 \times 16 \times 8 \times 16 = 34,359,738,368$ steps in order to scan all possible derivations with different features present or absent. This may obtain in the extreme case, given that the measurement of the complexity takes into account different possibilities for *types* of items (when 2 is raised to 4 or 2 at the first level of exponents, for example). This is only for a single clause (say, 'When did the man give girls flowers?'), but for k clauses the number of total steps would be $({}_2 4^n \times {}_2 2^n \times 2^n \times {}_2 2^n)^k$. With increasing k, the number of steps the algorithm will have to take in order to compute sentences of the length of k clauses will soon exceed the number of all elementary particles in the universe, and even the age of the universe will not be sufficient for the computation to terminate! At this point, one may now wonder where this formidable computational complexity comes from. Note that one of the sources of complexity is the number of choices varying with the presence/absence of the relevant features (or feature bundles) when juxtaposed with different combinations of these features (especially when the reference sets of all possible derivations are built so that the non-convergent and non-optimal derivations can be filtered out). This is so, because the presence or absence of a certain feature (or a feature bundle) cannot be prejudged by the computational system of the language faculty before the relevant phrases are constructed when syntactic objects are Merged. Even if one is inclined to maintain that the state of the computational system of the language faculty is set to a particular language, and by virtue of that, all the relevant settings for particular lexical items are already built into the knowledge base of the language faculty, this still does not rule out the possibility that T, C, v, DPs, etc. cannot be 'known' beforehand to have the relevant features present/absent. For example, not all DPs can be said to have the case feature (for instance, expletive DPs as well as indefinite nominals in languages such as Hebrew, Hindi, etc. (see for details, Danon 2006)), and the same thing can be said about T, v and C. Furthermore, if we deem that the computational system of the language faculty is a universal *minimal* system optimally built and mathematically elegant with no redundancy and underspecified with regard to semantic and indeed linguistic variation (see for details, Hinzen 2006; Burton-Roberts 2011), the gigantic growth of computational complexity in linguistic computations is destined to protrude from the abstract system of linguistic computations.[6]

Thus, narrowing the domain of the putative computational system of the language faculty by simply adopting the idea that semantic–conceptual systems and/or phonological/phonetic systems are mere realizations or representations of the abstractions generated by linguistic computations formidably expands the domain over which linguistic computations are supposed to be played out. That is, detaching the putative computational system of the language faculty in an essential way from the semantic–conceptual and/or phonological/phonetic systems that track much of the computational complexity of linguistic computations within the space of the putative computational system of the language faculty inexorably dislodges the complexity-impeding mechanisms from the putative computational system of the language faculty. This is simply because of the burden imposed on the putative computational system of the language faculty which is supposed to generate and thus deal with the enormous variety of natural language constructions, while the features of computational complexity manifest in those very natural language constructions can be reliably ascribed to the semantic–conceptual and/or phonological/phonetic systems. In all, the skyrocketing growth of computational complexity in linguistic computations is inevitable in the kind of a computational system of the language faculty that is not committed to tracking semantic–conceptual and phonological complexity of widely varied linguistic constructions. Therefore, such a computational system of the language faculty will be miserably crippled by as small a set as N = {T, C, v, Noun, Determiner, Auxiliary Verb, Noun, Verb, *Wh*-element, Noun}.

Moreover, this problem does not go away with the phase-theoretic architecture of Minimalism. The sine qua non of the phase-theoretic architecture of Minimalism is the Phase Impenetrability Condition (PIC) which states that in a phase α with head H, the domain of H is not accessible to operations outside α, only H and its edge are accessible to such operations. What this states is that in a simple monoclausal linguistic construction having the structure $[_{CP}$ C $[_{TP}$ T ... $[_{vP}$ v [VP ...]]]], the underlined computational spaces are complements of the phase edges, namely the little v and C, and when we move from the VP towards the CP the underlined part before the vP will be inaccessible to any operations beyond the little v, only v and its SPECIFIER being accessible to such operations; the same holds true for the next phase, that is, the CP phase. Similar considerations apply to DPs in which an NP – the complement of a D head – will be inaccessible to operations beyond D, except for the fact that D and its SPECIFIER can be available for such operations. Now let us take the same N that was taken up for illustration above, that is, N = {T, C, v, man, the, girls, give, did, when, flowers}. Since the computational domain in the phase-theoretic architecture has been drastically scaled down by having the entire domain over which linguistic computations run partitioned into smaller (sub)domains, we may expect to get the formidably daunting computational complexity considerably reduced. Let us see if this is really the case. Linguistic computations are to start from the DP phase in a configuration like $[_{CP}$ C $[_{TP}\underline{T}$ $[_{vP}$ v $[_{vP}\underline{V}$ $[_{DP}$ D [NP]] $[_{DP}$D [NP]]]]]] for a double-object construction that can be derived from N; so we may take a sub-numeration, say N1= {the, man, girls, flowers} and try to assess the computational complexity by starting with the DP phase and going all the way up to the CP phase. N1 = {the, man, girls, flowers} is sufficient for the DP phase, and hence we may consider just three (kinds of) features, namely definiteness, DP-internal φ-features (especially the number feature) and the focus feature (see e.g. Danon (2011) for a relevant discussion on DP-internal computations in Minimalism). Thus, these three features can be relevant to linguistic computations within the DP phase. Given that we have three nouns in N1, namely 'man', 'girls' and 'flowers', an algorithm that computes the DP phase will take a computational time of $_2 3^n = {_2} 3^3 = 512$ steps. Now moving up to the next phase, we can look at the computational complexity of the vP phase. The significant features (or feature bundles) are φ-features, and the case feature; here, the relevant subset of N would be N2 = {v, the, man, give, flowers, girls, when}. Since we have one little v, 3 DPs and a *Wh*-element in N2, a computational time of $_2 2^n \times 2 = {_2} 2^4 \times 2 = 512$ steps is required by an algorithm that executes the respective function(s) in the vP phase ($_2 2^4$ is multiplied by 2 because of the presence of the *Wh*-element with a

Q feature). In a similar way we now move into the last phase, that is, the CP phase. At this stage, the relevant subset of N is N3 = {T, C, did, when, 'the man'}, and the relevant features (or features bundles) are φ-features, the EPP feature, the case feature and the Q feature. An algorithm executing the function(s) in the CP phase will require a computational time of $_2 3^n \times {}_2 2^n \times 2 \times {}_2 2^n \times 2 = {}_2 3^3 \times {}_2 2^2 \times 2 \times {}_2 2^2 \times 2 = 512 \times 16 \times 2 \times 16 \times 2$ = 524,288 steps, since we need T, C and a DP (the man) (for φ-features), T and C (for the EPP feature), 2 steps (for the checking of the case feature of the DP against that of T), 'when' and C (for the Q feature) and finally, 2 steps (for the recognition of 'did' for its movement to the C head).

Since the phase-theoretic architecture of the language faculty must have *at least* two levels of linguistic computation – one at the level of independent phases and another at PF where all the pieces of structure Spelled-Out from the phases in a sequence are to be put back together for linearization – an algorithm that computes all the phases for a single clause like 'When did the man give girls flowers?' within the space of the computational system of the language faculty will run in a computational time of $512 \times 512 \times 524,288 = 137,438,953,472$ steps. Note that this figure is much bigger than the one for the non-phase-theoretic architecture of the language faculty, and with k clauses the number of total steps would be $(137,438,953,472)^k$ – which is so big as to definitely lead to intractability.[7] Therefore, it becomes clearer that the phase-theoretic system of linguistic computations does not seem to have an edge over the non-phase-theoretic architecture of the language faculty in terms of economizing on computational complexity, contrary to what is generally believed. Both models of the language faculty invite decision problems that require algorithms running in (non-deterministic) exponential time – which establishes their intractability. However, each phase when taken alone considerably scales down the relevant amount of computational complexity. But this does not make a significant difference, chiefly because a piece of structure Spelled-Out in each phase is not linguistically meaningful, insofar as the rest of the pieces of a construction in question are to be structurally related to that isolated piece of structure anyway. Any reduction of computational complexity in a phase does not *necessarily* correlate with a discount in the requirement to structurally piece together phasal outputs.

Another question seems pertinent here. Why do we bother about the computational complexity of linguistic computations, if complexity results are not necessarily insightful as to the real cognitive complexity of linguistic structures, as Berwick and Weinberg (1984) maintain? In fact, Berwick and Weinberg (1984) echo what Chomsky (1965) has stressed in connection with the generative capacity of linguistic theories, which is linked to a notion of structural descriptions as well as to the semanticity of linguistic structures. But one may note that matters of strong generative capacity do have a bearing on the requirement to structurally piece together phasal outputs, and if so, a linguistic theory that is complacent about the reduction of computational complexity, but not about the requirement to structurally piece together phasal outputs, becomes far removed from anything expected in a linguistic theory that is structurally grounded. Of course, the underlying presupposition is that the cognitive complexity of natural language may well look different from anything that an analysis of computational complexity of parsing procedures reveals, since any distinction in terms of efficiency between two different parsing procedures may not remain preserved over all implementations of the relevant procedures, and any such differences between the two different parsing procedures may not be reflected in the cognitive domain. It is thus believed that the computational system of the human mind or our brain may have certain 'operating characteristics' which are quite different from those which are assumed to be what different parsing procedures are more/less efficient in. This belief consists in the conjecture that the human mind/ brain may have quite differently specialized but unknown operations, structures and procedures which parsing procedures do not tap into. It is worthwhile noting that the present analysis of the computational complexity of linguistic computations in the putative computational system of the language faculty rides on the representational operations that are assumed to be beyond a level appropriate for any comparison and analysis of parsing procedures. This tension has been demonstrated to contain the germs of vicious riddles, inconsistencies and paradoxes, as also shown in Chapter 3. In the face of this problem, one cannot in any way appeal to any level beyond the computational level (in terms of Marr's schema) to locate the mental/neural operations with a view to grounding, in some way or the other, the plausibility of apparently intractable procedures in the computational system of the language faculty, because there does not exist any such level in Marr's three-level schema; nor can one go down the hierarchy of levels, having recourse to considerations having to do with the architecture of the computing machine that instantiates the relevant procedures at the computational level, because the putative computational system of the language faculty abstracts away from implementation details.

Beyond that, the functions specified by the generative procedure of the language faculty are by definition invariant over all parsing algorithms;

were it not so, they will not be functions in the first place. And it is not clear why the theory of computational complexity cannot apply to the domain of linguistic competence which is constituted and instantiated by a system of linguistic computations in the putative computational system of the language faculty (see Frixione (2001), who has made a similar point). Linguistic computations, by virtue of being computations that run over some version of a Turing machine, must be subject to restrictions imposed by computational complexity. Having said this, we cannot concomitantly assume that natural languages or natural language grammars in themselves must be similarly constrained so as to pave the way for efficiency in language processing, as Berwick (1991) seems to think. The reason is quite simple, yet not quite easy to see. Computations and natural languages or even natural language grammars belong to two different ontological domains, even if both computations and natural languages/natural language grammars are partly abstract and partly concrete. But this underlying commonality is not sufficient to support a common ontology for both, for computations are ultimately physical even if recursive procedures or computable functions are abstract mathematical objects,[8] while natural languages are not *strictly* physical objects although natural language has its manifestation in a physical medium through speech. By saying that the entire community of English speakers speaks English, we do not mean to say that English speakers use a specific physical object when they produce and comprehend linguistic utterances. This is not so in the case of computations which are such that they can only be located in a device or machine that executes computable functions. The problem of non-computability by way of intractability looms large in the case of computation (*especially* digital computation), while natural languages/ natural language grammars *need not* be so constrained by restrictions of computability/non-computability because no algorithmic description of natural language grammars is ontologically necessary.

In fact, the investigation of a number of linguistic phenomena including anaphoric dependency, agreement, morphological marking and also cases of ambiguity in natural language has revealed that natural language grammars invite NP-hard decision problems (see e.g. Barton et al. 1987; Ristad 1993). What this means is that problems in the NP class can be reduced to decision problems with programs for dealing with linguistic phenomena such as anaphoric dependency, agreement, morphological marking, ambiguity, etc., and that such problems in the NP class can be solved if, for instance, we have solutions to decision problems with linguistic phenomena such as anaphoric dependency, agreement, morphological marking, ambiguity, etc. However, natural language phenomena *may* well be more computationally complex, and any appeal to grammar-internal constraints that reduce complexity-producing processes (as Berwick (1991) argues) will not make any sense, since the phenomenon in question can be couched in terms that do not make reference to syntactic representations and constraints. The case of intensional emotive constructions that involve aspects of intensionality and predicates having an affective dimension is such a linguistic phenomenon. Intensional emotive constructions are thus associated with two different aspects of linguistic meaning: one mediates the expressive aspect of meaning and the other the referential and/descriptive aspect of meaning. Let us now move on to the relevant examples to illustrate what is at stake.

(114) Peter wants to put on an inexpensive coat.

(115) Sarah desires a job that suits her goals.

(116) He needs a car that he can repair.

(117) They long for a place where they can sustain themselves.

In (114)–(117), the intensional verbs ('want', 'desire', 'need', 'long for') denoting (emotive) affect create scopal ambiguities in terms of whether the existential quantifiers ('an inexpensive coat', 'a car that he can repair', 'a job that suits her goals' and 'a place where they can sustain themselves') get a higher scope than the intensional verbs or not. That is, there is an ambiguity in terms of whether the relevant affect the predicates incorporate can be about something specific (*de re*) or about something non-specific (*de dicto*); so a want or a desire can be of something specific or of something non-specific. Thus, for example, in (114) Peter wants to put on, say, a blue-coloured coat which he may have seen in a store and he saw that it was not expensive, or it could be that Peter wants to put on some inexpensive coat or other and he does not have any choice with regard to this. Additionally, the predicates in these sentences fulfil all the other criteria of intensionality as well (see for the notion of intensionality, Forbes 2001, 2006; Hallman 2004; Moltmann 2008, 2013), since the *lack of existential import* is also satisfied by virtue of the fact that we can say things of the sort: 'John longs for/wants/ desires water from the fountain of Paradise'; the reflex of this is that in (115), for example, 'a job that suits her goals' may not exist at all. Finally, *substitution failure* goes through as well, in that we may see that

Peter/Sarah may want/desire an (illusory) image of a situation which is actually a scenario in the real world but the substitution will fail here; the test of substitution failure may, however, turn out to be a bit murky with these predicates (Forbes 2006), though substitution failure more often than not obtains with the predicates in (114)–(117).

The situation differs with certain other emotive predicates. The following examples show this clearly.

(118) Sarah loves/idolizes/hates/is frightened of/fears/dislikes Clark Kent.

(119) Sarah loves/idolizes/hates/is frightened of/pleases/fears/dislikes a man.

As far as the mental state is concerned, the truth value may not be conserved if Clark Kent and Superman are interchanged in (118), despite the two terms being co-referential. On this construal, the predicates above pass the test of inducing substitution failure. Other than that, the example in (118) provides a clear case of lack of existential import; even if Superman does not exist in reality, it is possible for Sarah to love/hate/fear, etc. Superman. Interestingly enough in (119), the only reading available of the object quantificational noun phrase 'a man' is the specific/*de re*/relational reading – so this means that there is a specific man, say, Mr X, who Sarah loves/idolizes/hates/is frightened of/pleases/fears/dislikes. The non-specific/*de dicto*/notional reading – which essentially conveys the meaning that Sarah is in a relation of love or idolization with some man or the other as she does not have any choice concerning this, and *any* man fits the description of the person who she loves/idolizes/hates/is frightened of/pleases/fears/dislikes – is not available. Let us now consider another set of examples provided below.

(120) The businessmen are excited/thrilled about a merger plan.

(121) The public are disgusted/horrified/offended/outraged/surprised/pleased/grieved by a military operation.

These sentences do not have a non-specific/*de dicto* reading of the quantificational noun phrases. In addition, they also do not seem to satisfy the other criteria of intensionality. However, one may argue that substitution failure *may* be applicable in some cases of the predicates above. If somebody is thrilled/excited about/intend/aspire to see, say, the engulfing of the sun by a demon (which is actually a solar eclipse), is not the person really thrilled/excited about a solar eclipse or does not the person intend/aspire to see a solar eclipse? Maybe yes. Maybe no. Things are far from clear as far as intuitions go (Larson et al. 1997). Similarly, lack of existential import does not apply to most predicates belonging to this category. So for example, somebody is insulted; the person must be insulted by an entity of some existential import, barring other conditions.

Besides this, it is easy to show that emotive predicates in (118)–(119) and (120)–(121) do not stand up well to the diagnostic linguistic tests for intensionality described in Moltmann (2008). Thus, the following inferences by virtue of *identity conditions* do not go through for the predicates in (118)–(119).

(122) John loves/idolizes/hates/is frightened of/fears/dislikes a man.
Sarah loves/idolizes/hates/is frightened of/fears/dislikes a man.

---

*? John and Sarah love/idolize/hate/are frightened of/fear/dislike the same thing.

Similarly, *no support (non-special) anaphora* does not hold true of these predicates as well since the anaphora 'it' is compatible with these predicates.

(123) John loves/idolizes/hates/is frightened of/fears/dislikes a deserted house. Also, Sarah loves/idolizes/hates/is frightened of/fears/dislikes it/that/the same thing.

Significantly, similar considerations apply to the predicates in (120)–(121) too.

(124) John is disgusted with/afraid of/delighted with/ashamed of/angry with an employee.
Mary is disgusted with/afraid of/delighted with/ashamed of/angry with an employee.

---

*? John and Mary are disgusted with/afraid of/delighted with/ashamed of/angry with the same thing.

(125) John is happy/sorry/delighted about a proposal. Also, Bill is happy/sorry/delighted about it/that/the same thing.

Now compare what is shown above with what is provided below:

(126) John wants/needs an expert in wine making.
Mary wants/needs an expert in wine making.

John and Mary want/need the same thing.

(127) John desires/longs for a lover. Also, Bill desires/longs for * it/
that/the same thing.

In contrast to these constructions, the following sentences have independent intensional elements (marked in bold) that are decoupled or sort of *de-conflated* from the emotive predicates.

(128) The child is excited to **draw** a gold coin.

(129) Sam is annoyed at being **shown** in a portrait.

(130) He **could** be happy to execute a plan.

These constructions show variability in linguistic meanings; while (128)–(129) both have a specific/*de re* reading, (130) has only a non-specific/*de dicto* reading. One can now see that there is a gradation in intensional behaviour in different intensional emotive constructions, since the predicates in (114)–(117) satisfy all the criteria of intensionality, the predicates in (118)–(119) only two (*substitution failure* and *lack of existential import*) and those in (120)–(121) only one (*substitution failure*). So we get three classes of such predicates/constructions on a cline of intensional behaviour. This obtains when the predicates are both intensional and emotive; more significant variations in linguistic meaning arise when such predicates are used along with other intensional elements in the same linguistic constructions, as shown in (128)–(130). This adds to the complexity of patterns in linguistic meanings as a function of intensional elements and emotive content.

We are now in a position to articulate the nature of the computational complexity of the semantic contents underlying intensional emotive constructions. First, the semantic contents of intensional emotive constructions cannot be computed without taking into account the three criteria of intensionality in each intensional emotive construction. If so, supposing that n denotes the number of clauses linked in a sentence each of which contains an intensional emotive predicate allows us to say that the time complexity of an algorithm that may compute the semantic content of such a sentence will run in computational time of

3^n steps. Second, if we also factor in three different groups of intensional emotive predicates, the complexity will certainly increase further, albeit linearly. This will get us to add a computational time of $(3^n + n)$ steps to 3^n. This is because of the fact that for each clause we may also want to compute which of the three classes of intensional emotive constructions/predicates the clause conforms to, since just figuring out the number of criteria of intensionality for each predicate in each clause is not enough. And hence, for n number of clauses, we need an extra computational time of 3^n plus n steps (plus n, because the algorithm has to make reference to the satisfaction table of intensionality criteria in *each* of the clauses computed for the three criteria of intensionality in order to compute intensional emotive class memberships). Third, we shall have to consider the interaction of emotive predicates (which have their own intensional patterns) with other intensional elements (for example, 'could, 'draw' and 'show' in (128)–(130)). If we do that, the computational complexity can increase further as a polynomial function of $(3^n + n) + 3^n$ steps. That is, we get a computational time of $((3^n + n) + 3^n) \times 2^n$ steps. What we have here is that the individual functions $f_i(n) \dots f_k(n)$ have an exponential growth, while their *combination* has a polynomial growth. Hence the asymptotic time complexity would be *at least* $O(f_i^E(n) \times f_j^E(n))$, where f_i^E and f_j^E are exponential functions (since n will be washed out as n increases). Overall, this falls under exponential complexity at the first-order level of growth of functions, but the second-order level of growth of a combination of exponential functions is bound by *at least* polynomial time complexity (P). Many computationally hard problems are of $O(2^n)$ exponential time complexity – deterministic or otherwise; but the problem of computing the semantic contents of intensional emotive constructions appears to be much harder than them, and in fact, the time of the relevant function grows faster than that of any polynomial or exponential function. Therefore, it seems that computing the semantic contents of intensional emotive constructions requires an upper bound of superpolynomial time. This has serious consequences for the cognitive complexity of natural language grammars.

As has been shown in Mondal (2013b), the relevant generalizations about intensional emotive constructions cannot be couched in syntactic terms; nor do syntactic constraints neutralize complexity-inducing processes in the present case. The reason is that the semantic generalizations about intensional emotive constructions remain invariant over different possible syntactic representations of the constructions – whether at the surface or at the deep level. Since computational complexity problems with intensional emotive constructions are way harder than those in the NP-hard class in a strict sense, we strongly suspect that natural language grammars *can* have decision problems that are way beyond tractability. Thus, this reinforces the conjecture that no algorithmic description of natural language grammars is ontologically necessary. That is, either the property of computationality for natural language/natural language grammars may be completely irrelevant to natural language,[9] or the exact computational property of natural language/natural language grammars is a needless theoretical artefact and may well remain elusive forever. This echoes what has been emphasized in Mondal (2010). If so, the cognitive complexity of natural language grammars in no way points to the feasibility of any generative procedure of the language faculty that can have viable programs for running computable functions, since no such functions may exist for natural language/natural language grammars. This conclusion is different even from the view that Seuren (2013) has advanced when critiquing the view of an *autonomous* algorithmic rule system for natural language grammars, since, for him, natural language grammar can be reckoned as an *ancillary* algorithmic system that mediates between propositionally structured thoughts and phonologically structured recipes for actual sounds. But if the message to be taken from the whole exercise in this chapter is clearer, the algorithmic property of rule systems for natural language grammars even in its ancillary role is at best suspect. The next chapter (Chapter 5) will provide further evidence in favour of this conclusion.

4.5 Summary

In this chapter, we have made an attempt to make sense of the concept of linguistic computation in its various nuances when our goal is to have a serious understanding of how natural language relates to computation and vice versa. We have stumbled over many of the puzzles and conundrums in trying to plough through the mazes that the relationship between language and computation throws open. We have demonstrated that the problem of non-computability and intractability hovers around linguistic computations that either ride the operations obtaining within any postulated computational system of the language faculty, or are assumed to apply to properties intrinsic to natural language grammars. One should not, of course, confuse the property of computational complexity as arising from the former with that which happens to apply to the latter, in that linguistic computations in any postulated computational system of the language faculty may well be artefactual or arbitrary (a product of theoretical construction), whereas those inferred from the properties intrinsic to natural language grammars are at best presumptive (a matter of presuming something to be something else on the basis of a number of otherwise acceptable premises). It has also been argued in this chapter that any presumption about computationality drawn from the properties intrinsic to natural language grammars does not establish that the property of computationality is a *necessary* property of natural language grammars, and the supposition that computations run in a putative computational system of the language faculty is disastrously flawed. As a matter of fact, that the field of computational linguistics has long abandoned the Generative machinery of computations is not much of an antidote to the prevailing conception, and this state of affairs itself points to the gap between what theoretical linguistics builds and what computational linguistics adopts. Even though it is true that the theoretically formulated calculus is different from its practical applications, one must not confuse this difference *simply* with a gap between theory and practice. The theoretical machinery builds on a conception of computation which is distinct from that used in computational linguistics. Given this scenario, it behoves us to become alarmed when a conception of computation built into the theoretical machinery eats into the machinery itself, while this may not be that alarming in computational linguistics because the notion of computation in that field is not so much informed by theoretical developments concerning the notion of computation as by engineering challenges in real time. Chapter 5 will unearth far more intricate puzzles and paradoxes when language, mind and computation are placed together in the context of diverse linguistic phenomena.

5
Putting it all together: the Relation between Language, Mind and Computation

This chapter will investigate the relationship between language, mind and computation when they are put together in the broader context of the relation between language and cognition. We have observed that language when related to the mind or computation begets unusually damaging consequences for a linguistic theory that incorporates unexamined assumptions about this relationship between language, mind and computation. These assumptions have gradually hardened into axioms which are thought to form the conceptual basis of a theory that perpetuates the fallacy of extending these assumptions beyond a level necessary for justification. This has exactly happened in the case of modern linguistic theory. The endorsement of the relationship between language, mind and computation revealed a wide range of deep insights into the nature of natural language grammar, and the questions of adequacy for linguistic theory concomitantly became sharper and sharper, as is usual at a certain stage of scientific inquiry in any discipline. But apparently questions of adequacy concerning the empirical ramifications of theoretical tools in cross-linguistic contexts became a prime concern for theoretical linguists, and subsequently, the ontological foundations with regard to the relationship between language, mind and computation were rarely, or have not been, interrogated.

Yet, what we have seen so far challenges any simplistic conceptualization of the relationship between language, mind and computation, or rather problematizes any such relationship however construed. One the one hand, when natural language grammar is coupled to the mind, natural language becomes decoupled from the domain of psychological/ cognitive mechanisms. On the other hand, if the character of computation is ascribed to the linguistic system in the mind or to natural language grammar, this disintegrates the very nature of human language because natural language grammar (in a broader sense) becomes intractable, contrary to facts. Just as human cognition is viable, natural language grammars are also tractable. Our linguistic expressions of all our effable thoughts, ideas, beliefs, actions and the interpretations of those very expressions are *not quite* underdetermined by the grammatical machinery – nor is the grammatical machinery fully underdetermined by our linguistic expressions and interpretations of those expressions. Had it not been so, the grammatical machinery – whatever it actually turns out to be – would have been a system of erratic components that would be utterly flaky, not usable by our cognitive system. Given this situation, it now becomes increasingly clearer that the presupposition is not simply that the linguistic system must be usable by the cognitive system; rather, the cognitive system must also be configurable with respect to the aspects of the linguistic system in that the complexities and intricacies of natural languages must have to be viable within the set of constraints the cognitive system offers. When we make an attempt to accomplish this goal of such scope, we need to place language, mind and computation in the same context in order to see how language is computed in the cognitive system, given that a range of specific conditions which diverse linguistic phenomena contain are not barred from making contributions to any explanatory relation that holds true for natural language. On the surface, this sounds promising, for various natural language phenomena within and across languages appear to impose certain *sui generis* conditions on linguistic computations that are supposed to obtain in the mind. That is, the hope is that such *sui generis* conditions on linguistic computations can be discovered by way of examination of widely different natural languages, and these conditions constrain and also in a way constitute what is characterized as linguistic computation. Thus linguistic computation, to a certain extent, owes its natural character to these conditions which are supposed to not merely unlock properties of natural languages, but also project a window onto linguistic computation itself.

However, this chapter is aimed at demonstrating that this goal is not (onto)logically possible, let alone achievable. There is no common room for natural language grammar, the mind and computation all placed together in the same context. One may now wonder why this cannot be otherwise – that is, why the system of axioms that describe or encode the mentally represented rule systems of natural language cannot be such that principles of computation can be defined on them. This sounds plausible, given the notion of inferential calculations defined on the inputs and outputs of systems of logical reasoning that are constituted by sets of axioms, principles of deduction/induction and the relevant premises, for it may be analogously thought that inferential calculations can also be defined on the linguistic strings that are inputs and outputs of the system of grammatical principles which are ultimately instantiated in the mind/brain. Any such notion of computation that turns on the abstract notion of step-by-step calculation driving a sequence of operations is trivial and hence verges on overgeneralization. Thus, applying a concept of computation based on *merely* input–output mappings does not preclude one from wishfully, or even whimsically, applying it to any object we see or know of. Starting with strings, quarks, atoms, molecules, objects, animals, plants, groups, society, life – all of which can thus be supposed to be computing, we even say that the entire universe is computing. There are such speculations, generalizations and extensions aplenty in the academic pool of thinking. A notion of computation grounded in the concept of a set of calculations driving a sequence of operations can barely say anything substantive either about natural language phenomena or about mental phenomena, or even about the mentally represented linguistic system. Most importantly, natural language phenomena or even mental phenomena are different and may well be *sui generis* so that the extrapolation of the notion of inferential calculations valid in systems of logical reasoning may have nothing whatever to do with the form of natural language phenomena or mental phenomena. This is the line of reasoning that will be pursued in this chapter on the basis of careful scrutiny of different linguistic phenomena.

Additionally, the issue of whether the exact concept of computation has been employed in the pertinent theoretical context is equally important, as Piccinini and Scarantino (2011) have taken pains to emphasize. But why does this matter? As discussed at length in Chapter 4, this matters, inasmuch as adoption of one concept of computation, rather than another, affects the foundational assumptions on which a theory is built. Any assumption naively accepted may have repercussions – both conceptual and empirical – for other parts of a theory when applied to the domain to which it is supposed to apply. The divide between digital and analogue computation may not be so wide at a very low level of the brain, especially when neurons which act as digital machines (either firing or not firing) can also be considered to be analogue devices when the properties of neurochemical and neuroelectrical transmissions are taken into consideration, or the issue on the nature of information in any information-processing view of linguistic computation may not matter much when the concept of information is cashed out in terms of Shannonian entropy at the lower scale of neural pathways. Plus the digital versus analogue distinction also depends on the format of representations as well as on the system that uses the relevant information (see, for details, Katz 2008). But if the aim is to investigate the linguistic system that is supposed to be a cognitive structure cross-connecting many levels of detail, it would be an understatement on the part of a theory by not articulating in an adequate manner what exactly is involved in the conceptualization of linguistic computation if a lot more contribution from linguistic computation is claimed or even demanded to underlie much of the theoretical paraphernalia. Apart from that, natural language grammar may have many properties that are not in an intersective relation to those of either cognitive mechanisms or computational operations. In essence, this chapter will make an attempt to establish this view on firmer ground as we proceed to focus on some more linguistic phenomena that will be inspected for an exploration of the relationship between language, mind and computation.

5.1 Language, mind and computation put together

We may now try to articulate what occurs when the relationship between natural language grammar, mind and computation is probed in linguistic contexts that turn on the relevant connections pertaining to language, mind and computation. In order to demonstrate the perplexities, we will consider a range of linguistic phenomena from areas of syntax and semantics. A proviso needs to be made at this stage. No attempt will be made to bring out a comprehensive treatment of all the phenomena that will be taken into consideration in this connection. Rather, only the relevant matters of concern by attending so far as can be deemed fit for an exploration of the issues at the intersection of language, mind and computation will be spelled out.

We shall first look at the phenomenon of long-distance dependency. The details of the argument here come from Mondal and Mishra (2013). The examples (131)–(134) below show that any dependency should be local but long dependencies are possible as well in some circumstances, as in (131) and (133). Readers may note that such cases have already been discussed in Chapter 2 (in examples (37)–(41)).

(131) What does John think (that) he needed_?

(132) *Who/what did John ask why Mary looked for_?

(133) What did she walk to the campus to buy some stuff from_?

(134) *Which club did John meet a lot of girls without going to_?

The sentences in (131)–(132) show that *Wh*-movement or the dependency between the gap and the occurrence of the *Wh*-phrase should be local. In (131) the apparently long dependency between the gap and the occurrence of the *Wh*-phrase is actually summed over smaller dependencies/movements (through the CP of the embedded clause), while it is not so in (132) where the CP of the embedded clause already contains a *Wh*-phrase. The sentence (134), which is adapted from Cattell (1976), is ungrammatical because of a long-distance dependency between the gap in an adjunct and the *Wh*-phrase; but interestingly (133) is fine even though there exists a long-distance dependency between the gap in an adjunct and the *Wh*-phrase. Cases like these have puzzled linguists and have led to the refinement of much of the technology in the Generative linguistics paradigm (see for relevant conceptual and empirically motivated discussions, Postal 1998; Nunes and Uriagereka 2000; Sabel 2002). It is because if a dependency/movement is posited to be local, it is mysterious why some dependencies/movements are sometimes possible (as in 133) and sometimes banned (as in 134), when the establishment of locality through successive cyclic movement/summing over smaller dependencies is controlled. However, the domain over which smaller dependencies are summed may vary across languages; for example, languages such as German, Hungarian and Japanese have long-distance *Wh*-dependencies that are summed over domains the edges of which are located below the CP layer (Richards 2001).

Overall, the problem of why such long-distance *Wh*-dependencies between structures from within adjuncts and *Wh*-phrases are sometimes possible and sometimes not appears to be acute. In order to solve this problem, one proposal made by Truswell (2011) states the *Single Event Grouping Condition* which requires, in the case of a long-distance dependency of a *Wh*-phrase, two events described in the matrix verb phrase and the adjunct clause/phrase to form a single macro-event when the two events have a *causal* (direct or enabled) relationship and the causing event precedes the one caused, or to be two independent events that overlap spatio-temporally forming a conjoined event, and at most one of the events from a conjoined event or from a set of macro-events having an agentive character. The example of one single macro-event built from two causally related (sub-)events is this: 'John copied the papers to pass the exam', where John's copying of the papers is causally related to the (sub-)event encoding John's goal of passing the exam, whereas an example of a conjoined event with two events overlapping spatio-temporally is this: 'John works listening to Bob Marley', where the listening event and the working event *may* not be causally related, but rather are spatio-temporally connected. Furthermore, the agentive character of an event can be construed in terms of the goal-driven intentionality of agents participating in events; thus, for instance, in 'John built a house', 'John' is the agent of the action described in the event, *but not* in 'John knows the answer', which describes a state. More concretely, an event is agentive, in Truswell's sense, if and only if (i) the event concerned is such that it cannot be decomposed into sub-events and one participant in that event is the agent (which is what happens in the case of an event that is a part of a conjoined event), and (ii) the event concerned may be decomposed into a sequence of sub-events $e_1 \ldots e_n$ such that one of the participants in the initial sub-event e_1 is an agent (this is the case of a single macro-event with its constituent sub-events). As Truswell argues, this explains why a sentence like 'What did John die thinking about__?' is possible with the two events in the matrix and adjunct clauses forming an extended or conjoined event, given that the event of John's dying characterizes an achievement in the aspectual configuration of the verb 'die', as the achievement profile of an event specifies the culmination of a process, not the *agentive* process prior to the culmination. Hence the conjoined event has just one agentive event – that is, the one described by the event of John's thinking about something. In a similar manner, 'What did John eat his breakfast sitting on__?' is also fine because the conjoined event incorporates two events – namely John's eating his breakfast and his remaining seated on something – out of which only the latter is not agentive.

Now coming back to the examples (131)–(134), we shall verify whether the *Single Event Grouping Condition* can explain the data in (131)–(134). In the data (133) is fine but (134) is banned, since the (sub-)events in the matrix verb phrase and the adjunct clause/phrase in (133) form a macro-event while those in (134) do not, mainly because the two events in the matrix verb phrase and the adjunct clause/phrase overlap spatio-temporally but neither of the two events is agentive on the grounds that the event in the adjunct containing 'without' is not agentive in having not occurred at all, and the event in the matrix clause specifies an achievement which bleaches the event of its agentive character. This appears to explain a range of data that are otherwise unaccounted for, although there are many caveats that have been built into the *Single Event Grouping Condition*, which makes reference to the lexical aspect encoded in verbs/verb phrases as well as to the semantic structure of events of clauses. However, whether the *Single Event Grouping Condition* is adequate enough to cover all cases of long-distance dependency of *Wh*-phrases within the domain it is supposed to apply to is a question that the current study does not aim to address. We leave it open for further verification. Since the *Single Event Grouping Condition* obtains at the interface between syntax and semantics, it is assumed to be computed in cyclic manner – that is, at each step of the verb phrase building process in syntax in a schema: $[_S [_{CP1} \cdots [_{VP1} \cdots [_{VPn}]]]]$. If so, it would be interesting to see how this works in a situation where the issues involving linguistic computation and the mental grounding of linguistic computation come out clearly. In a way, this provides a good testing ground for an examination of linguistic computation that is supposed to be mentally grounded, primarily because the *Single Event Grouping Condition* is a condition at the syntax–semantics interface which is a part of the organization of the mental grammar, and this condition is supposed to be executed in a sequence of operations that can be formulated algorithmically.

Let us suppose that we have a program P (which is run on a machine, say, a version of the Turing machine, plausibly in the human mind[1]) that can determine which event causes which out of the two events in a sentence containing the matrix verb phrase/clause and the adjunct clause/phrase. Additionally, it can also determine which event has an agentive character. Now two sentences (i) 'This program P checks causal relations and the agentive character of events to determine which event causes which out of the two events in a sentence' and (ii) 'This program P determines which event causes which out of the two events in a sentence to check causal relations and the agentive character of events' are given simultaneously as input to P. In such a situation, the program P determines that the event, say e_1, in the matrix clause of the first sentence is the event that causes the one, say e_2, in the adjunct clause and hence the two events form a macro-event. But when the program moves over to the second sentence, the relationship is reversed, and it is e_2 that causes e_1. The problem for the program is that now both e_1 and e_2 mutually cause each other, and thus none precedes the other. If so, technically there does not seem to be a problem for the long-distance dependency formation of a *Wh*-phrase when moved to the front (as far as the *Single Event Grouping Condition* is concerned), in that the events in each sentence independently form a macro-event. But then the paradox that arises is this: on the one hand, the program P determines that e_1 causes e_2 and thus the first sentence can allow *Wh*-extraction from the adjunct satisfying the *Single Event Grouping Condition*, but then the same program finds that e_2 causes e_1 in the second sentence, and hence this violates the *Single Event Grouping Condition* on the grounds that the precedence relation among events must not be symmetric. So the program finds that long-distance dependency formation of a *Wh*-phrase is possible for each sentence taken alone, and at the same time, not possible for any.

To solve the problem posed by the paradox above, one may argue that the program P will differentiate the events in the first sentence with some index *i* from those in the second sentence with some index *j*. One possibility is to index each event or pair of events in a sentence differently from any other events in other sentences. If so, this gives rise to another paradox. One can note that each of the sentences is about the program P itself. Now P determines that e_1 causes e_2, given that P itself checks causal relations and the agentive character of its behaviour first and then this results in the determination of what causes what. But when P goes over to the second sentence, P finds that e_3, a new event, causes e_4, another new event, given that P's own determination of what causes what eventuates in the checking of the causal relations and the agentive character of its own behaviour. Now in this situation, P determines that the *Single Event Grouping Condition* is not violated in each sentence but still violated in each, again because of the symmetric precedence of the events concerned inasmuch as the set of events in the first sentence is the same as the set in the second. One cannot appeal to truth in this case since the program P does not have access to any relation in which truth/non-truth may obtain. Even if P has access to the truth about itself, P determines, upon checking the first sentence, that the causal/contingent relation between the events e_1 and e_2 (when e_1 causes e_2) is true of its behaviour. Next, it goes over to the second sentence and determines that the causal/contingent relation between the events e_3 and e_4 is false given its behaviour observed during the reading of the first sentence, but true on the basis of the structure of the second sentence (if the adjunct rationale clause is the resulting event). That is a contradiction! But have we not also stated that $e_1 \neq e_3$, $e_2 \neq e_3$, $e_1 \neq e_4$ and $e_2 \neq e_4$? If so, then this leads to another level of contradiction, for even though it is the case that $e_1 \neq e_3$, $e_2 \neq e_3$, $e_1 \neq e_4$ and $e_2 \neq e_4$, the events e_2 and e_3 refer to the same thing and so do the events e_1 and e_4, and on the basis of this fact, P finds something to be true of its own behaviour (upon reading the first sentence) and at the same time, false too (upon reading the second sentence). This is how all this begets one paradox after another when (linguistic) computation is assumed to apply to the mind. If this still does not leave one puzzled, some more cases from other linguistic phenomena can also be considered to make the overall argument convincing and sound enough.

We shall now concentrate on another phenomenon: gapping. Let us look at the examples below. Here we have two sentences with the verb missing (when matched in interpretation with the one in the matrix clause) in the second conjunct of each of the sentences (135)–(136).

(135) John wants to build a tower and Mary, _ a bridge.

(136) *John wants to erect a structure and Mary, _ a structure.

The ungrammaticality of (136) shows that the object of the missing verb, namely 'a structure', needs to be the FOCUS (*contrastive focus* – by virtue of being contrasted with the object noun phrase of the first clausal conjunct against the *common ground* which is constituted by the common verb complex 'wants to erect' missing in the second conjunct), whereas in (135) the common ground exemplified by 'wants to build' is missing in the second conjunct, and the noun phrase 'a bridge' is the FOCUS which is in contrast with the noun phrase 'a tower'. What is gapped in such constructions can thus be interpreted in the gap marked in (135)–(136) by being matched with the instance of the common ground that is present in the first conjunct. Overall, this is how gapping has been dealt with (Kuno 1976; Agbayani and Zoerner 2004; Johnson 2009). However, gapping does not interact merely with the information structure of clauses which encodes (discoursal) aspects of sentences, but also with features of scope quantificational or otherwise. The following examples, taken from Siegel (1984), illustrate what is at stake.

(137) Ward can't eat caviar and Sue, __ beans.

(138) Ward can eat caviar and Sue, __ beans.

Here, the negation present in (137) can induce two readings based on where the negation is located in our interpretations. One reading is that Ward cannot eat caviar and Sue cannot eat beans. This is called the *narrow scope* reading – which means that the negation is interpreted locally within the verb phrase/tense phrase of each clause. On the other hand, there is another reading in terms of which we say that it is not the case that they both eat the foods mentioned – that is, caviar and beans. This is the *wide scope* reading – which indicates that the negation is interpreted outside the boundaries of both clauses, and hence the word 'wide' in the wide scope reading. Likewise, (138) has two readings based on where we interpret the modal 'can' which specifies a notion of possibility. Hence we can say either that the individual called Ward can eat caviar and the individual called Sue can eat beans (narrow scope reading), or that it is possible that both individuals eat the foods, namely caviar and beans (wide scope reading). In addition, as Jackendoff (1971) points out, exactly what portion of a verb phrase can be missing in gapping varies in many cases. The following sentences (139)–(142) from Jackendoff exemplify this quite well.

(139) Arizona elected Goldwater Senator, and Pennsylvania___ Schweiker.

(140) Max writes poetry in the bathroom, and Schwarz___ radical pamphlets.

(141) Ralph told Dick Deadeye that Little Buttercup sold treacle, and Sir Joseph___ the Captain.

(142) Jack begged Elsie to get married, and Wilfred___ Phoebe.

In (139) the verb phrase containing a noun phrase ('elected Senator') is missing; in (140) the verb phrase containing a prepositional phrase ('writes in the bathroom') is not present; in (141) the verb phrase that contains an entire complement clause ('told that Little Buttercup sold treacle') is absent, and in (142) the verb phrase with its infinitival complement ('begged to get married') is missing. Overall, it becomes clear that gapping targets the head of a verb phrase (or a phrase, in general) with all the auxiliaries that mark modality, tense, aspect, finiteness, etc. as well as (some) complements of the verb in a clause which is identical to another clause conjoined to it only in these parts of a verb phrase.

Given this understanding of gapping, now it needs to be seen whether this phenomenon can also invite the sort of problems that we have encountered thus far. Once again we imagine that there is some program, let us call it G, instantiated in the mind by some Turing machine. Let us also suppose that G can determine which phrase is the FOCUS, since this is what turns out to be crucial in the examples of gapping above. Now a sentence 'Either John wants to erect a structure and Mary wants to erect a tower or Sony tries to destroy a structure and Amy wants to erect a structure'[2] is input to G. The relevant organization of the entire sentence can be schematized as follows:

(143) [$_S$ [$_{C1}$ Either John wants to erect a structure and Mary wants to erect a tower] or [$_{C2}$ Sony tries to destroy a structure and Amy wants to erect a structure]]

C1 is the first conjunct and C2 the second. The entire sentence S is thus composed of two major clauses which are in turn composed of two clauses each. Now let us move over to the main issue. Upon reading the first major conjunct (C1) of the sentence, G finds that 'wants to erect' is repeated twice in the two sub-conjuncts across the first major conjunct (C1) and thus determines that 'wants to erect' is the common ground and that 'a tower' is the FOCUS when contrasted with 'a structure'. But, when G scans the second major conjunct (C2), it determines that 'a structure' is the common ground and 'wants to erect' is the FOCUS contrasted with 'tries to destroy'. This gets G mired in a paradoxical situation. On the one hand, 'wants to erect' is the FOCUS and 'a structure' is the common ground (which is what the structure of C2 shows), but on the other hand, 'wants to erect' is not the FOCUS and 'a structure' is not the common ground (which is what can be seen in C1). Hence, this is a contradiction! To pull G out of the paradox, one can argue that G may scan each major conjunct separately and index the FOCUS and the common ground in the respective conjuncts. Even if this is allowed, the consequence would be damaging as this too will not save G from getting bogged down in another paradox. Here is how. Now suppose the sentence (135) is changed to 'John wants to build a tower and Mary wants to build a bridge' – that is, changed to a form that requires the presence of an instance of the common ground 'wants to build', and then is input to G. While scanning this sentence, G will determine that there is no common ground and there is no FOCUS in any of the conjuncts when independently checked. This is because of the fact that FOCUS and common ground are relational concepts in the sense that what is a FOCUS and what is the common ground can only be determined by means of an examination of the relation that obtains between at least two structures. If so, there is no gapping in (135), but at the same time, there is a gapping in (135), as a matter of fact! Because of such contradictions, G will either halt or loop forever. Such absurd paradoxes and inconsistencies are damaging for any naïve view of the relationship between language, mind and computation. Perhaps something more damaging than this may ensue from another linguistic phenomenon that connects aspects of form to meaning in more intricate ways.

It is quantification in natural languages that holds the prospect of unravelling a great deal of interesting stuff concerning the issue we are concerned about in this chapter. We shall first explore how quantificational scope relations affect the organization of forms in natural language. Quantificational scope relations are semantic relations which obtain when quantifiers (such as 'a', 'few', 'every', 'some', modals, etc.) stand in a certain relation with respect to each other such that the meaning of the relevant construction varies in terms of how the quantifiers

concerned stand in a specific relation. A brief discussion on quantificational scope was made in Chapter 2. Quantification has been handled
from a number of perspectives – set-theoretic, representational, derivational, etc. (see for details, Ruys and Winter 2010). Quantificational
scope is one of the most important marks that can betray form–meaning
divergence in a more perspicuous fashion, and natural languages vary
in terms of how quantification scope obtains in specific constructions.
Heim and Kratzer (1998) have argued that QNPs (quantificational noun
phrases) are interpreted not in a place where they appear on the surface,
mainly because they need their argument requirement to be satisfied.
The motivation behind this is simply that QNPs having the denotation
of second-order predicates (for instance, 'is true' is a second-order predicate which applies to a proposition when we say that the proposition
expressed in 'Earth revolves around the sun' is true) take predicates as
their arguments, but their arguments, that is, predicates which are in a
sister position in a tree are to be one-place predicates. If the arguments
in sister position are not one-place predicates, QNPs are to be displaced
to a position where this requirement can be satisfied. What this means
has emerged out of a long tradition in formal semantics and thus needs
a bit of elaboration. As was discussed in Chapter 2, a noun such as
'John' is of the type e, and an intransitive verb is of the type $e \rightarrow t$, since
an intransitive verb (such as 'smoke' as in 'John smokes', for example)
takes an entity e and maps it to a truth value t. Described in terms of
set-theoretic properties, an intransitive verb is a set of individuals; thus
the denotation of 'smoke' is a set of smokers. But the denotation of a
transitive verb is a set of ordered pairs – that is, a verb like 'love' will
have in its denotation the set of all pairs of the form $<x, y>$ when x is
the lover and y is the person loved. Now a transitive verb must be of the
type $e \rightarrow (e \rightarrow t)$, because it takes an entity e to map it to $(e \rightarrow t)$, thereby
turning into a type of intransitive verb. QNPs pose a specific problem
in this case, since they (such as 'a man', 'every teacher', 'some girl', etc.)
do not simply denote entities; rather, unlike other noun phrases, they
involve a specific quantificational *relation* among sets. For example, the
denotation of 'a man' in 'A man walks' will be such that the set of men
and the set of walkers must have an intersection that is not null. Given
this justification, a quantifier is construed to be of the type $(e \rightarrow t) \rightarrow$
$((e \rightarrow t) \rightarrow t)$, in that a quantifier takes an expression of the type $(e \rightarrow t)$ and
yields an expression of the type $((e \rightarrow t) \rightarrow t)$. For example, a quantifier 'a'
takes 'man' – which is a common noun and hence is of the type $(e \rightarrow t)$,
a set of individuals – only to yield a QNP which is an expression of the
type $((e \rightarrow t) \rightarrow t)$, which obtains when a QNP is to take an expression of

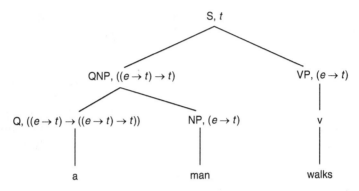

Figure 5.1 A type-logical tree for the sentence 'A man walks'

the type of an intransitive verb, that is, $(e{\rightarrow}t)$, and return a truth value t. Figure 5.1 makes it clear.

The symbol Q in Figure 5.1 denotes a quantifier. The argument $(e{\rightarrow}t)$ of Q and the type of 'man' are cancelled out in identity, and then at the next level, the argument $(e{\rightarrow}t)$ of the QNP 'a man' and the type of 'walks' are cancelled out to yield t for S at the top. Hence, if the arguments in a sister position are not one-place predicates (such as 'smoke'), QNPs are supposed to move to a position where this requirement can be satisfied (but see for an *in situ* approach to this problem, Keenan 2005). So, for example:

(144) John kicked every ball.

(144') [every ball]$_1$ [John kicked t$_1$].

As is evident in (144), the verb 'kick' is a two-place predicate because it needs two arguments – a person who does the kicking and the thing that is kicked, and hence the QNP 'every ball' moves to a position at which point the expression [John kicked t$_1$] is transformed into a predicate itself which means that for all x such that x is a ball, the property of John's kicking x is to be interpreted as a set of ordered pairs of 'John' and x, as shown in (144'). Since a typical transitive verb is of the type $e{\rightarrow}(e{\rightarrow}t)$, QNPs, being of the type $((e{\rightarrow}t){\rightarrow}t)$, give rise to a type mismatch (Partee and Rooth 1983), and hence the need of this operation which can be called *Quantifier Raising* (QR), which is assumed to be operative at LF in the minimalist architecture of the language faculty.

However, Fox (2003) has also argued that QR in many cases is sensitive to syntactic constraints such as the *Coordinate Structure Constraint* (which bans a sentence like 'John wonders who Mary likes__ and Max likes Sam'), *VP Parallelism* (to be discussed below), *binding principles*, etc. In addition, Sauerland (1999) has shown QR to be sensitive to constraints that ban longer displacement/movement of syntactic objects – that is, QR is also subject to conditions of minimality. Overall, this suggests that QR is syntactically constrained. Elsewhere Fox (1999a, 2002) has proposed another constraint, the *Economy Constraint*, which stipulates that a scope-shifting operation will be allowed only when that operation brings forth a (different) semantic interpretation, and if two scope-shifting operations can yield the same semantic interpretation, the one with a shorter movement or with no movement will be preferred. The examples below show this clearly:

(145) A man loves every girl.

(146) John loves every girl.

In (145), 'a man' can take scope over 'every girl' and vice versa, giving rise to two possible interpretations in terms of how the two QNPs stand in a relation to each other. On one reading, there is some specific man (say, Mr James) who loves every girl, and on the other hand, there is another reading in terms of which men can vary with the girls such that every girl is loved by some man or other. But two readings do not obtain in (146), precisely because the movement of 'every girl' will not lead to any new semantic interpretation, and so the *Economy Constraint* will ban this movement. Likewise, the following sentences (147)–(148), by way of the *Economy Constraint*, lead to a scope ambiguity only in (147), but not in (148).

(147) A boy admires every teacher. A girl does, too.

(148) A boy admires every teacher. Mary does, too.

This is because the reconstructed VP 'admires every teacher' can be interpreted with respect to a QNP 'a girl' in (147), by virtue of *VP Parallelism*, while this is not the case in (148) where 'Mary' is the subject of the second sentence. More importantly, the *Economy Constraint* bans the interpretation that every teacher has a distinct boy admirer in (148), since this interpretation (after the reconstructed VP is interpreted in the relevant position after 'Mary' in the second sentence of (148)) does not follow on from the quantificational scope readings that obtain with respect to 'Mary'. Simply phrased, a higher scope interpretation of 'every teacher' with respect to 'Mary' is the same as the lower scope interpretation of 'every teacher' with respect to 'Mary', and hence the higher scope interpretation of 'every teacher' with respect to 'Mary' – which can be derived through QR – is banned, in virtue of what the *Economy Constraint* dictates. Fox calls this generalization *Ellipsis Scope Generalization*. But there are other complications that Fox (2002) has attempted to resolve in a different manner. The examples (149)–(150) are disallowed by the *Economy Constraint*, but are otherwise valid.

(149) Every boy admires a certain professor and Mary does too.

(150) A guide accompanies every tour to the Eiffel Tower, and Jeanne does, too.

The example in (149) has an ambiguity in terms of how 'every boy' and 'a certain professor' scope over each other, despite a ban on this ambiguity, as warranted by the *Economy Constraint*. Following Reinhart (1997), Fox has proposed that the apparently problematic case the sentence (149) gives rise to can be resolved if this is interpreted in terms of *choice functions* applied to the bare indefinites (such as 'a', 'a certain', 'some', etc.). Formally speaking, if f is a choice function and A is a non-empty set, then $f(A)$ is an element of A. That is, if A is a set of countries in the world, for example, a choice function f maps the set A onto an element of A, say, France. Thus the apparent wide scope reading of the QNP 'a certain professor' is explained in terms of a choice function applied to the set of professors, but not through QR. In fact, many such cases of apparent wide scope readings of the QNPs in a range of constructions are explained in terms of choice functions (see for details, Reinhart 1997). However, the sentence in (150) calls for a different account, as Fox argues. It is *generic quantification* over time that comes to the rescue. The reading in which guides vary with respect to the tours to the Eiffel Tower – though apparently banned by the *Economy Constraint* owing to the presence of 'Jeanne' in the second conjunct of (150) – can be derived if we say that, instead of looking at the entire event of (150), we can slice the event into time intervals such that for each time interval some guide or other accompanies a number of tours. And thus we get the wide scope reading of 'every tour to the Eiffel Tower' with respect to 'a guide', only if the view of the event zooms out and guides vary *across* time intervals constituting the entire event. If, on the other hand, the view zooms in on each time interval of the event, a single guide accompanies every tour in a single time interval. This yields the other reading in which the wide scope reading of 'a guide' with respect to 'every tour to the Eiffel Tower' obtains – which can also be inferred from the order of QNPs on the surface structure.

Both choice function interpretations and generic quantification are thus supposed to interact with the *Economy Constraint*, rather than being antagonistic with one another.[3] But all three mechanisms are provided by the putative computational system of the language faculty, as Reinhart as well as Fox emphasize.

Interestingly, Fox (2002) also adds, in this connection, that syntax is not *fully* autonomous as it can see the effects of quantificational scope readings, in that syntactic constraints such as *VP Parallelism* in ellipsis (as in (147)–(148)), *Coordinate Structure Constraint*, etc. can affect QR as well as QL (Quantifier Lowering – the converse of QR). Looking at quantificational scope readings from another angle, Fox and Nissenbaum (1999) have posited that the output of QR can be taken as input to overt operations of Merge.

(151) We saw [a painting $\_\_\__i$] yesterday [from the museum]$_i$.

(152) We saw [a painting $\_\_\__i$] yesterday [by John]$_i$.

So in cases of (151)–(152), Fox and Nissenbaum have argued that the displaced/moved constituent ('from the museum' in (151) or 'by John' in (152)) is an adjunct, so it can be Merged late after the QR of the whole NP ('a painting (PP)') to a higher position on the right. By virtue of this, Fox and Nissenbaum claim that QR can obtain in the overt component of grammar (before Spell-Out), and there is no need for covert operations for QR that hold at LF. That is, a post-Spell-Out operation will be interspersed with the pre-Spell-Out operations; this can have a different description in the phase-theoretic architecture, though. It appears that this imposes more syntactic constraints on the derivation of quantificational scope readings. With a view to showing how tightly constrained by linguistic computation quantificational scope readings can be, Beck (1996) has, on the other hand, argued that quantified structures can block LF movement of *Wh*-elements, other quantifiers and also restrictive elements of DPs ('from Germany' in the noun phrase 'a car from Germany', for example). This is shown below in examples (153) and (154) from German, where at LF 'niemand' blocks the movement of 'wo' in (153), and so does 'nicht' to 'wer' in (154):

(153) *Wen hat niemand **wo** gesehen?
whom has nobody where seen
'Where did nobody see whom?'

(154) *Was glaubt Hans nicht, **wer** da war?
what believes Hans not who there was
'Who does Hans not believe was there?'

Negation is a different type of quantifier; it quantifies over propositions making a true proposition false by being applied to the true statement, or conversely turns a false one into a true statement. What Beck intends to demonstrate by means of (153)–(154) is that the readings that are paraphrased in the respective examples are blocked and would have otherwise obtained, if the negative quantifiers in question had not prevented the *Wh*-quantifiers ('wo' in (153) and 'wer' in (154)) from being displaced to the front at LF. The assumption is that whatever happens at LF is not supposed to be visible on the surface structure of a sentence, but its effects on interpretative possibilities can be detected. According to Beck, such intervention effects of quantificational structures can also explain quantifier scope in German (but see Beck 2006 for a different proposal).

There are also other approaches to quantificational scope that have shown how quantificational scope readings can be derived in more syntactically constrained fashion. Notable among them is the approach by Beghelli and Stowell (1997). Beghelli and Stowell have tried to account for quantificational scope patterns in terms of a (universal) functional hierarchical ordering of different QNPs. The fact that different quantificational scope readings obtain in different contexts hinges on the hierarchical projection of different phrases for different types of QNPs and also on how feature checking is done in such a hierarchical organization of different phrases for different types of QNPs. Thus on Beghelli and Stowell's approach, QNPs such as 'every boy', 'each lady', etc. are different from QNPs such as 'some guy', 'a car', etc. which are in turn different from *Wh*-QNPs like 'how many'. While Beghelli and Stowell's account crucially relies on a range of features *intrinsic* to specific types of QNPs that drive the feature-checking process, Aoun and Li's (1993) account of quantificational scope traces the displacement of QNPs to general feature-checking processes that drive linguistic computation. They have provided an account of quantificational scope interpretation across languages such as Chinese and English in terms of two principles: the *Minimal Binding Requirement* (which stipulates that variables must be bound by what binds such variables in the most local context) and the *Scope Principle* (which states that a quantifier A may have scope over a quantifier B iff A c(onstituent)-commands a member of the chain containing B, given that a chain is a sequence containing the item moved and the trace from where the item is moved, and that A c(onstituent)-commands B iff the first branching node above A in a tree dominates B). Readers may note that this *Scope Principle* is in many respects similar to the one by May (1985), as discussed in Chapter 2.

(155) Every man loves a woman.

So for a sentence like (155) the two possible scope interpretations can be derived. On one interpretation, the QNP 'every man' c(onstituent)-commands the QNP 'a woman' on the surface structure in a tree, so the former can scope over the latter. In the second case, the QNP subject 'every man' will move overtly from within the verb phrase leaving a trace behind, and then the QNP 'a woman' will move covertly (at the post-Spell-Out stage) to get adjoined to the VP, thereby landing up in a position to c(onstituent)-command the trace of the QNP 'every man', which is a member of the chain containing the QNP 'every man'. So 'a woman' can scope over 'every man' as well. This follows straight from the *Scope Principle*. This is shown in (156).

(156) $[_{TP}$ every man$_i$ $[_{VP}$ a woman$_j$ $[_{VP}$ t$_i$ loves t$_j]]]$

Chinese is a language that has a fixed surface scope for QNPs in general cases. Hence a sentence of the type (155) in Chinese will look like:

(157) Meigeren dou xihuan yige nuren.
     everyone all   like   one women
     'Every man loves a woman'

(158) $[_{TP}$ meigeren$_i$ $[_{TP}$ x_i $[_{VP}$ yige nuren$_j$ $[_{VP}$ dou xihuan x_j $]]]]$
     QNP$_i$ x_i QNP$_j$ x_j

The *Minimal Binding Requirement* applies here, in that the variables x_i and x_j which are actually traces are each bound by the most local variable binders. As is evident in (158), x_i is bound by 'meigeren', and x_j by 'yige nuren'. Readers may note that 'meigeren' originates in a TP,[4] not in a VP, as is the case with English shown in (156), because the TP in Chinese is believed to be degenerate. So the schema looks like (158). However, Chinese passives of sentences like (157) give rise to scope ambiguity, and the *Scope Principle*, which we have observed is handy for effects of displacement of QNPs, can be easily applied to such cases, as Aoun and Li argue.

To recapitulate, these approaches to quantificational scope readings are all aimed at uncovering tight constraints imposed by the nature and form of linguistic computation in the putative computational system of the language faculty. Whether they are sufficient to provide a justified account of a diverse range of variations in quantificational scope readings across and within languages is a question that requires a serious investigation.[5] Insofar as the mechanisms proposed by these accounts are those that the putative computational system of the language faculty is supposed to make available, it would be good to see what this reveals when we test the relevant mechanisms in a setting that draws on the very context in which they are deemed to operate.

Let us now construct a program Q, which is instantiated in the mind. We can also suppose that this program Q has access to set-theoretic semantic properties of QNPs and can determine scope relations between QNPs when it takes linguistic structures involving QNPs as inputs. That is, Q incorporates properties of the *Scope Principle* and *Economy Constraint*. Q is thus a program which is a part of the mental organization of the system of rules, principles and constraints of grammar. So far so good. A sentence 'EITHER a student becomes every teacher and an apprentice does, too OR a student becomes every teacher and every apprentice does, too' is now input to Q. Here the correlative conjunction 'OR' (in association with 'EITHER') conjoins the first major conjunct 'a student becomes every teacher and an apprentice does, too' and the second major conjunct 'a student becomes every teacher and every apprentice does, too'. Thus 'EITHER' and 'OR' are ordinary conjunctions marked with upper-case letters in order to make the two major conjuncts appear distinct. For simplicity the entire sentence can be schematized in the following way.

(159) $[_S$ $[_{C1}$ EITHER a student becomes every teacher and an apprentice does, too] OR
$[_{C2}$ a student becomes every teacher and every apprentice does, too.]]

After scanning the sentence in (159), Q determines that *Ellipsis Scope Generalization* by virtue of the *Economy Constraint* rules out within the (sub)conjunct of C1 the interpretation in which apprentices vary with respect to teachers. The second (sub)conjunct of C1 is in fact grammatically deviant on this reading, and hence this will necessitate banning a similar reading for the first (sub)conjunct in C1, that is, for 'a student becomes every teacher'. When Q switches over to C2 and zooms in on it, a disastrous paradox crops up. Q finds that *Ellipsis Scope Generalization* by dint of the *Economy Constraint* goes through in C2, then it follows that 'every teacher' cannot scope over 'a student' in the first (sub)conjunct so long as the scope relation between 'every apprentice' and 'every teacher' in the second (sub)conjunct does not lead to an ambiguity. But note that the reading on which 'every teacher' cannot scope over 'a student' does not, by default, obtain in the first (sub)conjunct of C2 taken alone because the first (sub)conjunct of

C2 is grammatically deviant on this reading, and if so, *Ellipsis Scope Generalization* does not in itself block this reading. Therefore, *Ellipsis Scope Generalization* does not, as a matter of fact, go through in C2, nor does the *Economy Constraint*. This is a contradiction! The other horn of the dilemma is that *Ellipsis Scope Generalization* by virtue of the *Economy Constraint* applies to C1, as we have just seen. And if this applies to C1, it cannot, as far as the facts are concerned, apply to C1. A contradiction again! Note that neither the first nor the second (sub) conjunct of C1 lends itself to a reading on which a student/an apprentice turns into multiple teachers. This reading is *pragmatically* deviant. If this is the case, *Ellipsis Scope Generalization* can never apply to C1 simply because *Ellipsis Scope Generalization* allows for, or rather does not block, the pragmatically deviant reading. Besides, the interpretation in which apprentices vary with respect to teachers within the first (sub) conjunct of C1 is otherwise unavailable when the first (sub)conjunct of C1 is considered in isolation, and this unavailability is not triggered by *Ellipsis Scope Generalization* anyway. This reinforces the conclusion that *Ellipsis Scope Generalization* does not apply to C1, even though we have observed that it holds in C1 by virtue of the fact that the scope relation which warrants the interpretation in which apprentices vary with respect to teachers does not have a semantic effect in the second (sub) conjunct of C1, thereby leading to unambiguousness in the first (sub) conjunct of C1. Hence the contradiction.

With a view to circumventing this inconsistency, one may insist that a separate pragmatic component embedded within the C-I system which interfaces with LF can eliminate the readings that are not viable in terms of world knowledge after the outputs of *Ellipsis Scope Generalization* are fed into the C-I system.[6] If this is permitted, this paves the way for another level of paradox. Let us see why and how. Consider the sentences (160)–(161) below; the sentence (160) is taken from Fox (2002) and (161) is a modified form of (160).

(160) A Canadian flag is in front of many buildings and an American flag is too.

(161) Many Canadian buildings are in front of a flag and many American buildings are too.

As Fox argues, the interpretation that for many buildings there is some Canadian flag or other such that it is in front of those buildings holds true for (160), and if so, it must have been triggered by a similar reading in the second conjunct, that is, by the reading on which for many buildings there is some American flag or other such that it is in front of those buildings. The reading on which there is a single Canadian or American flag in front of many buildings is pragmatically dispreferred, if not impossible.[7] *Ellipsis Scope Generalization* cannot block this reading in (160) anyway, regardless of whether or not we assume that this reading will be eliminated later by a pragmatic component. Overall, it is clear that *Ellipsis Scope Generalization* triggers (at least) one reading in (160) which has the desired semantic effect and which happens to be pragmatically viable too. Now if we look at (161), the reading on which a single flag is in front of many buildings – whether American or Canadian – is pragmatically deviant, yet it is supposed to be derived by *Ellipsis Scope Generalization* inasmuch as this reading is construed to be a semantic effect only to be later ruled out by a pragmatic component. Now we have stepped in a whirlpool of inconsistencies. If a pragmatically deviant reading is identified with a semantic effect, the pragmatically deviant reading has to have a truth-conditional import which contributes to the relevant semantic effect. This is inconsistent on the grounds that if an interpretation is pragmatically deviant, it is also truth-conditionally deviant. For instance, if it is not pragmatically possible for a single buck to be killed as many times as there are hunters, as in a sentence such as 'Every hunter kills a buck', it is not also truth-conditionally possible to derive this reading precisely because such a state of affairs cannot hold true in the world we live in.

Furthermore, even if we grant that a pragmatically deviant reading *can* be identified with a semantic effect by simply assuming that a semantic component is oblivious to pragmatic deviance or well-formedness, this will do no good in dispelling the inconsistencies. Because, if a semantic component is said to be oblivious to pragmatic deviance or well-formedness, this presupposes that the distinction between what can be construed to be semantic and what is pragmatic is *pre-theoretically* built into the putative computational system of the language faculty. Had this been so, the sentence (159) would not at all be grammatically deviant since a semantic component oblivious to pragmatic deviance or well-formedness will not filter out (159) in the first place. This is inconsonant with facts, as we see. In all, whatever stipulation we make to save the whole idea ends up getting bogged down in paradoxes and inconsistencies. Essentially, the same kind of paradoxes will (re)appear if the respective examples are formulated in terms of Beghelli and Stowell's feature-checking account or *Scope Principle*, as many readers may have observed by now.

In fact, the example in (159) can be traced to a puzzle first noted by Gruber (1965), who came up with the following pairs:

(162) a. Every acorn grew into an oak.
  b. An oak grew out of every acorn.

(163) a. Every oak grew out of an acorn.
  b. *An acorn grew into every oak.

What the pairs (162) and (163) show is that (163a) cannot be paraphrased as (163b), while (162a) can be paraphrased as (162b). Jackendoff (2002) maintains that a solution to this puzzle that does not stipulate the asymmetry in the pairs of (162) and (163) does not exist. Ter Meulen (1997) believes that this asymmetry has something to do with the dynamic interpretation and eventive structures of verbs of change, such as 'grow', 'develop', 'make into', 'become', 'turn', 'transform', etc., while Fillmore (1970) has related this asymmetry to some more linguistic cases that do not have the import verbs of transformation give rise to. Fillmore's examples are thus worth (re)visiting.

(164) a. A Sunday follows every Saturday.
  b. Every Saturday is followed by a Sunday.

(165) a. Every Sunday follows a Saturday.
  b. *A Saturday is followed by every Sunday.

(166) a. A Saturday precedes every Sunday.
  b. Every Sunday is preceded by a Saturday.

(167) a. Every Saturday precedes a Sunday.
  b. *A Sunday is preceded by every Saturday.

The most significant aspect that is the running thread through the puzzle as a whole is that all scope relations in which a universal quantifier (for instance, 'every') has a higher scope than an existential quantifier (such as 'a/an', 'some', etc.) are valid (Seuren 2004). That is, a scope relation in which a single entity X stands in a specific relation – dynamic or otherwise – to all other entities, say, a set of Ys, is both syntactically and semantically deviant. It is not the case that such a reading is otherwise implausible. We find scores of such cases; the sentence 'A vendor proposes to every woman in this town' is just such an example. It appears that much of our world knowledge about what kind of relations a singular entity can stand in with respect to certain other entities underlies whatever can solve this puzzle. Additionally, universal quantifiers in many linguistic structures of the type provided above to exemplify the puzzle seem to inevitably give rise to a wide scope reading in a way that cannot be traced to effects of generic quantification. We may leave this matter open for further investigation.

What is, however, more important for us is that a mere incorporation of eventive structures into lexical items that are part of an N will not serve the purpose. The reasons are far from simple, and hence require an elaboration. One plausible attempt to circumvent the paradoxes that have been laid bare is to endow lexical items with the relevant lexical–conceptual information. That is, lexical items as part of an N will not be dummies; rather, lexical items, especially verbs, will carry information about the event structure encoded in verbs as well as any associated conceptual information so that a difference between a verb like 'grow' and another verb such as 'hate' can be deduced from the lexical items in question.[8] The problem becomes apparent when one notes that the minimalist architecture of the language faculty locates the C-I system at a position where lexical items are not selected. And if so, it is not clear how lexical items selected in N can participate in structure-building operations impregnated with the relevant pieces of conceptual and event-structural information. One of the ways of achieving this desired result is to propose that the C-I system needs to be split into two parts – one for the conceptual structures of lexical items and the other for discoursal–intentional properties of meaning and interpretation. That is, there would be two systems for two different ontological domains of mental organization. The conceptual system, which needs to be positioned at the top of the architecture of the language faculty connected to the lexicon from which N is drawn, will encode the event-structural information of predicates, selectional requirements and theta-properties of lexical items, while the intentional system is supposed to deal with discourse–structural properties (properties of topic and focus, for example), properties of mood, evidentiality, matters of reference, etc. Such a proposal can be found in Uriagereka (2008), Munakata (2009) and also in Borer (2005), albeit in a different way. Thus it appears that this proposal can help get around most of the paradoxes and puzzles we have observed thus far in this chapter, insofar as the underlying assumption, one may believe, warrants that the event-structural information of predicates and the selectional properties of other types of lexical items drawn from the conceptual system would be sufficient to eliminate the inconsistencies uncovered here.

However, this assumption is mistaken, as we shall soon see. Note that it is not solely the event-structural and selectional properties of verbs that are responsible for the interpretations which obtain in the sentence (159). In other words, the event-structural and selectional properties of verbs cannot exclusively determine what interpretations obtain in examples (159)–(161) and what do not. Consider, for example, the difference between C1 and C2 in the example (159). How can the interpretative differences between C1 and C2 taken in isolation be cashed out merely in terms of the event structure of the verb 'become'? All that the lexical entry for the verb 'become' specifies is that it is a verb of transformation which encodes a state, rather than a process or event, requiring a source argument, which can be either animate or inanimate, and a goal argument the source is transformed into or comes to be. This conceptual–structural information, in no way, serves to illustrate the differences between C1 and C2 in (159) on the grounds that this does not predict or determine the nature of the QNPs that go with the verb 'become' any more than the event-structural and selectional properties of the verb 'hate' determine the appearance of the QNP 'not more than twenty things about Google' in 'I hate not more than twenty things about Google'. The difference between C1 and C2 in (159) – and for that matter, between (160) and (161) – is a property of the interpretation of the overall construction to which the event-structural and selectional properties of the verb, among many other kinds of structural factors, are a party. Beyond that, it is evident from Fillmore's examples in (164)–(167) that the puzzling properties of scope relations cannot perhaps be traced merely to the event-structural and selectional properties of a certain class of verbs demarcated on grounds of semantic conformity. Nothing in the lexical structures of the verbs or from the syntactically relevant structural conditions such verbs exploit can solely guarantee what interpretations are to be assigned to linguistic structures, as is the case in (159)–(167). No arbitrary stipulation, as a matter of fact, can be imposed on any of the principles or generalizations for quantificational scope readings, by merely incorporating into those principles or generalizations the assumption that all cases in (159)–(167) form a special class, for there must be countless such cases across and within languages and treating all of these as an exceptional class is a fallacy. Even if one comes up with a different account of these cases, the requirement licensing a special condition for these cases in itself needs an explanation. In essence, there do not appear to be any principled grounds for cordoning off (159)–(167) as a special class.

Another disastrous problem, especially with *Ellipsis Scope Generalization*, or rather with the *Economy Constraint* per se, is that the putative computational system of the language faculty has to run through an enormous space of computational steps for any quantificational scope reading that matches the correct interpretation. Note that the availability of a wide scope reading of the QNP 'a certain professor' in (149) and of the QNP 'every tour to the Eiffel Tower' in (150) has been accounted for in terms of two mechanisms other than *Ellipsis Scope Generalization*, namely choice functions (as in (149)) and generic quantification (as in (150)). This is computationally cumbersome, if the putative computational system of the language faculty is supposed to make all these mechanisms available. The paradoxes and inconsistencies uncovered in this chapter indicate that there cannot be any algorithmic way of determining beforehand which mechanism fits a condition at hand. Even if there exists any plausible algorithm for this, the problem of computational intractability looms large in any condition that involves the three principles for quantificational scope readings in a restricted range of cases alone. Let us suppose that we have a sentence S consisting of two clauses with QNPs. If we consider the three mechanisms, that is, *Ellipsis Scope Generalization*, choice function and generic quantification alone, the number of computational steps to derive the correct scope reading for S will be at least $_2 3^2 = 64$. We need 2 at the innermost base because the presence or the absence of any of the three principles will add up to two possibilities, and 3 is an exponent at the next higher level because of the three principles at hand. And finally, we require $_2 3$ to be raised to 2 because for simplicity we have assumed that the sentence S has only two clauses. An important clarification is in order here. It may be noted that the number of computational steps is calculated to be $_2 3^2 = 64$, but not simply 3^2. Why is that? The reason why the presence or absence of any of the three principles has to be taken into consideration is that having two possibilities – the presence or absence – for each of the three principles will amount to considering two possibilities for each of the three principles taken together. If, on the other hand, we have 3^2 steps for S, we cannot see what happens to the third possibility at any stage while we zoom in on the clauses in S. This requires further elaboration. Suppose that the sentence S looks like [S [X ...] [Y ...]]. Here, X and Y are the clauses in S. Also, let *Ellipsis Scope Generalization*, choice function and generic quantification be E, C and G respectively. If the number of computational steps is $_2 k^n$ rather than 3^n when n is the number of clauses in a sentence and k is the number of principles/generalizations, for the former case we have the following range of possibilities that constitute the required computational steps at the first level, that is, for $_2 3$ since $k = 3$:

(168)   (i) $E^+ C^+ G^+$
        (ii) $E^+ C^- G^+$

(iii) E⁻ C⁺ G⁺
(iv) E⁺ C⁺ G⁻
(v) E⁺ C⁻ G-
(vi) E⁻ C⁻ G⁻
(vii) E⁻ C⁻ G⁺
(viii) E⁻ C⁺ G⁻

Since $_2{}^3 = 8$, we have (viii) possibilities when we consider the presence ('+') or the absence ('–') of the three principles taken together. Now 8 raised to n should be $8^2 = 64$ because $n = 2$ in S. If so, 8 possibilities have to be checked for each of the clauses (X and Y) in S. This can be schematized in (169), as shown below.

(169) (I) $X^{(i)} Y^{(ii)}$
      (II) $X^{(iii)} Y^{(viii)}$
      (III) $X^{(iv)} Y^{(v)}$
      ...
      (LXIV) $X^{(v)} Y^{(iv)}$

Note that this helps review the broadest range of possible sets of applications of the three principles in any clause, as is evident in (168)–(169). But if the number of steps is 3^n, we simply check whether the three possibilities represented by E, C and G hold in each of the clauses (X and Y) in S, as shown in (170).

(170) (I) $X^E Y^C$
      (II) $X^G Y^C$
      (III) $X^G Y^E$
      (IV) $X^E Y^G$
      (V) $X^C Y^C$
      (VI) $X^E Y^E$
      (VII) $X^G Y^G$
      (VIII) $X^C Y^G$
      (IX) $X^C Y^E$

As can be observed in (170), any possibility from among (I–IX) lets us review only two options from the set of E, C and G while the status of any application of the third option remains unknown in any of (I–IX). This is not so in (169). There is another stronger reason why (169) adequately represents the computational complexity of the application of the principles E, C and G in a sentence composed of two clauses containing QNPs. As has been described earlier, *Ellipsis Scope Generalization* is not exactly an alternative to choice function or to generic quantification; rather, *Ellipsis Scope Generalization* seems to be the default option whereas choice function and generic quantification are alternative strategies within the putative computational system of the language faculty which can be applied in a case which is not covered by *Ellipsis Scope Generalization*. Hence we cannot have a wide scope reading of the QNP 'every teacher' in (148) by means of an application of generic quantification. For convenience, the sentence (148) is repeated below as (148').

(148') A boy admires every teacher. Mary does, too.

Therefore, it is more appropriate to check the status of the application of *Ellipsis Scope Generalization* in any possible step in which a clause is scanned in order to verify whether the principles E, C and G apply or not. This explains why (169) is the more appropriate method of calculating the computational complexity of applying the relevant principle(s) to derive the correct scope readings for sentences containing QNPs. Computational intractability results when n in $_2k^n$ grows bigger. If, for example, $n = 10$, a total of $_2k^{10} = _23^{10} = 1,073,741,824$ steps will have to be scanned for the correct scope reading in a sentence with 10 clauses (when the number of principles/generalizations to be checked for applicability is three). Other than that, if, for instance, $k > 3$ in $_2k^n$, $_2k^n$ will asymptotically grow bigger and bigger, because for simplicity only three principles/generalizations have been taken into account in the present case in hand. Thus it follows that the computation of scope relations with *Ellipsis Scope Generalization* is intractable. It is also worthwhile pointing out that Collins's (1997) proposal for reducing computational complexity does not apply here. An evaluation of economy considerations, as in *Ellipsis Scope Generalization*, in each step of a derivation rather than in whole derivations is not of much help, especially when only whole derivations give rise to the relevant interpretative effects. As has been stated above, smaller domains of a sentence with QNPs cannot be considered to lead to the range of available interpretations in a sentence, precisely because the reference sets of scope relations for any sentence containing QNPs cannot be evaluated in something smaller than the clausal domain, regardless of whatever way a local step of the derivation of a sentence is cashed out. On top of everything else, the examples in (159)–(167) clearly show that the relevant interpretations permitted by the available scope relations are properties of whole sentences; any partitioning of the entire sentence into smaller domains for what is called 'efficient computation' is destined to run into vicious paradoxes. Overall, this seems to have something to do with the nature and form of interpretation itself. This is what we turn to now.

The present discussion has perhaps left us with a question that has appeared throughout but has not been addressed. Hence, at this juncture, a question may arise as to whether interpretation in itself derives from linguistic computation such that it coincides with semantic effects and in what ways. What is it about interpretation that linguistic computation per se takes as an input or yields as an output? This is a thorny and bewilderingly complex question – something that has the potential to shed light on the issues so far dealt with in this chapter in particular and in this book in general. We now move on to disentangle the logic from the complex question surrounding the relationship between linguistic computation and interpretation. Needless to say, all the knots may not be unfastened. However, we may hope to at least loosen some of the knots that have muddled the issues of concern. One may certainly sense a bit of finicky playfulness in the attempt to disentangle the notion of interpretation from everything else that constitutes something other than interpretation. Be that as it may, this attempt can unravel the relationship of interpretation with semanticity, linguistic computation and the mind all in the same context. The property of interpretation has played a key role in any linguistic account that traces semantic effects of linguistic constructions to the specific conditions warranted by the relevant interpretations. But what is it about the property of interpretation that something seemingly ineffable becomes an abstract entity detectable or discernible within the linguistic system so that it can run computational operations on it?

In fact, the notions of logical form – whether in logic or in formal linguistics – have built on the idea that the property of interpretation can be represented in form. As discussed in Chapter 2, this particular idea actually dates back to philosophers like Frege and Russell. All these scholars were concerned about the real form hidden beneath the surface structures of natural language constructions. That is, they believed that the surface form of natural language sentences does not always match the real form which is invariant across languages. This real form is nothing other than universal structure of thought rendered as logical form. This idea has remained hugely influential and forms the bedrock of much of formal linguistics, especially of formal semantics. But there are significant differences, apart from the obvious commonalities, between the logical form in logic and the one in formal linguistics.

In formal linguistics, the real form beneath the surface structures of natural language constructions corresponds to the semantic structures as they are interpreted. What this means is that semantic structures characterize aspects of meaning which are subject to interpretation by another system formal or otherwise. Construed this way, semantic structures are representations of meaning as they are to be interpreted by a system that can read those relevant aspects of meaning off the representations. Whereas the system that reads aspects of meaning off semantic representations to assign the right interpretations to them is a formal system in the logical tradition, this system in formal linguistics, especially in Generative linguistics, is the C-I system, which is believed to be instantiated in the mind. However, one needs to be cautious in bringing out the differences in views within formal linguistics on the formal system reading off from semantic structures. In formal semantics which is foundationally based on Montague Grammar, the notion of the system that reads off from semantic structures is that of a formal system which is a 'model'[9] (in its technical sense) of the formal system defining semantics in the sense that some system has to interpret natural language structures so that structural properties of the interpreting system can be extrapolated to the linguistic system formally defined (Potts 1975). In other words, semantics considered to be an algebraic system which is isomorphic to the syntactic system contains formally structured representations which sort of have meanings in need of an interpretation by something other than the system defining a tight correspondence between syntax and semantics.

The necessity of grounding in the mind the system reading off from semantic structures differentiates the stance in Generative Grammar from that in formal semantics. The system of linguistic representations incorporating aspects of meaning is related to the C-I system, which is a mental system, and therein lies the crux of the issue that matters in the present context. The question of why semantic structures need to be related to another system that interprets those structures still remains, clearly because semantic structures contain or are the meanings anyway. That is, it is not clear why we require an intermediate representation that mediates between the strictly linguistic system and a non-linguistic formal model or a mental system when the property of interpretation is already present in semantic structures. One of the underlying reasons for having an intermediate representation mediating between the strictly linguistic system and a non-linguistic formal or mental system is that the semantic structures present at the level of the intermediate representation are not exactly meanings that we can verify. Rather, they are expressions carrying aspects of the linguistic system over to the non-linguistic formal or mental system that fully interprets those intermediate expressions rendering them verifiable for truth conditions or making them available for mental processes including inferences. In simpler terms, semantic structures present at the level of the intermediate representation can be mapped either onto cognitive representations, as in Relevance Theory (Sperber and Wilson 1995) or onto truth-conditional structures, as in formal semantics. The former view harmonizes well with a translational view of intermediate semantic structures or simply, logical forms, and the latter with a referential view. As Recanati (2004) argues, these two views need not be incongruent with one another, insofar as nothing precludes one from believing that semantic structures evaluated for truth-conditions are to be ultimately related to mental structures anyway.

This suggests, among other things, that the intermediate representation of semantic structures in logical forms requires further operations to yield *real* semantic interpretations. This is indeed the case, irrespective of whether the intermediate representation is in logical form (as in logic) or in LF (as in Generative Grammar). In Generative Grammar it is supposed that these operations are computational in character and have the grounding in the mental substrate. Logical forms in logic, on the other hand, need not be grounded in the mind, but computable functions can be defined on them as far as the effective procedures for the manipulation of logical forms are precisely determined. Operations on logical forms of sentences can be given an algorithmic description in terms of Foster's (1992) notion of algorithms, given that logical forms of sentences of natural language determine their logical properties and logical relations. A simple example can be provided for illustration.

(171) John walked and Mary laughed. ~ $[W(j) \wedge L(m)]$

(172) Mary laughed. ~ $[L(m)]$

The logical forms of the sentences (171)–(172) rendered in first-order logic[10] are placed alongside the sentences. The upper-case letters W and L represent the predicates 'walked' and 'laughed' respectively; the lower-case letters 'j' and 'm' denote the singular terms, that is, the names 'John' and 'Mary' respectively. One can easily observe that the formula $[L(m)]$ can be deduced from the formula $[W(j) \wedge L(m)]$, insofar as the sentence (171) entails the sentence (172) on the grounds that if it is the case that John walked and Mary laughed, it must be the case that Mary laughed in virtue of the understanding that both the event of John's walking and the event of Mary's laughing obtained. This relation between (171) and (172) is a matter of entailment – a case of logical relation. Likewise, the logical property manifest in the logical form of each of (171)–(172) determines whether each of them can be true or false given the state of affairs in the world out there. Thus (172) is true if and only if Mary laughed. So far so good. We are now in a position to articulate how an algorithmic description of the operations on logical forms that yield semantic interpretations can be sketched out. Let us suppose that we have a morphism Ψ such that $\Psi: L^f \rightarrow L^p \times L^r$ where L^f denotes a set of logical forms (say, in first-order logic), L^p a set of logical properties, and L^r a set of logical relations. A morphism is a kind of function with the added advantage that morphisms associate two objects within a category that the relevant morphisms define. In the present context, the relevant category may constitute, intuitively speaking, the category of logical objects which can be logical forms as well as forms that are derived from operations on logical forms. This can help embed this notion of category in the algorithmic description of logical form. The following, which is in line with Foster, can be shown.

(173) $[LO_1: L^f_i \; LO_2: L^p_i \; LO_3: L^r_i] \rightarrow [LO_1: L^f_i \; LO_4: L^p_i, \; L^r_i \;] \rightarrow [LO_1: L^f_i \; LO_4: (L^p_i, \; L^r_i) \;] \rightarrow [LO_5: (L^f_i \; (L^p_i, \; L^r_i))]$

In the schema (173) above, LO is a logical object, L^f_i is a logical form with an index i, and finally, L^p_i and L^r_i refer to a logical property and a logical relation respectively both carrying an index i. The algorithmic characterization in (173) will turn out to be handy enough in projecting a window onto the nature of the relationship between interpretation, linguistic computation and the mind. We may now proceed to see what this reveals.

One of the most puzzling aspects of the nature of semantic computationality has been noted in Mondal (2013a), who has shown that there is no determinate sense in which semantics is computational or can be computationally realized in the mind/brain. This requires further clarification. Logical form and LF have a range of similarities in many respects. They are both 'paraphrases of natural language sentences', to use Quine's words (1970), and are aimed at uncovering the semantic/ logical properties masked by grammatical forms. The following examples show the parallels between logical form and LF. The logical form of the sentence 'Every girl likes a toy', for example, is represented in (174), and the corresponding LF in (175).

(174) **Logical Form (Logic):**
   (i) $\forall x \; [Girl(x) \rightarrow \exists y \; [Toy(y) \wedge Likes(x, y)]]$
   (ii) $\exists y \; [Toy(y) \wedge \forall x \; [Girl(x) \rightarrow Likes(x, y)]]$

(175) **Logical Form (LF):**
   (i) [$_S$ every girl$_1$ [$_S$ a toy$_2$ [$_S$ e$_1$ likes e$_2$]]]
   (ii) [$_S$ a toy$_2$ [$_S$ every girl$_1$ [$_S$ e$_1$ likes e$_2$]]]

Since the sentence 'Every girl likes a toy' is ambiguous, each of (174)–(175) has two representations. The logical form in (174i) corresponds to the one in (175i), and similarly, the one in (174ii) corresponds to (175ii). What (174i) specifies is the interpretation that for every girl there exists some toy or other such that the girl likes that toy; Likes(x, y) represents the predicate 'like' with two of its arguments and has the denotation of a set of pairs of x and y such that x likes y. On the other hand, (174ii) represents the other interpretation on which there is a single toy which every girl likes. The correspondences in (175i–ii) now become much more evident.

However, logical form and LF are in many ways distinct both in form and in purpose. Logicians devised the notation of logical form in order to draw relevant inferences involved in logical and/or arithmetical reasoning, whereas LF was devised in order that semantic aspects syntactic structures contribute to can be represented in an intermediate form which the C-I system can read off from. Many such differences are well known in the literature (see for details, Heim and Kratzer 1998). What is more interesting is that such differences can tell us something about the property of being computational which one may ascribe to semantics. We have already seen in an earlier chapter (Chapter 4) that the notion of linguistic computation builds on the notion of digital computation in the syntactic system. The question is whether the same can be said about the semantic system given the presupposition that the semantic system is an ontologically distinct system of language. But one may wonder how the differences between logical form and LF can have something to illuminate about the property of semantic computationality. It needs to be stressed that the nature of linguistic meaning is such that it cannot be touched or seen. It is intangible and natural language users understand or mean it without much difficulty. When characterizing the linguistic system, a linguist faces the problem of representing linguistic meaning which constitutes the semantic system. Logical form and LF are two different representations or notational variants that sort of reify (aspects of) semantics by embodying it in a form that can be manipulated. And if this is the case, the properties of what the metalanguages – logical form and LF – represent, when logical form and LF are said to represent semantic structures, can reveal something about the property of semantic computationality on the grounds that what logical form and LF represent are the formal objects computation is defined on. An analogy may be helpful in this case. Take the example of colour which is ultimately an abstract property, although colour is visible on objects around us. The colour space can be represented in colour wheels or diagrams or even in tables specifying colour dimensions. Now suppose that we wish to know about the property of spatiality that can be ascribed to the abstraction called colour, that is, whether colour is spatial or not. In such a case, the representational formats of colour space can be useful for figuring out how to understand the property of spatiality that can be ascribed to colour, since surely we do not perceive colour the way we perceive, say, water.

The question of whether semantics is computational or not is a question about whether the structured forms of linguistic meaning *can* be manipulated in accordance with well-defined rules that operate on those structured forms. This can be investigated by taking examples from a range of natural language phenomena, and this has been elaborated on in Mondal (2013a). Some relevant examples, however, can be provided to make the point we would like to demonstrate. The following examples are from binding.

(176) His$_i$ teacher appears to every student$_i$ to be conservative.

(177) Mary$_i$'s mother seems to her$_i$ to be weird.

The logical forms of (176) and (177) are shown in (178) and (179) respectively:

(178) $\exists y$ [Teacher(y) $\wedge$ $\forall x$ [Student(x) $\rightarrow$ Teacher-of (y, x) $\wedge$ Appears-to-be-conservative(y, x)]]

(179) $\exists x$ [m's mother(x) $\wedge$ Seems-to-be-weird (x, m)]

What (178) says is that there is a teacher y and every student x is such that y is x's teacher and the teacher y appears to be conservative to x, while (179) says that there is somebody x who is Mary's mother and who seems to Mary to be weird. Importantly, (178) does not capture the fact that the LF for the sentence (176) is derived from a *reconstruction* of the noun phrase 'his mother' in the place where it is moved from, that is, where it is interpreted, as shown in (180) below.

(180) [$_S$ appears to every student$_i$ [[his$_i$ teacher] to be conservative]].

On the other hand, (179) does not encode the fact that the surface form and LF coincide with each other in (177). No reconstruction of the noun phrase 'Mary's mother' below the pronoun 'her' is allowed because this would trigger a violation of the binding principle C which prevents the referring expression 'Mary' from being lowered below the pronoun 'her'. This shows that LF is sequence-dependent and thus sensitive to levels of representations in the (putative) computational system of the language faculty, whereas logical forms are not sequence-dependent in this way and are self-contained. In simple terms, logical forms do not reflect structural distinctions of linguistic representations.

Moreover, another related point has been emphasized by Jackson (2007), who has cast doubts on the system of logical forms, especially in the context of the Davidsonian framework of truth-conditional semantics. His observations are noteworthy in the present context. Now consider the following sentences in (181a–c):

(181) a. Mary felled the tree into the lake with the axe.
   b. The tree fell into the lake.
   c. The tree fell with the axe.

The sentence (181a) entails the sentence (181b) because if it is the case that with an axe Mary felled the tree into the lake, it follows that the tree fell into the lake. But the same thing cannot be said about the logical relation between (181a) and (181c), insofar as (181c) sounds odd with an instrumental reading of 'with the axe'. That is, (181c) does not have a reading on which the tree was made to fall with the axe used as an instrument. This observation relates to another point that Jackson makes when he provides another example (182), the logical form of which is given below the sentence in question.

(182) *Bart sneezed with the pepper
   $\exists x \, [\text{Pepper}(x) \land \forall y \, [\text{Pepper}(y) \leftrightarrow y=x] \land \text{Sneezed-with}(B, x)]$

Note that the fact of entailment from the putative logical form of (181a) to the putative logical form of (181b) does nothing to guarantee that (181a) will also entail (181c), just as (181a) does not do so in the case of (182) where the logical form does not make the sentence in (182) a grammatical sentence of English. Clearly, the mapping from object-language sentences (from English) onto the formulas of the metalanguage (logical forms) comes a cropper. This shows that logical forms face the problem of overgeneration, while LF does not since the derivational sequences of which LF is a part can block (182) by means of selectional restrictions.

Overall, the observations made above underline the pivotal differences between logical form and LF which can be brought forward for the exploration of the issue of whether semantics is computational or computationally realized in the mind/brain. Before we proceed further, there is another piece of evidence that can be put forward to cast doubt on the postulation that links logical forms of propositional attitudes (which relate a person having a propositional attitude to the proposition that the propositional attitude concerned contains; beliefs, desires, thoughts, etc. are such propositional attitudes) to the syntactic properties of mental representations corresponding to propositional attitudes. This is relevant in that this can unearth another insight into the issue of whether semantics is computational or computationally realized in the mind/brain with respect to the differences between logical form and LF. We already know that LF is a part of the mental organization that instantiates the putative computational system of the language faculty. But what about logical forms? Here is a suggestion. Logical forms can be mentally grounded by assuming that propositional attitudes have logical forms which equate to the syntactic properties of the corresponding mental representations, and that these syntactic properties explain why mental representations corresponding to propositional attitudes cause mental processes and behaviours/actions. In fact, this idea is part of what is called the *computational theory of mind* (mentioned in Chapter 4) the recent version of which is clearly presented in Fodor (2000), who identifies the logical form of a thought, for example, with the syntactic properties of that thought. This identification is also called *supervenience*, or rather a sort of isomorphy; whatever the nature of the logical form of a propositional attitude (such as a thought) is, the corresponding mental representation will have the same syntactic property as the logical form. We shall now see that this has its deleterious consequences. The insight in essential details comes from Mondal (2013a).

(183) a. M1 ~ John walks. $\longrightarrow$ F(j)
b. M2 ~ Max walks. $\longrightarrow$ F(m)

(184) a. M3 ~ Crystal is bright. $\longrightarrow$ G(c) / $\lambda x\, \forall y\, [^\cup x(y) \wedge G(y)]$
b. M4 ~ John is bright. $\longrightarrow$ G(j)

(185) a. M5 ~ Crystal is bright. $\longrightarrow$ G(c)/$\lambda x\, \forall y\, [^\cup x(y) \wedge G(y)]$
b. M6 ~ Summer is bright. $\longrightarrow$ G(s)

M here refers to mental representation, and F = the predicate 'walks', G = the predicate 'bright', $^\cup x$ = the predicate 'crystal/summer (the property of being crystal/summer)'.[11] The English sentences in (183)–(185) can be taken as beliefs, thoughts or whatever propositional attitudes one may like. The logical forms of the sentences are placed alongside the sentences in question, and this is indicated by means of arrows. In (183), the logical forms of the sentences are different because (183a) contains the term 'John' while (183b) has 'Max'; the predicate F is predicated of 'John' (as in (183a)) or of 'Max' (as in (183b)). Hence the corresponding mental representations M1 and M2 will also be different in virtue of the different syntactic properties aligned with the respective logical forms of the sentences. The case in (184) is interesting for our purpose; (184a) will have two possible logical forms (indicated by means of a slash separating the two logical forms) based on whether 'Crystal' is interpreted as a common noun or as a proper name. Note that (184b) does not pose any such problem. What is noteworthy is that the indeterminacy present in (184a) cannot be resolved from within the sentence in question; it needs context for disambiguation which is *not* a syntactic property per se. The problem (184) poses is this: on the one hand, the logical form does not supervene on the syntactic property of the mental representation, as (184a) shows, and on the other, the logical form *does* supervene on the relevant syntactic property, as in (184b).

The case in (185) gives rise to a recalcitrant inconsistency. It can be observed that each of the sentences in (185) has a logical form different from that of the other. But at the same time, the sentences in (185) share the same single logical form, as indicated with a slash. This inconsistency arises (again) owing to the unavailability of context which is *not* a syntactic property. The question is: how do we decide between these logical forms? Since logical forms are assumed to be isomorphic to the syntactic properties of mental representations that correspond to the relevant propositional attitudes, propositional attitudes, especially in (184)–(185), having different logical forms, cannot be different mental representations or simply different 'mental particulars', to use Fodor's words. Given that logical forms can be identified with the syntactic properties of mental representations corresponding to the relevant propositional attitudes, as in (183), but at the same time, they cannot be so identified due to indeterminacy, as in (184)–(185), propositional attitudes having different logical forms cannot be *ipso facto* different mental representations or mental particulars of different types.

The inconsistency leading to a contradiction stems from the supposition, explicitly made in the *computational theory of mind*, that logical forms of propositional attitudes are *intrinsic* properties of propositional attitudes, and no appeal to anything beyond the syntactic properties of mental representations corresponding to propositional attitudes is to be made. That is, a reference to anything over and above logical forms, or rather over and above the syntactic properties of mental representations, is banned, and if so, contextual intrusion is thereby banned too. What is, however, allowed is the possibility that two thoughts have different contents, but share the same logical form. To establish that this is indeed the case, Fodor provides the following example. The belief that there is no Santa Claus has the same logical form as the belief that there are no unicorns even though they are different beliefs in virtue of having different contents. Both these beliefs can have a form like $\neg\exists x\,[Z(x)]$ where Z can stand for the predicate referring to the set of Santa Clauses or the set of unicorns. However, on Fodor's account that two thoughts, for example, have two different logical forms and yet possess the same mental content seems to be a spurious possibility, for if two thoughts have different logical forms, they must be different mental representations having different syntactic properties. This is because it is not clear how two different mental representations can have the same content. At this juncture, one may try to overcome the difficulty here by positing that the non-linguistic domain of the mind that runs the computations can make reference to the linguistic system because the propositional attitude sentences, after all, have a linguistic structure that cannot be eschewed. So the computations that operate on the logical forms of propositional attitudes, one may think, have access to the LFs of the linguistic instances of the relevant propositional attitudes.

This possibility cannot even get off the ground. There are two reasons. First, LF, in virtue of being connected to the C-I system, does not deal with (all) aspects of contextual disambiguation since the crucial information required for the contextual intrusion that the examples in (184)–(185) demand cannot be handled by LF, as LF has to ship the LF representations of the examples in (184)–(185) to the C-I system for later disambiguation through adequate enrichment. As May (1985) has made clear, surely this is not something that LF does. Labelling words such as 'crystal', 'summer', etc. with different indexes in the lexicon itself in order to pave the way for different interpretations for items with different indexes will also not eliminate the trouble. After all, there would be many words that have to be pre-indexed in the lexicon, thereby building up a huge amount of redundancy, and this presupposes that we already know how – and also in how many ways – different words including names are interpreted by people. This is impossible. There does not exist any way different interpretations of a single word which can also be a name can be known beforehand and controlled. Consider, for example, the word 'will', which can mean a legal document of property transfer or determination or wish, as well as being interpreted in countless other ways – a name of a person, the name of a movie, the name of a company, the name of a club, the name of a TV channel and so on. The same holds for words such as 'hero', 'baker', 'eve', 'fox', etc. It is also hard to imagine that a competent native speaker of a language knows all such interpretations. Similar arguments can also be found in Fiengo and May (1996), who have questioned the status of interpreted logical forms proposed by Larson and Ludlow (1993) which too sort of reify semantic interpretations. Besides, the suggestion above risks making the lexicon suck the entire mind into it – which is as absurd as imagining the syntactic system of the language faculty running all computations in the physical universe. Second, it should be borne in mind that the kind of contextual intrusion the examples in (184)–(185) demand is a case of *abduction* that the modular mind which is computational is not supposed to deal with, as is made clear in Fodor. The kind of indeterminacy present in (184)–(185) requires access to inferences drawn from the relevant domain of context and settings in the world as well as information from a body of knowledge that a person may not even contain in their head. Nor does the putative computational system of the language faculty incorporate or represent within it such *holistic* aspects of semantic interpretations. Needless to say, both the putative computational system of the language faculty and the modular non-central system of cognition will fail to resolve the puzzles from within their internalized knowledge bases. Also, it is to be noted that this issue is independent of whether one holds on to the computationalist thesis of symbol manipulation yet recognizes that mere association of symbols cannot ground meaning, for one could accept the possibility that symbols can be grounded in the perceptual system[12] without abandoning the thesis of the *computational theory of mind* (see for details, Shapiro 2008). It needs to be emphasized that a solution to the grounding problem of symbol manipulation may not *ipso facto* solve the problems of semantic interpretation with LF or logical forms.

The long and the short of it is that LF and logical forms project distinct scenarios of semantic computationality. To the extent that logical forms are mentally grounded, semantics appears to be *minimally* computational on the grounds that structured forms of linguistic meaning cannot be manipulated in accordance with well-defined rules which, when operating on those structured forms, do not always yield correct outputs or even do not produce any outputs due to indeterminacy. This is so regardless of whether logical forms represent or encapsulate syntactic properties of propositional attitudes or of natural language sentences.

And, on the other hand, to the extent that LF is *intrinsically* a part of the mental organization realizing the putative computational system of the language faculty, semantics seems to be *maximally* computational in virtue of the rule-bound faithfulness to the syntactic properties of natural language sentences across a range of linguistic phenomena. The mind included, logical form resists rendering semantics computational, while LF makes semantics maximally computational. Conversely, minus the mind, logical form is maximally computational (as per the formulation in (173)), and on the other hand, the question of judging, on the basis of an examination of LF, whether semantics is computational or not becomes meaningless precisely because LF is intrinsically a part of the mentally grounded language faculty. Which scenario is truer of semantic interpretations, given that the property of semantic interpretation is supposed to be encoded or represented in both logical form and LF? The problem becomes more severe, especially when we observe that semantics or the realization of semantics in the mind is computational to a certain extent and yet it is not so to that extent. This looks like a contradiction, although in a relativized condition. Looking at LF, we come to believe that computational operations on the structured forms of semantic interpretations can be defined in order that they are exploited for cognitive interfaces. But we tend to resist this conclusion as soon as we look at the consequences that derive from logical form being made subject to the same constraints and restrictions as LF is.

This relativism immanent in the computational nature of semantics certainly seems hard to swallow, as it does to Borg and Lepore (2002), because certain constraints must be placed on the choice of the formal representation (which we use to unmask the logical properties of natural language sentences) in such a way that the formal representation guarantees a *unique* logical form of each sentence over a vaster range of natural language expressions. Borg and Lepore think so, primarily because natural language expressions are unbounded in nature, and multiple possibly valid formal representations undercut the possibility of deriving logical inferences over a vaster range of natural language expressions. Thus the emerging picture appears to be more damaging from this perspective. Faced with this dilemma, we may abolish either the apparent fact that natural language expressions are unbounded in nature, or the traditionally inherited assumption that LF or logical form encodes or represents properties of semantic interpretation. Whatever option we choose, we end up losing both ways. The abandonment of the apparent fact of unboundedness of natural language expressions will render natural language expressively crippled, and eschewing the assumption that LF or logical form represents properties of semantic interpretation will make the prospect of a semantic theory far dimmer than is generally supposed. To understand the nature of this dilemma far more deeply, we shall have to scrutinize a number of other related assumptions that underscore the set of presuppositions and assumptions entertained thus far.

One of the deeply entrenched assumptions is that semantics is like arithmetic or algebra such that logical formalisms are used to express facts about natural language meanings just like they are employed to express facts about arithmetic or algebra, and LF constitutes a model of those facts, that is, facts about natural language meanings. Implicit in this is another assumption that LF models facts about natural language meanings which are as real as facts about the natural world, in that such facts are supposed to be out there in the world. In other words, this belief presupposes that logical form does not in fact model aspects of natural language meanings, but rather expresses objective facts about natural language meanings just like set theory, for example, expresses arithmetical facts when it is used to describe mathematical facts and generalizations. In addition, this also presupposes that the model of facts about natural language meanings, that is, LF, is distinct from the facts about natural language meanings in themselves. That these assumptions are fallacious can be revealed by carefully inspecting the underlying analogy drawn between semantics and any branch of mathematics.

In this context the case of physics serves as an appropriate example because the basis of the analogy lies in physics. First of all, facts, or rather the description of facts, about physical reality in terms of geometrical (or mathematical) formalisms/structures are identical to and not thus *separable* from the model(s) of these facts in theoretical physics. What this means is that there is no transition from a level/stage of description of physical facts in mathematical structures to a level/ stage of construction of a model of these facts about physical reality. Had it not been the case, mathematical structures would perhaps be considered to be representational metalanguages in which physicists tend to couch, by convention or otherwise, their physical facts, and for this very reason, physical facts can be couched in other possible representational metalanguages (such as natural languages or programming languages or codes, etc.). But this is certainly not true of physics. Abstract physical descriptions are in themselves mathematical objects; the mathematical descriptions, say, in quantum mechanics or relativity theory or even in string theory are all mathematical structures, not models derived from descriptions of physical facts. Thus mathematics is not a special garb that physical facts wear to become visible; rather, physical reality itself is a mathematical reality.

Second, what holds true in the context of theoretical physics is not true of the relationship between logic and meaning in natural language. Logic is a well-defined system of axioms which help derive certain theorems from those axioms based on inferences (inductive or deductive or abductive) through human interpretations. One can thus use the logical metalanguage to represent meaning in natural language (as formal semanticists do using set-theoretic structures and truth-conditions). But then one can also use, with equal ease, conceptual schemas (in Cognitive Grammar, for example) or conceptual spaces/graphs (as in artificial intelligence) to represent the very meanings in natural language. Hence logic or logical formalisms (that is, logical forms) are not the *only* metalanguage in which meanings or facts about meaning can be described. Within the Generative tradition, LFs constitute another metalanguage that represents aspects of meaning expressed syntactically. However, one may now complain that this does not correctly describe the role of LF since the derivation of logical relations and logical properties from LF representations cannot be executed, except by making a reference to the logical structures. And if so, LF as a model of facts about natural language meanings must rely on logical formalisms that express the logical relations and logical properties of natural language sentences. Hence, for example, the logical relation of entailment from (175ii) to (175i) can be deduced from (174) by means of the calculation of the relevant truth-conditions. One may check that if there is a single toy that every girl likes, it must be the case that every girl likes some toy or other, regardless of whether the toy happens to be the same toy or not. The situation described by (175ii) is a more specific scenario subsumed under the more general one described in (175i).

(175) (i) $[_S$ every girl$_1$ $[_S$ a toy$_2$ $[_S$ e$_1$ likes e$_2$]]]
     (ii) $[_S$ a toy$_2$ $[_S$ every girl$_1$ $[_S$ e$_1$ likes e$_2$]]]

In this sense, one can make the reasonable claim that logical relations and logical properties can be deduced from facts about natural language meanings which LF models in virtue of those facts objectively present in natural language sentences. But then LF as a model of facts about natural language meanings becomes *intrinsically* linked to the formalism of logical forms, which is disastrous because the grounding of logical forms in the mind has its deleterious consequences, as observed above, which can eat into the relation of conceptual dependence between LF and logical form. Apart from that, if logical relations and logical properties deduced from facts about natural language meanings can be represented or modelled in formal representational notations other than LF, the possibility of having different equivalently valid models for the same set of semantic facts is at odds with the state of affairs in theoretical physics, for this goes against the requirement that there should be a unique correspondence between a formal representation and any natural language sentence. For example, the theory of conceptual spaces (see Gärdenfors 2004; Warglien and Gärdenfors 2013) can represent many aspects of logical relations and logical properties that can be deduced from facts about natural language meanings, while, on the other hand, it is nonsensical to say that Maxwell's equations describing the properties of electromagnetism can be expressed with the same degree of faithfulness in formats other than mathematics.[13] We have to keep in mind that the goal of constructing logical forms or LF is to have a separate metalanguage for semantic structures which can help tell the surface syntactic form apart from the logical and/or semantic structures. Only in this sense are LFs aligned with logical forms in virtue of both being models of linguistic/semantic facts.

Furthermore, the differences between LF and logical form are not akin to those between different formats for representing number. Even if it is true that one can write numbers in binary or decimal or countless other ways, and that this does not of course change the fact that arithmetical operations are algorithmic because the details of the algorithm just vary appropriately based on the representation used, this is not equally true of semantics. Again, the assumption that semantic objects are like mathematical objects and semantic facts are like mathematical facts plays a large part in getting it rooted in our linguistic inquiry. Had this supposition been true, we would not have found mutually opposite consequences in two different conditions (a condition that includes the mind and a condition minus the mind). This is not true of mathematical objects or facts, since numbers written either in the binary format or in the decimal format do not thereby lead to different consequences in the faithfulness with which the decimal format or the binary format can represent numbers. Nor do numbers vary based on where they are grounded – whether in machines (such as calculators, elevators, mobile phones, etc.) or in human minds, for instance. The ontology of semantics is way different from that of mathematics both in form and in nature. The latter may lie in the Platonic realm, whereas the former cannot perhaps be of such a nature, given that the very metalanguages

that encode or represent semantics are not uniform in their representational faithfulness, and that semantic objects are not merely reified
representations, they subsist on human contexts and interpretations.
For example, the property of being a prime number may be independent of human cognitive processes that conceptualize the property of
being a prime number, but the property of semantic interpretation in
a sentence such as 'John smokes every day' is not independent of the
human interpretation process. Of course, not all of semantics may be
computational. Also, one should note that the differences between LF
and logical form do not simply reduce to differences in algorithmic
details; rather, the differences point to the sizable dissimilarity in the
computable functions which can be defined on them in that the differences rest on unmistakable alterations in the functions that map
relevant inputs onto outputs over the domain of structured forms of
semantic interpretations.

In short, it becomes conspicuous that there cannot possibly be any
determinate sense in which the property of computationality can be
attributed to semantics. If this is right, then this strengthens the conclusion made in Chapter 4 that the property of computationality may be
completely irrelevant to natural language/natural language grammars.
Given that structured forms of meaning need to be manipulated for
further mental and/or logical operations, one may find it striking that
no determinate sense attaches to the notion that computational operations can be defined on structured forms of semantic interpretations.
Recall that the property of semantic interpretation is thought of as an
object that is implicit in logical forms or LF representations as a kind
of what Cresswell (1985) calls 'structured meaning', which is composed
not merely of the individual semantic values of the parts that make up
the meaning of the whole structure but also of the semantic value of
the entire syntactic structure. The notable point in making the property
of semantic interpretation recognizably distinct from the inferences
that operate on the semantic interpretations relates to the concern
that one may mistake the property of semantic interpretation for the
inferential processes that execute operations on structured forms of
semantic interpretations, or vice versa. Such concerns have been force-
fully highlighted by Bach (2013) and Devitt (2013), to name just two.
Indeed, such concerns are otherwise justified on the grounds that the
distinction between the properties of semantic interpretation – which
pertain to the hearer and derive from the metaphysical properties of
interpretation – and inferential interpretative processes operating on
the objects of semantic interpretation – which link to the epistemology

of interpretation and hence connect to the hearer – helps draw a conceptual boundary between what is said and what is contextually connoted. This very distinction, however, has been obliterated in Recanati (2004) as well as in Sperber and Wilson (1995).

Against this background, the observation that has come to the fore in the present context is that it is not clear how to make sense of the way in which computational operations can be defined on forms of semantic interpretations. If this is the case, it may not be hard to see that the underlying reason behind the perplexing results uncovered in this chapter has some fundamental connection to the nature of interpretation itself. The message to be driven home is simple. If a determinate sense cannot possibly attach to the notion that computational operations can be defined on structured forms of semantic interpretations, it may then be the case that there does not exist any determinate way in which the distinction between the properties of semantic interpretation and the interpretative processes that operate on structured forms of semantic interpretation can be reliably drawn. That is, the distinction between semantic interpretation as an abstract entity and semantic interpretation as an inferential or abductive process of the human mind by which one tries to understand the meaning of linguistic expressions in real time ceases to exist. That is not so much to say that such a distinction cannot otherwise be drawn, as to bring into focus the point that we can never possibly know whether something is an abstract entity of semantic interpretation or the mental process of semantic interpretation that takes as input the information encoded in the 'objectified' property of semantic interpretation. It is ontologically impossible to draw a boundary between the two because semantic interpretation as an abstraction is a property which can become a property *only* by virtue of being a part of the psychological process of interpretation by which one tries to understand the meaning of linguistic expressions. The psychological process of interpretation is an *intrinsic* part of the abstraction of semantic interpretation since the property of semantic interpretation taken as an abstraction cannot assume the form it assumes, minus the psychological process of interpretation.[14]

Significantly, this dilemma also has its trace in the Gricean demarcation between what is said (specified in terms of the truth-conditional content) and what is meant (by way of employment of pragmatic inferences). In order to overcome the dilemma, Dascal (2003) makes a distinction between the 'diachronic' aspect of meaning and the 'synchronic' aspect of meaning, the former having something to do with how semantic interpretation as a property of linguistic expressions is *grounded in* or *derives from* the meaning in the speaker's mind and the latter with the *function* of semantic interpretation as part of the formulation and interpretation of speakers' communicative intentions. As Dascal argues, these two perspectives of meaning can be thought of in independent terms, inasmuch as the theory of pragmatics concerns the way communication functions. It is important to underline the fact that even this distinction for the theory of pragmatics is a distinction to be kept in principle, not in practice. For the very notion of the function of semantic interpretation as a property owes its intrinsic character to the grounding relation that obtains between semantic interpretation and speakers' meanings. Additionally, the grounding relation itself need not be merely logical, it is chronological as well, as Dascal emphasizes. This appears to dilute the demarcation, however drawn, between semantic interpretation as an objectual property and semantic interpretation as a psychological process, even when one wishes to pull the cart of any conceivable pragmatic theory of semantic interpretation. This re-encodes the line of reasoning we have been pursuing in this section.

To make this point much easier to grasp, a phonological example borrowed from Ohala (2010) can be provided. The point that Ohala takes pains to make is apt enough to elucidate the matter the conclusion drawn above points up. Ohala argues that the phonological tendency for obstruent sounds – which are produced by means of an occlusion of air within the vocal tract and its consequent sudden release in the form of a burst – to be voiceless can only make sense if this process is not just stipulated as a rule of the mental organization of phonological rule systems. For example, sounds such as /k/, /p/, /t/ (which are voiceless) are commoner across languages than sounds like /b/, /d/, /g/, which are all voiced. The underlying reason for this is not to be found in the abstract rule that merely stipulates this pattern. Rather, this phonological process can be fundamentally traced to the underlying physiological aerodynamics of sound production within and through the vocal tract. The air pressure in the oral cavity needs to be greater than the subglottal pressure for the voicing of obstruents to obtain. If it turns out that the air pressure in the oral cavity is approximately or exactly equal to the subglottal pressure, there is a high degree of likelihood that air flow will fall below the threshold which is necessary to maintain vocal vibration. In such a case the oral tract has to suck in extra air to propel the voicing of obstruents. A phonological rule that simply represents this process as an abstraction borders on a triviality, since the reified abstraction is *intrinsically* a physical constraint constituted by aerodynamic and kinetic factors of speech production. The representation of this constraint as an abstraction encoded in notations misses the internal content of the constraint in question. Similar arguments have been raised about the process of *assimilation* in sound sequences. The insertion of an obstruent sound /p/ between the sound /m/ and the sound /s/ in the name 'Thomson' – (that is, Thom + /p/ + son) – is a matter of assimilation of the features of the neighbouring sounds into the sound that is inserted in a sound sequence. Such assimilation can in fact be traced to the process involved in the transition from the sound /m/ to the sound /s/ during the utterance of 'Thomson'. Note that the sound /m/ is a nasal obstruent sound in the production of which the nasal cavity remains open but the oral cavity remains closed before the final burst, whereas the sound /s/ is an alveolar voiceless sound during the production of which the nasal cavity is closed and the oral cavity remains open enough to cause a friction. During the utterance of the word 'Thomson' the closed states of two exit channels – one from the sound /m/ and the other from the sound /s/ – give rise to an obstruent sound /p/, which is what is inserted in between (Ohala 2005). Again, this process derives from physical and physiological constraints which cannot be represented as an abstract property. These concerns have been expressed rather strongly in Ohala (1990).

These examples are provided in order to state the point we aim to drive at. It seems that phonological phenomena have a similar reflex of the ontological difficulty in drawing a boundary between semantic interpretation as an abstraction and semantic interpretation as a psychological process of interpretation. That is, in the case of phonological phenomena too, there cannot possibly exist any determinate way in which a boundary between phonological abstraction as a property and phonological process as a physically grounded physiological process can be drawn. A phonological abstraction is an abstract property/feature that exists as an abstract property/feature, however postulated, only in virtue of the phonological process which intrinsically carries the content of that phonological abstraction. Again, this is not to exactly mean that such a distinction cannot otherwise be made; rather, the nature of the process is such that it defies any postulation of an ontologically grounded split.

5.2   Summary

This chapter has attempted to establish that the combination of language, mind and computation is not an innocuous combination. Any postulation that brings into its ambit the triumvirate is doomed to run into crippling inconsistencies and paradoxes. The problems cut across many domains of cognitive sciences touching on problems of linguistic knowledge, the relationship between mind and language, the form of cognition, the nature of computation vis-à-vis natural language, etc. But is there any way to get around such inconsistencies and paradoxes? In fact, there is no simple way. There are a plethora of assumptions and presuppositions that provide scaffolding for much of the technology and machinery of mainstream theoretical linguistics. No direct anti-dote to this fundamental problem is at hand though. However, a path which is basic and tentative enough can be outlined. This is the task of the next few chapters. Let us see how we can go about this formidably complex task.

6
The Emerging Connection

The preceding chapters have so far thrashed out some of the deepest problems and puzzles that lie at the heart of the connection between grammar, mind and computation. It has been shown that virtually all the problems and puzzles spring from quite a number of apparently harmless assumptions about the nature of the relationship between a mental grammar and computation. If this is so, it appears that the elimination of these assumptions along with a consequent sharpening of the suppositions that a linguistic theory is based on can perhaps clear up much of the mess. It may be noted that many of the suppositions pass for methodological pillars on which the superstructure of linguistic theory is built, and for that reason, it becomes difficult to impugn a set of suppositions that support linguistic inquiry at a relatively preliminary stage of development. This is, in a certain sense, a justifiable stance in that any rational inquiry has to proceed with a basic set of assumptions and presuppositions. However, if it turns out that the methodological base itself is constituted by shaky structures, it would be worthwhile re-examining the foundational assumptions supporting the methodological base. But in doing so, one needs to be cautious about any step one may consider taking to make sure that this concern does not become simply tangential to the efforts to pull the theoretical cart. That is, any attempt to purge the theoretical superstructure of the disastrous presuppositions that tend to corrode the superstructure itself must also be aimed at avoiding the same presuppositions. Furthermore, to treat the mental grammar as something that intentionality is not directed at is an assumption that introduces a kind of homunculus intentionality into the mental system at lower levels of organization. We have already observed the paradoxes of interpretation that appear when interpretation as a mental process is miniatured at the level of a component that represents meanings given by grammar. In fact, as we have seen throughout this book, any attempt at eliminating intentionality at the level of the linguistic system ends up reintroducing it on a much lower scale. This constitutes the crux of most of the puzzles, paradoxes and problems discussed in this book.

Consider, for example, the problem of undecidability that Chomsky (1980) discusses in the context of some puzzles with 'any' pointed out by Hintikka (1977). What Hintikka says is that the replacement of 'every' by 'any' in two different linguistic contexts produces two different consequences which are significant, insofar as the grammaticality of sentences matters to a grammar that generates only grammatical sentences. For example, the substitution of 'any' for 'every' in a sentence such as 'Jerry likes everything' renders the sentence ungrammatical although the meaning is preserved, whereas the same operation in a sentence such as 'Jerry does not like everything' does not render it ungrammatical but rather changes the meaning. The change in meaning in the latter case can be stated as: the sentence 'Jerry does not like anything' means that for all x it is the case that Jerry does not like x, while the sentence 'Jerry does not like everything' has a reading on which it is not the case that for all x it is true that Jerry likes x. On the basis of this, Hintikka concludes that there is no decidable procedure, that is, an effective procedure, for determining whether a substitution of 'any' for 'every' in a sentence will change meaning. The indeterminacy introduced by any such replacement of 'every' by 'any' militates against the construction of any algorithm that can determine when such an operation changes meaning, given that the preservation of meaning due to such a replacement triggers ungrammaticality. This problem arises mainly because, as Hintikka points out, natural language expressions are such that it becomes hard – and in many cases impossible – to determine what the appropriate component expressions of a larger expression are, especially when the larger complex expression has an ambiguity in meanings. Assuming that both 'any' and 'every' are quantifiers, one may thus find it surprising how a generative grammar can generate sentences with 'any' so that an effective procedure would tell the grammatical sentences apart from those ungrammatical. Chomsky responds to this by stating that the problem can be simply solved if the meaning differences, if any, due to replacements of 'every' by 'any' are all *syntactically* represented at LF, which is a syntactic level after all. And if so, the meaning representations in virtue of the forms at LF can be checked and so determined.

This issue has serious repercussions for the matter we are concerned about. First, if indeterminacy obliterates LF itself, it makes no sense whatsoever to appeal to LF representations with a view to making the syntactic forms of meaning representations at LF checkable. That is, if there cannot be any decidable procedure for ontologically differentiating between semantic interpretation as a formal/syntactic object and semantic interpretation as a mentally grounded process, there cannot exist, in the absence of any intentional grounding of the internalized mental grammar, any decidable procedure for determining any distinction, however conceived, between formal representations of meaning differences and the psychological process that engages in the relevant meaning interpretations. And if this is so, the syntactic forms of meaning representations at LF may not be distinguishable from the mentally grounded process of interpretation, thereby making the determination of syntactic forms of meaning representations at LF in purely intentionality-independent terms collapse. Second, related to the first point, is the issue of how the determination of changes in meanings due to the replacement of 'every' by 'any' is done at LF. It must be nothing but some form of homunculus intentionality that appears to make the relevant meaning distinctions at LF, which is a syntactic level per se. Beyond that, the intrusion of any intentional process from the C-I system is disallowed too, because this will render the mentally internalized grammar an object of one's knowing. As has been emphasized all throughout, the mentally represented grammar is *not* subject to conditions in terms of which the notion of a relation between the represented and the mental state that represents it can be cashed out. In such a case, it seems pointless to stick to the claim that meaning differences can be formally tracked. The problems with 'any' in fact run much deeper. Surely 'any' and 'every' as universal quantifiers match each other in many respects. However, there are sundry differences between these two universal quantifiers; many linguistic contexts make the subtle differences evident enough. Below are such examples.

(186) We have cheese, butter, mayonnaise and ketchup. You can take anything you want.

(187) You are requested to talk about travelling, bird watching, or anything else you like.

(188) Steve ate everything apart from the noodles.

(189) Everything is fine right here and right now.

As can be seen in (186)–(189), the replacement of 'any' by 'every' leads to changes in meanings as much as a replacement of 'every' by 'any' does. Even if 'any' and 'every' are similar in having the meaning of a universal quantifier, that is, 'for all x', it is not true that they behave the same way in contexts that do not involve negation. We have observed that in linguistic contexts not involving negation, the replacement of 'every' by 'any' leaves the meaning intact but the sentence in question becomes ungrammatical. As the examples (186)–(189) show, this is not quite true. While the replacement of 'every' by 'any' in (188) renders the sentence grammatically deviant, this is not the case with (189) in that both 'every' and 'any' are compatible with the context described in (189). On the other hand, the replacement of 'any' by 'every' in both (186) and (187) alters the meanings that are available. The restricted interpretation of 'anything (…)' in the sense of a selection out of a set of given choices changes to the usual meaning of the universal quantifier 'every' (which is 'for all x'), if any replacement of 'any' by 'every' is done. In all, linguistic contexts not involving negation also give rise to a kind of indeterminacy since neither of the replacements – the replacement of 'any' by 'every', and the replacement of 'every' by 'any' – guarantees a preservation of the available meaning(s). Therefore, it is not clear which aspects of form in the examples (186)–(189) contribute to the changes in meanings and which do not, because the presence of negation in 'Jerry does not like everything/anything' is a formal marker, which is absent in (186)–(189). One can easily verify that a substitution of 'every' for 'any' in (186) may preserve the meaning if the first sentence 'We have cheese, butter, mayonnaise and ketchup', which provides the context for a set of choices, were missing because the sentence 'You can take anything you want' taken in isolation can have the meaning of a universal quantifier. And in fact, there is another context to which the interpretation of 'any' is specifically suited, and which unveils a great deal of indeterminacy ensuing from any replacement of 'any' by 'every'. This linguistic context involves *downward-entailing* structures; they are so called because the relevant inferences go from sets to subsets. Here are some examples (taken from Chierchia 2013 with slight modifications) that suffice to make the point.

(190) If there is any food in the fridge, please bring it.

(191) Everyone who still maintains any car should come forward.

(192) Nobody buys any book.

In all the cases above, inferences from the superset to a subset are valid; for instance, if nobody buys any book (as in (192)), it must be the case that nobody buys any book by Milton, given that the set of books written by Milton is a subset of all books. Now if the quantifier 'any' is replaced by 'every' in each of the examples in (190)–(192), certain significant changes follow from this. The sentence (190) will be ungrammatical, although for independent reasons;[1] the sentence (191) will have its meaning changed because of the universal reading of 'every'; and the meaning of the sentence (192) changes too, in a different way though. Note that the meaning of 'any' in (190)–(191) is that of an existential quantifier, that is, 'for some x', which changes to the reading of a universal quantifier if 'every' replaces 'any' in those examples. The case of (192) is more complex in that the sentence in the original form reads like 'for all x such that x belongs to the set of books, it is not the case that there is someone who buys x'. The crucial point is that the replacement of 'any' by 'every' in (192) does alter the meaning of (192), which reads like 'it is not the case that for all x such that x belongs to the set of books, there is someone who likes x'. This means that the replacement of 'any' by 'every' in (192) gives rise to a scalar implicature (which consists in a set of alternative implications positioned on a *scale* of strength) that someone buys some, if not all, books. Plus the downward entailment fails to hold in (192) if 'any' is replaced by 'every'; thus, if nobody buys every book, it does not necessarily follow that nobody buys every book by Milton because someone may still buy some books which happen to be all the books (written) by Milton. In sum, 'any' as a quantifier suits downward-entailing structures in being sensitive to polarity, that is, to the distinction between negation and non-negation (see Krifka 1991 for a critical account), and it is intertwined with interpretative complexities arising from certain specific replacements of 'any' by 'every'. In no sense can these interpretative complexities be predicted from formal representations at LF, solely in terms of the syntactic computations and without thereby incorporating some form of homunculus intentionality.

In what follows a meta-theoretical reorientation of linguistic theory will be attempted. The reason why the task will involve an attempt at providing a meta-theoretical reformulation is that the problems are fundamentally rooted in the foundational assumptions about what a theory for linguistics should aim at. The requirement of explanatory adequacy, which connects the logical problem of language acquisition, has been one of the driving forces behind the adoption of assumptions about the mental representation of grammar and computation. What this says in essence is that the problem of how children learn language, given impoverished inputs, can be solved if a general theory of language, that is, UG, specifies what grammars can be acquired such that any such grammar yields structural descriptions of sentences that cohere with the individual linguistic competence constituted by the mentally grounded grammar. As we proceed, we shall see that this problem, in whatever form, can be best approached if the grounding assumptions about the mind, interpretation and computation are reformulated. Given that Generative Grammar treats UG as a meta-theory with generative grammars specified by it being theories, the notion of a meta-level theory in the present context is different. The meta-level theory to be outlined here will be a theory of the language faculty at a level of abstraction way beyond what individual linguistic theories apply to. In other words, the meta-level theory to be enunciated will certainly be a theory of the language faculty, but it will be rendered in terms that subsume, or in a certain sense unify, aspects of linguistic theories.

6.1 Architectures of grammar and linguistic formalisms

The relationship between the architecture of language and a linguistic formalism specifying rules of syntax, semantics, morphology and phonology is not very straightforward. Different linguistic theories have approached this issue in different ways. In fact, Chomsky's (1975b) work on an axiomatic system for rules of grammar within a system of levels of representation was not specified in terms of levels of details (computational, algorithmic and implementational levels), since the axiomatic system was not intended to be psychologically grounded. However, it is not necessary that a correspondence between an axiomatic system for language and an architecture of language grounded in the mind has to be drawn. This point has also been made by Kracht (1998), who has argued that a translation between logics and grammar can be achieved without making a reference to any architecture of language; the reduction of a gap between the principles of grammar and linguistic rules, he believes, can accomplish this.

In particular, theoretical linguistics has two extreme positions on this issue, with a few in-between. On the one hand, mainstream Generative Grammar posits rules and constraints which are assumed to be directly represented in the language faculty (Chomsky 1980, 1995), and on the other hand, Head-Driven Phrase Structure Grammar (Pollard and Sag 1994) characterizes the system of signs independently of any conceivable architecture of the language faculty in order to maintain a neutrality on the issue of realization of the system of grammar in the mind. Optimality Theory (Prince and Smolensky 1993), which is a representational theory of grammar specifying linguistic structures in terms of a competition of a set of violable constraints, has also followed a path similar to the one by Head-Driven Phrase Structure Grammar (but see Smolensky and Legendre 2006 for cognitive grounding of Optimality Theory). Lexical Functional Grammar (Bresnan 2001) in its formalism adopts a somewhat similar stance, although the foundational assumptions underlying Lexical Functional Grammar incorporate a homomorphism between the system of rule types of grammar and processing functions in the mind (Bresnan 1982). The only difference that comes to mind is perhaps Jackendoff's Parallel Architecture (Jackendoff 2002). On this proposal, the system of rules and constraints is non-intentionally represented in the architecture of the language faculty which incorporates syntax, semantics and phonology as parallel systems of grammar which are connected to each other through interfaces and have independent rules and representations each. In many ways similar to Jackendoff's Parallel Architecture is Sadock's Autolexical architecture of the language faculty (Sadock 1991), which is massively parallel in having modules for different systems of grammar, namely syntax, semantics, morphology and phonology with lexicon being the interface connecting them all. However, the assumption that such a distributed massively parallel architecture makes each module computationally tractable, at least in a sense, presupposes that operations on linguistic representations are judged to be computational (see Sadock 2012).

The present meta-theoretical proposal will make an attempt to unify these distinct aspects of the relationship between the system of grammar and an architecture of the language faculty.[2] Therefore, the aim is *not* to replace current theories; rather, the aim is to place them where they belong. Given that the problem of homunculus intentionality relates readily to the problem of interpretation with respect to the computational basis of the operations obtaining within the fabric of the mentally grounded linguistic system, a description of the linguistic system in terms that *at least* avoid these problems by specifying the abstract properties of the rules of syntax, semantics, morphology and phonology will be outlined. This description will then be related to an architecture of language which is sufficiently general to encode what the description describes. To put it a different way, we aim at a translational transparency between the operations of a general architecture of language and (linguistic) rules of syntax, semantics, morphology and phonology. The translational transparency will be such that the (linguistic) rules of syntax, semantics, morphology and phonology will constitute and thus correspond to the operations of a general architecture of language. So we shall have two different levels: a level of description of the abstract properties of the rules of syntax, semantics, morphology and phonology, and a level of the operations of a general architecture of language. The most significant point is that the description is *intentional* in that the system of rules of syntax, semantics, morphology and phonology is *not* represented or instantiated in the general architecture of the language faculty any more than the binary number system is represented or instantiated in the decimal system when translated from it. This is so because any translation of the operation of a general architecture of the language faculty into a system of rules is ultimately a description, and any description is by definition intentional. The system of rules along with all associated axioms and constraints that govern and restrict the application of rules is *intentionally* grounded by human beings, whenever any operation in the general architecture of the faculty of language is related by human beings to a system of rules, axioms and constraints. This system of description resides in and derives its character from, inasmuch as it is related to a general architecture of the language faculty, the nature and form of the language faculty. We may now move on to present the general architecture of language in rudimentary details.

6.2　A general architecture of language

The overall idea of having a general architecture of language is to construct a model of the language faculty which is architecturally general enough to express various possible distinctions and connections among the systems of grammar. For the most part the description that follows will be borrowed from the specification of a general architecture of language, as detailed in Mondal (2012). The structures and formal principles of the operations within the general architecture of language are also general in nature; however, this generality, as we shall see, can be understood to have a *sui generis* character. Importantly, the operations of the general architecture of language to be outlined below are not (linguistic) computations, although the word 'computation' as shorthand for 'operation' was used in Mondal (2012). Because of the damaging connotations and consequences that computation leads to, this term has been subsequently eliminated in Mondal (2014b).

The general architecture of language is *maximally* interconnected with fluid interactions among the systems of language, namely syntax, semantics, lexicon, morphology and phonology. Fortunately, a range of studies on linguistic phenomena in areas as diverse as syntax, semantics, morphology and second language acquisition (Neelman and Weerman 1998; Hengeveld et al. 2004; Van Valin 2005; Montrul 2011;

White 2011) also point to this direction. What this amounts to in concrete terms can be measured in terms of the way this handles – and can perhaps resolve – many theoretical and empirical issues of linguistic phenomena. The schematic representation of the general architecture is given in Figure 6.1.

This is a representational level architecture of language in the mind/brain. The nodes representing systems or components of grammar are functional modules having functionally coherent units of representational resources realized in diffuse and often shared networks of brain regions. Thus they are not fully encapsulated modules in the sense described by Fodor (1983). The bidirectional arrows stand for connections or simply 'interfaces' connecting the components/domains of grammar, and hence operations can run in any direction involving any number of components of language, namely syntax, semantics, morphology, lexicon and phonology. Different linguistic phenomena will involve different sets of interactions among the systems of grammar. The architecture is *flexible* or *elastic* in the sense that the architecture can contract into differential interfacing configurations involving only one linguistic component or two or three or four, or conversely, the architecture can also expand into interfacing configurations involving two linguistic components or three or four or five. This is necessitated by the presence of various idiosyncratic items in natural languages such as 'ouch!', 'dammit!', 'hmm', 'abracadabra', etc. as well as linguistic signs some of which can involve only one system of grammar (see Jackendoff 2002). At this stage, one may now see how the general architecture can mirror the Parallel Architecture as well as the Autolexical architecture of grammar. Other relevant properties of representational linguistic theories can also be expressed in terms of the general architecture once the system of rules, axioms and constraints of different components

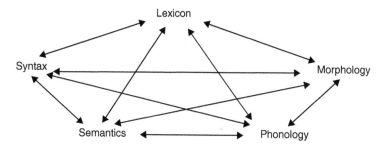

Figure 6.1 A general architecture of language

of grammar is adequately described – a task to be taken up in the next section. The reason why lexicon in the general architecture is endowed with the status of a system just like morphology or phonology is that lexicon may be thought of as an algebraic system in the sense described in Kornai (2010). Thus, being an algebraic system, lexicon can have its idiosyncratic properties not reflected by generative or predictive rules in any of the other systems of grammar – syntax, semantics, morphology and phonology.

It is important to stress that any interaction in the architecture is subject to a number of linguistically *sui generis* constraints operating over the architecture, which do not merely restrict the power of the architecture, but also cause *elasticity* to obtain so that the geometry of the architecture is warped or distorted. It may be argued that these constraints are the ones that are *epigenetically* encoded in our language faculty in that these constraints are constituted by and emerge through a complex coupling between genes and environments (whether internal or external to the body). The form of these constraints renders the language faculty *unique*, thereby making it distinct from, say, the visual faculty. Many of these constraints have been presented in Jackendoff (2002) in the context of a discussion on the restrictive properties of interfaces that connect two systems of grammar. For exposition, some of these constraints are mentioned below.

(i) Syllabification which is a matter of phonology is not of concern to syntax, and it is generally irrelevant to semantics as well. Thus, why the phonological structure of the word 'dictate' is broken up into syllables as /dIk/ and /teIt/ has nothing to do with the meaning of the word 'dictate'.

(ii) (Multiple) embedding in syntax is not relevant to phonology which deals with segments, suprasegments, syllable structure, intonation, etc.

(iii) Hierarchical organization of syntactic structures is not accessible to phonology which does not relate to how hierarchical organization underlies syntactic structure building. This explains why long-distance dependency is not available in phonology. However, word boundaries and edges of phrases may be relevant to the organization of major (prosodic) phrases in phonology on the grounds that subject noun phrases, verbs, object noun phrases and adjuncts can form major (prosodic) phrases when they are at the edge of a noun phrase or a verb phrase (Selkirk 2006). Phonology can thus have access *at least* to the lowest level of syntactic organization.

(iv) Argument dropping under some interpretative conditions is opaque to the internal structure of phonology. For example, the object argument in 'John left early' can be dropped, but this does not have anything to do with phonology per se.

(v) Matters of quantification and variable binding in semantics are not properties of lexicon; rather, they matter to syntax and semantics.

(vi) Many things from semantics are not visible to syntax, or vice versa. For example, many cases of ambiguity or vagueness have nothing to do with syntactic organization. Examples of this kind we have already seen in the case of 'any' above. Syntax does not *fully* determine how (at least certain cases of) ambiguity is (are) formed in sentences or how vagueness arises in syntactic structures.

Different constraints may affect the coordinated interactions among the components of language in such a manner that one constraint may inhibit interaction between two components, thereby enhancing interaction among some other components. Take the case of (iv), for example. In this case interaction between phonology and semantics gets blocked, but at the same time, an interaction between semantics, lexicon and syntax is facilitated. Overall, it is now evident that there is one-to-many mapping between constraints and the linguistic components or domains. Let these constraints be described as a set $\Phi = \{C_1 ... C_n\}$. The exact number of such constraints is unknown, but surely there can be more that may be discovered as we examine more and more languages.

Moreover, every interaction in a linguistic phenomenon must also be governed by a *structural mapping condition*, which has to be compatible with Φ as well. Thus every interaction in the general architecture is doubly restricted – once by Φ and then by the *structural mapping condition*. The *structural mapping condition* requires the mapping of as much linguistic information at the interfaces between the components/ domains of language as demanded by a given linguistic phenomenon. Thus, for example, a sentence like 'John loves the dog he has brought' will involve an overlapping range of linguistic phenomena. For the sentence at hand, there will be an involvement of the phenomenon of agreement (to account for the agreement between 'John' and 'loves'), the relation of tense and aspect (the sentence is in the present tense and the aspect of the event is durative), the phenomenon of relativization (it tells us that 'John loves the dog' and 'he has brought' are two different clauses linked via the internal argument of 'brought' by means of a null relative pronoun), the phenomenon of displacement (the internal argument of 'brought' does not appear where it is interpreted), the semantic composition of the parts of the sentence (involving the meaning of 'the dog' that is restricted by the relative clause 'he has brought' along with the anaphoric link between 'John' and 'he'), the case of mapping major (prosodic) phrases and intonational phrases to relevant syntactic structures ('John' may be a different major (prosodic) phrase from that contained in 'loves the dog' and the relative clause may well be a different intonational phrase) and so on. Note that all these diverse phenomena may or may not intersect with each other. Significantly, all that the *structural mapping condition* dictates is that each such phenomenon must be constituted only by the amount of linguistic information which the relevant mapping between the components/domains of language involved requires.

Within the present proposal, the construction of any sentence in a language ensues from a coalescence of a range of interfacing conditions of the general architecture of language. The *elasticity* of the architecture of the language faculty makes this viable. In a sense then the *structural mapping condition* is an outcome of the *elasticity* of the general architecture of language. The *structural mapping condition* may thus be conceived of as a function that takes as input all possible interactions (in a given linguistic phenomenon) and restricts them to only those that make a contribution to structural difference, but it does not guarantee that it may not be overridden by Φ. For example, the phenomenon of agreement in the case of the example sentence 'John loves the dog he has brought' is irrelevant to intonational phrasing, and hence this must be subject to Φ, even though pieces of information from both the phenomenon of agreement and intonational phrasing are to be culled given the *structural mapping condition*. In sum, the *structural mapping condition* is relative to a linguistic phenomenon in a language, while the constraints in Φ are absolute within the architectural specifications. The former is all about bringing structural pieces into a space that fits the phenomenon at hand, whereas the latter is about the intrinsic fit between components or domains of grammar from which the structural pieces are drawn. An analogy will serve to illustrate the difference. Let us imagine writing an article on the political system of Britain. In such a case, all *relevant* pieces of information gathered from different books, papers, magazines, newspapers, etc. help write the article in question. Now it should be noted that it is not necessary that the sources from which the pieces of information are culled are *in themselves* compatible with each other. The issue of intrinsic compatibility relates to Φ, whereas the matter of bringing the relevant pieces together pertains to the *structural mapping condition*.

Now something about the cognitive grounding of the general architecture needs to be mentioned. The architecture as a whole can be reckoned as a system which has three degrees of freedom, that is, three dimensions along which the general architecture of language can be positioned. These are function, representation and mental processing: function is about both language use and the functions of linguistic communication; representation denotes linguistic representations, and mental processing involves perceptual, memorial, conceptual and inferential processes engaging various mental systems. At any point of time, the general architecture of language can be in a state determined by the position configured in terms of the three dimensions. For instance, if the architecture is in a state pulled towards the dimensions of representation and processing, we have the architecture confined to the boundaries of the cranium. But if it is in a state drawn towards the dimension of function, the architecture sort of projects outward for language use. The rationale for rendering function, representation and mental processing as three abstract dimensions, instead of having a larger architecture of the mind in which the general architecture of language can be shown to be grounded, is to simply describe the conditions or parameters that impact upon whatever the architecture does and how it operates. And the advantage of such a description in a continuous space resides in the obliteration of any *strict* partitioning between linguistic function, linguistic representation and the psychological processing of language, although surely all three of them can be *conceptually* distinguished from each other, which explains why we have three dimensions rather than just one. We cannot say anything more concrete about how the general architecture of language connects to other domains of cognition, given that we have a very faint grasp of this matter at the current stage of our scientific inquiry.

6.3 Axioms, rules and constraints

The level of the operations of a general architecture of language has now been characterized, but this level has to be related to another level at which the description of the abstract properties of the rules of syntax, semantics, morphology and phonology can be couched. But why does the level which makes a reference to the general architecture of language need to be related to a level of the abstract properties of the rules of syntax, semantics, morphology and phonology? The reason is far from simple, and hence deserves a clear articulation. The switch from a symbolic system (the level of the general architecture of language) to an analogue system, or rather to a continuous state-space (constrained by the dimensions of function, representation and processing), is made possible by the *intentional* projection of the linguistic system which can be conscious or unconscious. The *intentional* projection of the linguistic system grounds the linguistic system in the cognitive substrate, and the level at which the description of the abstract properties of the rules of syntax, semantics, morphology and phonology is couched expresses the axiomatic properties of rules and constraints as well as the grounding relation itself. In saying this, we certainly do not intend to mean that the linguistic system accepted as such derives from the mind, or that it is located in the Platonic realm. The switching between the symbolic level and the continuous space caused by the *intentional* projection of the linguistic system makes the linguistic system straddle the boundary between an architectural level of mental organization and a level of description.

We may now explicate the form of rules and constraints of grammar in relation to the faculty of language, as articulated in the section above. Let $D_1, D_2, D_3, \ldots , D_n$ be the components/systems/domains of grammar, namely syntax, semantics, phonology, lexicon and morphology. Let us start with the following fundamental axioms.

Axiom 1

Let there be a set of linguistic domain functions $\kappa = \{LD_1 \ldots LD_k\}$ such that for each D_i there is some set $\pi_i \subseteq \kappa$ and LD: $\alpha \to \beta$ where α is a graph in D_i and β is an n-tuple of binary relations $<R_1 \ldots R_n>$ for D_i.

Axiom 1 is a descriptive statement about the constitutive elements of linguistic component/domains each of which incorporates some subset of the set of linguistic domain functions (that is, $\kappa = \{LD_1 \ldots LD_k\}$). In other words, what Axiom 1 ensures is that for each linguistic domain out of $D_1, D_2, D_3, \ldots , D_n$ there must be a subset of κ. Thus there will be a subset π_1 for lexicon, another π_2 for syntax, π_3 for morphology, π_4 for phonology and π_5 for semantics such that $\pi_1 \ldots \pi_n \in \mathscr{P}(\kappa)$ (the power set of κ). To be clearer, it is possible that $\pi_1 \ldots \pi_n$ are intersective with each other, since some of the linguistic domain functions (LDs) may be shared by some of the linguistic domains/components from $D_1, D_2, D_3, \ldots , D_n$. This paves the way for parallels in rules and structures among $D_1, D_2, D_3, \ldots , D_n$, given that different components/domains of grammar may have similarities in organization (see for details, Anderson 2011). It should be made clear that the possibility of having different but partially overlapping LDs for the linguistic component/domains carries no assumption as to whether all the different components/domains of the general architecture of language should be ontologically different or not. As Cann et al. (2012) distinguish *levels of analysis* in linguistic descriptions from *levels of representation*, as discussed in Chapter 4, there is no presupposition that different linguistic components/domains are either ontologically different or level-wise distinct. This is primarily because the distinction between *levels of analysis* and *levels of representation* cuts across the general architecture of language. For example, linguistic form, which is ontologically distinct from meaning, is distributed across a number of linguistic component/domains, namely syntax, lexicon, phonology and morphology, whereas meaning is restricted to semantics. And at the same time, syntax, lexicon, phonology, morphology and semantics are not different levels of analysis either, since the notion of an essentially uniform LD across the entire extension of the set of linguistic components/domains, and an acknowledgement of a difference in the formative elements and their relations of constitution in each linguistic component/domain go together.

More concretely, the LD maps a graph structure onto an n-tuple of binary relations $<R_1 \ldots R_n>$ such that the graph can vary in structure from one linguistic domain to another, and similarly, the binary relations $R_1 \ldots R_n$ can also vary from one linguistic domain to another. Whatever properties are relevant to the specification of the syntactic, semantic, morphological, lexical and phonological structures, insofar as they identify different aspects of linguistic structures, will be a part of the formal structure of graphs or relations that relate properties of the respective structures. This has been followed all throughout this chapter. Hence, for syntax, we might need a tree structure in α and dependency or/and constituency or/and command relations (or whatever the case may be) in β. An example may illustrate this properly. Suppose that we have a sentence 'John knows that Mary is beautiful'; in terms of an LD_i: $\alpha \to \beta$ in syntax α can be taken to be a tree graph as schematized in Figure 6.2, and β can be a 2-tuple of binary relations R such that we have $<R1, R2>$ where R1 = {<(NP, VP), S>, <John, NP>, <(knows, CP), VP>, <that, C>, <Mary, NP>, <is, V>, <beautiful, AP>, <(is, beautiful), VP>} is a syntactic constituency relation (in which the first element constitutes the second), and R2 = {<John, knows>, <that, knows>, <beautiful, is>, <Mary, (is, beautiful)>, <CP, knows>} is a dependency relation in which the first element in each pair depends on the second. For clarity, NP = noun phrase, VP = verb phrase, CP = complementizer phrase, V = verb, AP = adjective phrase, C = complementizer and S = sentence.

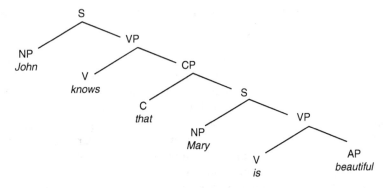

Figure 6.2 A tree for the sentence 'John knows that Mary is beautiful'

Similarly, for lexicon we may need a tree structure or a lattice for α, and conceptual relations or/and relations of qualia structures (see Pustejovsky 1995) or/and relations of features, attribute–value pairs, etc. for β. Thus, for the sentence in Figure 6.2, we need lexical items – 'John', 'Mary', 'know', 'that', 'be', 'beautiful' – each of which can be characterized in terms of another LD_j: $\alpha \rightarrow \beta$ such that α is tree graph of the form shown for 'John' in Figure 6.3, and β is a 2-tuple of binary relations <R1, R2>.[3]

R1 = {<John, object>, <John, name>} is a conceptual relation containing binary pairs, and R2 = {<John, FF>, <John, CF>, <John, AF>, <John, TF>} constitutes a qualia relation specifying *formal features* (FF) of 'John' ('John' is animate and a human being), *constitutive features* CF (John's physical features and appearances), *agentive features* AF (John's personal history and his personal relation to Mary) and *telic features* TF (characteristic activities and actions of John). Similar kinds of LDs of the same index *j* can be used for other lexical items as well.

For phonology α would include trees or lattice, and β will incorporate relations of articulatory, auditory and perceptual features in association with dependency or constituency roles. Thus a different LD_k: $\alpha \rightarrow \beta$ for phonology will include a mapping for each of the lexical items in 'John knows that Mary is beautiful'; so 'John', for instance, will have a α that will look like that shown in Figure 6.4.

And β will be a 2-tuple of binary relations <R1, R2> such that R1 = {<John, SF>, <John, AP>} is a relation that specifies the *segmental features* (SF) of the segments of 'John' and the *articulatory–perceptual features* (A-P) of the syllable of 'John', and R2 = {< John, σ>, <dʒ, Onset>, <ɒ, Nucleus>, <n, Coda>, <{ɒ, n}, Rhyme>} specifies the combinatory relation for the syllabic elements of 'John'. Importantly, within phonology

Figure 6.3   A tree for the noun phrase 'John'

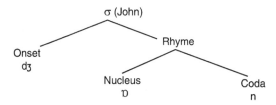

Figure 6.4   A tree for the syllable structure of 'John'

we may also need another LD: $\alpha \to \beta$ of the same index k that will determine how major (prosodic) phrases and intonational phrases can be assigned to the sentence 'John knows that Mary is beautiful' as a whole. In that case a reference to the syntactic LD_i may be necessary, and hence the LD for syntax (LD_j) and the LD for phonology (LD_k) can be shared across the interface linking syntax and phonology if and only if this is compatible with the constraints Φ that determine how much from either phonology or syntax (what subset(s) of LD_i and what subset(s) of LD_k) can be mutually shared. Likewise, another LD with a different index incorporating features and combinations of morphemes will be required for morphology such that trees or lattice would serve as what α is supposed to be, and β would contain relations between stems, infixes, prefixes and suffixes. We shall leave out the details because essentially similar principles apply here. Finally, for semantics α would be a graph, as shown in Figure 6.5.

And β will represent relations of semantic tiers (in Jackendoff's (2002) sense) or/and relations of cognitive structures/schemas (as in Cognitive Grammar) or/and logical representations in set-theoretic structures.[4] This will generally yield a 3-tuple of binary relations <R1, R2, R3> such that R1 = {<'John knows that Mary is beautiful', DT>, <'John knows that Mary is beautiful', MT>, <'John knows that Mary is beautiful', RT>} is a relation that specifies the sentence here in terms of three tiers. These are: the *descriptive tier* (DT) specifies the two linked *states* one of which

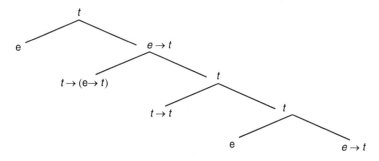

Figure 6.5   A type-logical tree for the sentence 'John knows that Mary is beautiful'

has 'John' as an object/individual and the other has 'Mary'; the *macro-role tier* (MT) specifies the property of 'John' as an EXPERIENCER of a stative proposition which contains 'Mary' as the THEME, and the *referential tier* (RT) specifies that there are two referential NPs, namely 'John' and 'Mary' having different indexes and are dependent on the event[5] indices of 'know' and 'be beautiful' respectively. On the other hand, R2 = {<'John knows that Mary is beautiful', C-schema>, <John, Trajectory/Focus>, <knows, Process>, <'that Mary is beautiful', Landmark/Ground>, <Mary, Trajectory/Focus>} is a relation encoding cognitive/conceptual schemas (C-schema), and R3 = {<John, a set of individuals who know that Mary is beautiful>, <(John, 'that Mary is beautiful'), a set of ordered pairs of individuals who are in a state of knowing and the propositions known>, <Mary, a set of individuals who are beautiful>} is a relation specifying set-theoretic properties (of membership); for example, John is a member of the set of individuals who know that Mary is beautiful.

Overall, it can be observed that the characterization above is independent of any (specific) linguistic formalism, as well as of any specific language. The exact graph (whether it is a tree or a lattice) in α, and the exact relations (the tuples in the relations) in β may vary across and within languages for various linguistic phenomena.

Axiom 2

Rules for linguistic phenomena across and within languages will be a mapping of the form:

ψ: < $LD_1, \ldots, LD_k$> $\rightarrow$ < $LD_1, \ldots, LD_m$> when it is not necessary that $k = m$.

All that Axiom 2 states is that rules for linguistic phenomena will have a sufficiently general character such that a tuple of LDs will be mapped onto another. The much debated problem of linguistic universals or principles of Universal Grammar versus linguistic variation is neutralized in the present context, so long as *all* linguistic rules, regardless of specificity or universality, involve operations on tuples of linguistic domain functions. Additionally, the specific character of rules is underscored by the range and domain of an LD which is constructed relative to particular linguistic domains/components and linguistic phenomena across and within languages. An example can make this clearer. Let us take the case of *Wh*-questions, which is perhaps one of the most investigated linguistic phenomena in mainstream theoretical linguistics (see for a discussion, Aoun and Li 2003). Consider, for example, *superiority* effects in both *Wh*-movement structures and non-movement *Wh*-structures which determine which *Wh*-element out of a number of candidates ends up creating a dependency between the gap and the position where it is interpreted. We shall take some relatively simpler cases from English that suit the discussion at hand:

(193) a. Who__ saw what?
     b. *What did who see__?

(194) a. Who__ came after what?
     b. *What did who come after__?

(195) a. Who did you convince__ to see what?
     b. *What did you convince who to see__?

The gaps are shown through dashes. Such cases are commoner in languages like Lebanese Arabic, etc, as Aoun and Li show. Superiority effects have been associated in Generative Grammar with principles such as *Subjacency* or *Attract Closest* or the *Minimality Condition on Movement* all of which, in essence, consist in the requirement for a movement of an item to the closest possible target. Such cases can have a straightforward representation as a mapping from some tuple $<LD_1,... , LD_i>$ (with the $LD_1,... , LD_i$ from syntax, lexicon and perhaps morphology) onto another tuple $<LD_1,... , LD_j>$ when $i \neq j$ and $LD_1,... , LD_j$ are within syntax and semantics.[6] Tree graphs with the associated constituency/dependency relations from $<LD_1,... , LD_i>$ will be mapped onto the tree graphs with the associated dependency/constituency relations and conceptual relations taken from $<LD_1,... , LD_j>$ with the smallest edge distance (relative to other candidate trees in surface form) between two vertices V′ and

V" such that V′ represents a *Wh*-occurrence, and V″ represents what V′ depends on (for instance, a verb or a preposition, etc., as in Dependency Theory discussed in Chapter 2) or the co-indexed expression of that *Wh*-occurrence (resumptive pronouns, for example). Note that this characterization is independent of any assumptions about movement, and whatever dependency/constituency relations are associated with tree graphs by a given LD are, as a matter of fact, specific to that LD.

However, this characterization leaves open other possibilities. For example, Pesetsky (2000) has argued that superiority effects do not obtain in the case of *Which*-phrases.

(196) a. Which police officer__ raided which house?
     b. Which house did which police officer raid__?

Plus, on the other hand, Hofmeister et al. (2013) have shown that superiority effects also do not obtain in many potential cases, and the criteria pointed out above seem to be violated.

(197) What did who read__?

(198) What rules should who follow__?

Such cases as (196)–(198) will have LDs in the tuple $<LD_1,... ,LD_j>$ different from those for (193)–(195) when ψ maps the tuple $<LD_1,... ,LD_i>$ onto $< LD_1,... ,LD_j>$, on the grounds that the cases in (196)–(198) owe their structural and semantic differences to the difference in the tuple $<LD_1,... , LD_j>$. But, as far as the character of generality or specificity is concerned, the status of LDs for cases in (196)–(198) is akin to that of LDs in (193)–(195). The same point can be elucidated with another example. We may take up Beck's (1996) examples of intervention effects discussed in Chapter 5. The examples (153)–(154) are repeated below as (199)–(200).

(199) *Wen   hat niemand **wo**   gesehen?
      whom has nobody where seen
      'Where did nobody see whom?'

(200) *Was glaubt   Hans nicht, **wer** da   war?
      what believes Hans not   who there was
      'Who does Hans not believe was there?'

According to Beck, such intervention effects of quantificational structures apply to most cases of quantifier scope in German. This can be represented in the following way. There will be a mapping ψ from some tuple $<LD_1, \ldots, LD_i>$ (the relevant $LD_1, \ldots, LD_i$ being from syntax, lexicon and perhaps morphology) onto another tuple $<LD_1, \ldots, LD_j>$ when $i \neq j$ and the relevant $LD_1, \ldots, LD_j$ are from syntax and semantics. Tree graphs with the associated constituency/dependency relations from $<LD_1, \ldots, LD_i>$ are to be mapped onto tree graphs paired with associated dependency/constituency relations and conceptual relations from the tuple $<LD_1, \ldots, LD_j>$. This mapping is executed with the condition that some LD from the tuple $<LD_1, \ldots, LD_j>$ will have in β conceptual/cognitive structures not encoding/representing bindings of variables represented by Z (Z = *Wh*-elements, other quantifiers and also representations of restrictive elements of determiner phrases (DPs)) iff Z is a vertex in a tree graph in α and Y (= quantified elements including negative elements) is another vertex in the same tree graph and a relation R ('precedes') holds between Y and Z (YRZ).

If there are other languages that also fall in line with such rules for the same phenomenon, the same kind of mapping will be preserved across *at least* a number of languages. That the LDs for (193)–(195) or for (196)–(198) have no privileged status over those for (199)–(200) dismantles the distinction between principles of UG and ordinary rules, as it is assumed in Generative Grammar. That is, the linguistically relevant cut is not between language-universal rules and language-specific rules, but rather among rules of different types of generality.

Axiom 3

An $I(\chi)$ among $D_1, D_2, D_3, \ldots, D_n \in$ Lc (= set of components/domains of grammar) is a set of ordered pairs $<a, b> \in I(\chi)$ such that a is a member of the set of ψs and b is a member of $\mathscr{P}(\Phi)$, and therefore, $I(\chi) = \{<a_1, b_2>, \ldots, <a_n, b_n>\}$.

Here $I(\chi)$ is an interaction for a linguistic phenomenon χ within a language or across languages. Axiom 3 is a statement about the interaction within the general architecture of language. It says that any interaction $I(\chi)$ in the general architecture of language must conform to the requirement that every rule be paired with the relevant constraints from $C_1 \ldots C_n$. In other words, every rule for any linguistic phenomenon must satisfy a (sub)set of constraints that determine the form of interactions among the linguistic components/domains. Thus, for example, a rule for assimilation of two segments, say, *x* and *y* in a word or across words to be defined at the suprasegmental level, if we posit such a rule for phonology, will be a mapping ψ from some tuple $<LD_1, \ldots, LD_i>$ (with the $LD_1, \ldots, LD_i$ from phonology and lexicon) onto another tuple

<LD$_1$,... ,LD$_j$>, where $i \neq j$ and LD$_1$,... ,LD$_j$ will include morphology. Thus, tree graphs with the associated segmental and syllabic constituency/dependency relations from <LD$_1$,... , LD$_i$> will be mapped onto the tree graphs with the associated dependency/constituency relations and morphological relations from <LD$_1$,... ,LD$_j$>. This is based on the understanding that phonological processes may affect morphological processes (as in English plural morphology that manifests the distinction between {roses, boxes...},{boys, cows ...} and {cats, laps ...} which is grounded in the phonological assimilation of voicing/non-voicing across morphemes). Besides, the relevant rule for assimilation of the two segments x and y may affect meaning, insofar as the concept of plurality is different from that of singularity. However, a process of (re-)syllabification stemming from phonological assimilation may be irrelevant to semantics – which is thus in consonance with some subset from $\mathscr{P}(\Phi)$. For example, the word 'handbag', after undergoing assimilation, changes to /hæmbæg/ and may thus be (re-)syllabified as /hæm.bæg/ or /hæmb.æg/.

Another relevant example can be provided from raising/control to illustrate how Axiom 3 works in the context of constraints that operate on the general architecture of language. Since the case of raising/control has been discussed in Chapter 3, we shall take up a small sample from the set of examples given there.

(201) John seems to be worried about his wedding.

(202) Ray is likely to retire soon.

(203) Steve believed the guy to have justified his case.

(204) Mary loves playing baseball.

(205) John tried to flee to France to pursue his passion for art.

(206) We have asked him to step down.

The examples (201)–(203) are cases of raising, whereas (204)–(206) are examples of control, as we have seen in Chapter 3. It is clear that control is the obverse of raising, and vice versa, because control consists in the sharing of the same argument or (the set of arguments) among a number of predicates across clause boundaries, whereas raising involves the sharing of many forms with a single semantic element/structure.

(207) a. There are likely to be some volunteers in the hall.
    b. *There hope to be to be some volunteers in the hall.

(208) a. They believe close tabs to have been kept/*placed/*maintained on her movements.

b. *They convinced close tabs to be kept/placed/maintained
on her movements.

Let us now consider the examples (94)–(95) from Chapter 3 repeated
here as (207)–(208). Clearly, control disallows – or in many ways resists –
any integration or coalescence of further forms from syntax or lexicon
or morphology when a single form can be semantically linked to many
predicates, thereby leading to a proliferation of semantic links. That is,
semantics can afford to have a multiplicity of meaning links hooked to
a single form, but does not otherwise tolerate such proliferation from
any of the formal components – syntax, lexicon, morphology. This is
essentially similar to what happens in cases of semantic ambiguity. For
example, a sentence 'John left his university' can have two meanings:[7]
(i) John physically moved out of the physical boundaries of the university building and (ii) John finished his studies at his university. The constraint at the interface between syntax and semantics makes this viable
when semantics goes its own way in having more meanings than are
visible in syntax. The interface in such a case cannot extract much from
semantics as syntax cannot access many LDs in semantics. This holds true
for control as semantics projects many LDs many of which are not accessible to syntax at all owing to an interface constraint, which is a part of Φ
or $\mathscr{P}(\Phi)$. What raising, on the other hand, reveals is that this specific constraint, which is a member of Φ or $\mathscr{P}(\Phi)$, has a dual. Note that any constraint can *potentially* be bidirectional or symmetric in that if something
is not accessible from X to Y it is quite likely that something is also not
accessible from Y to X. Given that linguistic form in the current context
is distributed among syntax, lexicon, morphology and phonology, any
duplication or proliferation or spreading of forms when keyed to a single
meaning can have a *balancing* effect on the architecture of the language
faculty when its obverse/dual already exists. Raising allows for a proliferation or integration of further forms with no concomitant proliferation or
spreading on the part of semantics. This explains why reduplication or
agreement marking across a number of parts of a single constituent
or across constituents is pervasive in natural language (consider, for
example, the sentence 'These boys are very efficient volunteers').

Axiom 3 thus helps determine that a rule for raising/control as part of
ψ must be consistent with relevant member(s) of $\mathscr{P}(\Phi)$ which will block
some LDs or some subsets of LDs from being mapped onto some others.
This can be schematized as in Figure 6.6.

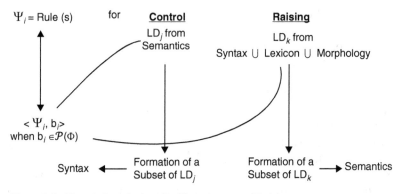

Figure 6.6   How Axiom 3 plays itself out in control/raising

As Figure 6.6 shows, as per Axiom 3 only a subset of an LD from semantics will be mapped onto syntax for cases of control in order that those
subsets of LDs which specify that an argument X – which is an argument
of some predicate Y – is also an argument of other predicates are blocked
from being mapped onto syntax. Only the part of the LD that specifies
that X is an argument of Y will be mapped onto syntax, and the rest will
remain enveloped within semantics. This is consistent with $\mathscr{P}(\Phi)$. That
is why we do not have a sentence like 'John tries John doing the work'.
Conversely, in raising some subset of an LD (or some subset of LDs) from
a union of syntax, lexicon and morphology – especially the part associated
with the form displaced – will not be mapped onto semantics, thereby
yielding a raising construction. This too is compatible with $\mathscr{P}(\Phi)$, which
is indicated by curved arrows in Figure 6.6 oriented towards LD_j and LD_k.

What are the consequences that can be deduced from these axioms?
In fact, one of the conclusions that can be deduced from them is that
the outcome of every application of a constraint from Φ is identical to a
pairing of a rule and its associated interaction in the general architecture
of language. Since an interaction (given Axiom 3) is itself a pairing of a
rule and a member of $\mathscr{P}(\Phi)$, the outcome of any application of a constraint is equivalent to the application of a rule such that the procedure
of applying the rule has been conditional upon the relevant constraints.
This sounds reasonable, given that a constraint is a constraint only by
virtue of being a part of an interaction within the general architecture
of language. Another conclusion to be drawn from the axioms is that
every rule can be defined by making reference only to the interaction
(within the general architecture of language) considered all by itself.
This too makes sense when we note that a rule which is not defined

in terms of an interaction within the general architecture of language ceases to be a rule for the language faculty. These conclusions are actually theorems the proofs of which are provided in Mondal (2014b). Also, an interesting corollary emerges from all this. If a constraint is what it is only by virtue of being a part of an interaction, any warped/distorted configuration of the architecture of the language faculty (due to the application of some constraint(s)) is identical to a relation containing ordered pair(s) of linguistic interaction ($I(\chi)$) and rule (ψ). Note that if we plot all the pairs of linguistic interactions and rules on a Cartesian two-dimensional graph, we would get a geometrical equivalent of the warped/distorted configuration of the architecture of the language faculty. Other ramifications that follow from these consequences will be spelt out in the next chapter (Chapter 7).

6.4 A subtle view of language, mind and computation

There are a few things that we can say about the emerging connections with respect to the relevant consequences that have come to the fore. If operations in a general architecture of language can be faithfully and transparently translated into axioms, rules and constraints of grammar, the translation made possible by an intentional projection shifts between two levels – the level of mental organization in which the language faculty is instantiated and the level of description. The finite capacity of the mind is thus restricted to the level of mental organization, whereas the axiomatic properties of natural language making a way for infinite extensions can be couched at the level of description. It may be observed that an intensional description of, say, the set of odd numbers as {x: x is not divisible by 2} *sort of* captures the infinite extension of the set of odd numbers, and if so, the intentional projection giving rise to the level of description which is intensional as well helps encode and fully express the infinite extension arising out of the axiomatic system of natural language. Beyond that, the determined neutrality on the notion of computation applied to the language faculty puts aside problems of non-computability, or rather of computational complexity because computation may be completely irrelevant to natural language grammar, however construed. In addition, the present meta-theoretical formulation highlights the shift from a preoccupation with universal/language-specific rule systems to the way rules of grammar covering syntax, semantics, morphology and phonology fit the specifications of the form and operations of the general architecture of language. This will help reconcile and also intertwine axioms, rules and constraints as part of the linguistic system with pragmatic reasoning, as we will see.

6.5 Summary

In this chapter a meta-theoretical reformulation of linguistic theory has been attempted in order to show how the puzzles and problems encompassing the relationship between grammar, mind and computation can be dissolved, if not entirely abolished. Relevant repercussions for the foundations of linguistic theory have been suggested. Chapter 7 will elaborate on further consequences for linguistic theory.

7
Linguistic Theory, Explanation and Linguistic Competence

This chapter will aim at underlining the ramifications of the new view of the relationship between grammar, mind and computation. In this connection issues of explanation in linguistic theory in association with the notion of linguistic competence will be touched upon, since the challenge of describing linguistic competence per se in a manner that answers to explanatory import will put the emerging view to the test. The relationship between language, mind and computation that obtains has a direct bearing on how to describe linguistic competence, and also on how such description leads to or falls out of linguistic explanation. As we proceed, these questions will be further refined so that the concern about explanatory value and a description of linguistic competence that answers to explanatory significance can be properly addressed.

The meta-level theoretical approach outlined in the last chapter (Chapter 6) provides the ontological space in which formulations of representational theories can be easily expressed. The added advantage of this approach is that it also helps (re)conceptualize the relationship between grammar, mind and computation present, implicitly or explicitly, in any version of derivational linguistic theory. Note that a translation between the operations of a general architecture and the rules of grammar (that is, rules of syntax, semantics, morphology and phonology) is much broader in scope and more general in its ontology than the usual conception of type transparency between a grammar and a parser which has always been a moot point since the advent of Generative Grammar (Berwick and Weinberg 1984; Stabler 2010). Of course, the issue of translational transparency between the operations of a general architecture of the faculty of language and rules of grammar is tangential to the notion of type transparency between a grammar and a parser, insofar as a relation defined so as to translate the axioms of grammar into a statement of the parsing mechanisms and procedures is something that can be covered by a translational transparency between the operations of a general architecture of the language faculty and rules of grammar. Undoubtedly, the presence or the lack of type transparency between a grammar of the language faculty and a parsing grammar has architectural repercussions on the grounds that some architectures of the language faculty may disallow the construction of a correspondence between a grammar and a parser. This concern has been more palpable in mainstream Generative Grammar than elsewhere. Clearly, the operations involved in parsing, just like those in language production, are just a subset of the entire range of operations the general architecture of language presented here can yield to. Thus translational transparency between the operations of a general architecture of language and (linguistic) rules of syntax, semantics, morphology and phonology is not simply about finding out a homomorphism between a competence grammar and a grammar for processing. The former relates to the concern about how to provide an ontological space so as to bring the axiomatic properties of language into correspondence with the concrete realization of those properties in finite mental/neural structures, while the latter pertains to the issue of how grammar as a formal object can lend credence to the idea that the hypothesized grammar itself is used for parsing. The present proposal has also not been about specifying structural universals of language in the sense articulated in Keenan and Stabler (2010). This discussion is meant to clarify the exact role of explanation that the present proposal will attempt to point at. That is, the present proposal does not aim at showing how a specification of the structural universals of language can explain many linguistic phenomena; nor does it claim to fix the *actual* homomorphism between a competence grammar and a grammar for processing. We have much more to unveil.

7.1 Explanation in linguistic theory

The nature of explanation in linguistic theory has not been a matter of much concern, despite the fact that explanation is very much the thing that every linguistic theory aims to arrive at. Linguists' data come from linguistic examples, and the methodology largely involves the collection of such data from native speakers and their subsequent analysis for hypothesis construction, theory building or for typological observations. But then what is the role of explanation in linguistic theory?

Admittedly, this question is more complicated than it appears, and the present chapter would do no more than pull together the significant strands that cohere to make up a viable story of explanation.

Surely explanation must be more than a mere description. Since if we have described some facts that are aspects or features of a linguistic phenomenon, we have to furnish something more than what the description in itself provides so that it counts as an explanation. The explanation in question must be such that the aspects or features of a linguistic phenomenon can be deduced from it. Unfortunately, most linguistic accounts do not meet this desideratum. Most linguistic proposals or approaches are nothing more than redescriptions of the phenomenon, or rather the explanandum. Some examples can clarify what is at stake. Let us take the case of argument structure which partakes of both syntactic and semantic properties. Bowers (2010) has provided a wholly different account of thematic/argument structure. His approach is aimed at projecting a unified theory of argument structure. Bowers has argued that the thematic hierarchy currently accepted among linguists is actually the reverse of what this hierarchy actually is. Traditionally, it has been assumed that *agents* come first in the thematic hierarchy followed by *recipient, theme*, etc., which helps see why we can say 'John (AGENT) sold his house (THEME) to the man from Spain (RECIPIENT)', but not 'to the man from Spain his house John sold'. Bowers argues that it is actually the reverse order of the actual hierarchy. So his proposed hierarchy called the *Universal Hierarchy of Projections* (UHP) looks like the following:

(209) C > T > Participle > Voice > Theme > Source > Goal/Applicative > Instrument> Beneficiary > Agent > Manner > Time > Place > Purpose > Root (V) (where '>' = precedes; C = complementizer; T = tense)

On this proposal, all thematic roles and modifiers are functional features selected by the verbal head called the root, and specific lexical items are supposed to be Merged in the SPECIFIERs of these functional phrases, as required by the light verb (little v) in the verb shell. The order of these functional phrases is stipulated to be universal and so cross-linguistically valid.

Let us now consider the difference, as pointed out by Jackendoff (2002), between a sentence like 'John became furious/an actor' or 'John grew/got furious', which is fine and '*John got/seemed/grew an actor', which is not grammatical. To explain this asymmetry in the selection of arguments, we may now appeal to the hierarchy in (209). Note that verbs such as 'become', 'grow', 'got' can behave as copulas ('be' verbs, for example) which often need two THEMEs and can also subcategorize for adjectives instead of a THEME, for this reason we require two Theme Phrase (ThP) shells as well as a functional phrase called a State Phrase (StP), which has the same status as phrases of Manner or Time. Also, stative and intransitive sentences will not contain both the Voice Phrase (VoiP) and the Agent Phrase (AgtP), and one of the THEMEs must exercise the option of being caseless in this hierarchy since only TP and VoiP heads can act as Probes for case valuation under the operation AGREE, as discussed in Chapter 3. Now let us look at the structural schema in (210), which represents the situation with the verb 'become'. X and Y marked in bold are the two THEMEs one of which can go up to the SPECIFIER of the TP for the assignment of *nominative* case. The other THEME will remain caseless; this situation does not arise when 'become' takes an adjective, as in 'John became furious'. This optionality is represented by means of the parentheses around the StP. ThP and ThP' are two Theme Phrases in a shell in (210).

(210) $[_{TP} \ldots T \ [_{PrP} \ldots Pr \ [_{ThP'} \mathbf{X} \ Th' \ [_{ThP} \mathbf{Y} \ Th \ ] \ become]]]$
$([_{StP} Z])$

For a verb like 'get' or 'grow' or 'seem', the structural representation available would look like (211). Here, X marked in bold is the THEME and Y is the adjective describing the state.

(211) $[_{TP} \ldots T \ [_{PrP} \ldots Pr \ [_{ThP} \mathbf{X} \ Th \ [_{StP} \mathbf{Z}] \ get/grow]]]$

Now the crucial question is whether this explains why '*John got/seemed/grew an actor' is not possible. Note that there does not appear to be any reason why an otherwise possible meaning that obtains in the case of 'become' does not hold in constructions involving 'grow' or 'get' or 'seem'. Certainly, the account of the syntactic–semantic mismatches in terms of the hierarchy of syntactic configurations in (209) does *not* explain why we find this asymmetry. Rather, such an account redescribes the problem; that is, it is a restatement of the problem. Merely restating in a syntactic hierarchy the fact that certain verbs allow certain kinds of argument structural frames and certain others do not, can have no explanatory value. Besides, if we try to account for cases of such mismatches, we get nowhere near the real core of the problem itself! We end up moving in circles around the problem. Similar considerations apply to the notion of a *Universal Extended Projection* of different functional categories such as light v, T, C, D, N, V, etc. A *Labelling Transition Function*, which makes available all possible mappings of functional labels, is determined with respect to the *Universal Extended Projection* in a manner that the question of acquisition of language-particular categories of functional items reduces to the question of which portion of the extension of the *Labelling Transition Function* consistent with the *Universal Extended Projection* is acquired (see for details, Adger 2013). Note that the *Universal Extended Projection* is a universal sequence of different functional projections; for example, the order C–T–v–V is universally fixed and based on what comes before what. Similar ideas can also be found, notably, in Kayne (1994) and Cinque and Rizzi (2010). Given the notions of the *Universal Extended Projection* of functional categories and the *Labelling Transition Function*, Adger tries to account for the optionality of arguments of certain relational nouns such as 'hand', 'edge', 'picture', as in (212)–(214) which have been taken from Adger.

(212) It had the same contours as a hand.

(213) The physics of colour is misunderstood.

(214) I was aware of sharpness.

These relational nouns ('hand', 'colour' and 'sharpness') are conceptually associated with another entity in an intrinsic sense, and if so, it is surprising how they can appear in syntactic contexts without the arguments they are predicates of (that is, 'colour' is the predicate taking a coloured entity as the argument). Adger's explanation of this phenomenon is that such relational nouns have a different syntax that determines their semantics. On his proposal, there must be a specific functional category, say, P^1 drawn from the *Universal Extended Projection* such that it first combines with a root lexical item ('part'/'representation'/'kin'), and then the structure so built combines with the argument of the relational noun. Finally, the whole structure combines with the relational noun itself. That is, for an example like 'mother of two children', the functional category **P** combines with 'kin', which is the root lexical item, and then combines with 'of two children'. Then the structural result of this combination combines with 'mother'. Here, the notion of combination reflects semantic composition. Adger believes that this explains why relational nouns in cases like (212)–(214) can drop arguments on the grounds that the meaning of the argument is not syntactically specified either in the nominal root ('kin', for example) or in the relational noun ('mother', for

222 Language, Mind and Computation

example). Thus he draws a distinction between such cases of argument dropping and those with verbs in sentences such as 'I ate in the morning'.

Again, let us ask the question: does this explain why relational nouns in (212)–(214) can drop arguments? The syntactic procedure of combination of a functional category (that is, **P**) with the argument of a relational noun divorced from the procedure of combination with the relational noun itself does no more than restate the features of the explanandum. The explanandum in question consists of two facts: (i) relational nouns may or may not allow arguments to appear in constructions, (ii) the arguments of relational nouns appear independently of the relational nouns or even the nominal roots (specifying the semantic property of the relation) in syntactic structures. The proposal in question would not have been circular, if the forms of relational nouns and their arguments described in the facts (i)–(ii) were not defined in terms of the proposed explanation itself.

Similar lines of reasoning can also be found in Borer (2004), for example, when she incorporates a functional head ASPQ (Aspectual Quantity Phrase) into the representations of sentences like the following in order to drive home the distinction between telicity (boundedness in temporal interpretation) and atelicity (unboundedness in temporal interpretation). It is like saying that elephants have something in them called 'slow' and tigers 'fast' when we see tigers running faster than elephants. Clearly this is nonsensical.

(215) John moved the piano in two hours (telic)/for two hours (atelic).

(216) John noticed the mistake *in three minutes (telic)/*for three minutes (atelic).

In fact, Chomsky's (2000b) Merge-over-Move account to explain why (216) is ungrammatical while (217) is not makes the same mistake. The items displaced/moved have been marked in bold. The assumption that Merge, which is about the combination of syntactic objects, is to be preferred over Move (that is, Internal Merge) reflects the features of the facts in (216)–(217). The Merge-over-Move account is in no way an explanation, regardless of whether it is applicably valid or not.

(216) *There is likely **a clue** to be discovered__

(217) There is a possibility that **clues** will be discovered__

Many such explanations in linguistic theory come in the form of redescriptions. In other words, a series of redescriptions passes for explanations in much of theoretical linguistics. Linguistic accounts in representational theories (such as Head-Driven Phrase Structure Grammar or Lexical Functional Grammar) also face the same problem, by virtue of being representational. So does formal semantics, although the problem as described is recognized by certain linguists (Ohala 1990; Carlson 2003). Plus serious discussions on the nature of explanation in linguistic theory have also somehow bypassed this problem (see Bromberger 1992, for instance). One of the apparently compelling arguments has been that the relation between tokens (concrete events) and types (abstract entities) in linguistics is not similar to that between tokens of physical events and invisible things (such as electrons, quarks), given that the former cannot be rendered in causal terms, while the latter can be. The problem becomes more crippling when the accounts assume omniscience on the part of the grammar machinery, inasmuch as the procedures appear to apply everything that we as humans know, but the grammar machine cannot, by definition, know anything. The next section will explore how the notion of explanation can be approached in connection with the conception of linguistic competence.

7.2 Explanation and linguistic competence

The meta-theoretical reformulation provided in Chapter 6 has a number of advantages. It locates the role of explanation within the entire system of descriptions that relate the level of the general architecture of the language faculty to the level of description. Admittedly, the description of different linguistic phenomena in connection with the illustration of the axioms in Chapter 6 is simply nothing more than a description, not explanation. To think otherwise is to commit the mistake of confusing one species with another. Since we need explanation to serve as something more than what a description does, the locus of explanation should reside, as the meta-theoretical proposal suggests, within the whole system encompassing both the level of the general architecture and the level of description of axioms of rules and constraints. Only then can we approximate what explanation is supposed to do. Importantly, under the present conception, linguistic competence is but one of the states in the state-space projected by the dimensions of representation, function and mental processing. If this is the case, linguistic competence, by riding on intentional projection, situates itself both in the domain of the level of the general architecture and in the domain reflected by the level of description of axioms of rules and constraints. This adds to the richness in the way we may view linguistic competence which answers to explanatory significance in that whatever account we may provide for linguistic phenomena must make reference to the two levels which are levels linguistic competence is wedged between. In fact, linguistic competence mediates between the two levels, insofar as the switch from one level to another contributes to what we explain and how we explain matters of linguistic interest. It needs to be clarified that linguistic explanation within the present meta-theoretical view upholds the notion of *reason*, as opposed to the concept of *cause*. Reason is different from cause in that the former predicts what the explanandum describes, whereas cause merely forecasts what happens or will happen (see for details, Dodwell 2000). For example, light in my surroundings is the cause of, say, my seeing a tree before my eyes; it is not so much of a reason, since my seeing what I see is not predicted by the surrounding light which does not *explain* why I saw the tree that I saw. The light present, in virtue of being a cause, provides the empirical conditions for my seeing the tree. Redescriptions are a species of causal descriptions, for if A causes B, A can be a part of the description of B, the explanandum. The reason for my seeing what I see, on the other hand, must involve certain axioms and constraints that derive my seeing what I see as the *necessary* consequences.

What this means has far-reaching consequences deriving from the nature of elasticity of the general architecture of the language faculty. Some examples can clarify what is at stake here. Let us take the case of subject extraction. Displacement of an item from within subjects is generally banned (Hornstein et al. 2006). Thus (218)–(219) are not grammatical. This is called *subject extraction*.

(218) *Who did stories about upset him?

(219) *Who did shadows of lurk behind the tree?

Chaves (2013), after surveying a huge literature on this, comes to the conclusion that subject extraction is rare yet possible. Thus he has provided the following fairly acceptable examples, among many others, in order to argue his case. In particular (223) shows that extraction from a subject clause is also possible.

(220) Which disease will the cure for never be discovered?

(221) Which question will the answer to never be known?

(222) Which problem will a solution to never be found?

(223) There are people in this world that – for me to describe as despicable – would be an understatement.

Finally, he argues for a parsing principle-based account of the widely varied cases of extraction from subjects. That is, *expectation* of no form–meaning mismatch in subjects is the primary parsing principle that, he believes, can account for the diverse range of cases of subject extraction across languages, by allowing for degrees of acceptability. This can have a straightforward and much simpler account in terms of the elasticity of the general architecture of the language faculty. In fact, such empirical data can provide strong support for the elastic property of the general architecture of the language faculty.

If the elasticity of the general architecture of the language faculty emanates from some constraints imposed on the interaction among the linguistic components, such elasticity ensures that some linguistic component(s) may not have access to representations in some other linguistic component(s). It may be noted that extraction from subjects, in general cases, derives from a proliferation or spreading of forms with no concomitant proliferation or spreading on the part of semantics – which explains why resumptive pronouns are often used in some cases of extraction. In such a case, some subset of an LD (or LDs) from a union of syntax, lexicon and morphology is not mapped, as was argued for raising in Chapter 6, onto semantics, and hence semantics is blocked from partaking of *all* of syntactic representations. This situation does not seem to be generally valid in English, but is marginally possible, as in (220)–(223) as well as in other languages such as Russian, German, Hungarian, Hindi, etc. Extraction from adjuncts in English enjoys the same status as subject extraction; it is not valid in general cases, but is otherwise acceptable in many others (as in 'What did she walk to the campus to buy some stuff from_?'), also discussed in Chapter 5. When elasticity holds in the general architecture of the language faculty, extraction from subjects, adjuncts (and also complements) occurs, and this is certainly a matter of some linguistic interaction $(I(\chi))$ being related to rules (ψ). Any weakening of elasticity in the general architecture of the language faculty reinforces form–meaning convergence, thereby ensuring transparency among the linguistic components. This situation can be equated with the obtaining of some linguistic interaction among the linguistic components (which may well involve a null element from $\mathscr{P}(\mathbf{\Phi})$, given that $I(\chi)$ is a set of ordered pairs $<\psi, b>$) – which exactly reflects the case when extraction is disallowed.

The reflex of this idea can also be detected in other linguistic cases. Take the example of gapping discussed in Chapter 5. Let us consider the examples of gapping in (224)–(226) taken from Jackendoff (1971).

While (224)–(225) are banned, (226) is perfectly fine. It is not clear why this is so, given that all the three sentences involve an infinitival clause.

(224) *I want Bob to shave himself, and Mary to wash himself.

(225) *Bill is depending on Harry to find the way to the party, and Sue to find the way home.

(226) Bob tried to wash himself, and Mary to read the funnies.

The nature of explanation under the present proposal can project the reason for this apparently bizarre behaviour of certain cases of gapping. Recall that some subset of an LD (or LDs) from a union of syntax, lexicon and morphology is not mapped onto semantics in the case of raising, which leads to a proliferation or spreading of forms with no concomitant proliferation or spreading on the part of semantics. The examples in (224)–(225) are cases of raising; 'Bob' is semantically the subject of the infinitival clause [to shave himself], or of [to wash himself], even though 'Bob' appears as the object of 'want' in the respective clauses. The same thing can be said about 'Harry' in (225). Note that if raising by its very nature blocks LDs from semantics and maps a portion of an LD (or LDs) to semantics from a union of syntax, lexicon and morphology, gapping cannot *ipso facto* obtain because gapping requires a semantic category (in the sense described in note 2 of Chapter 5) to be dropped. The dropped parts 'want Bob' in (224) and 'is depending on Harry' in (225) each contain a verb followed by a noun phrase, and the noun phrase is not a semantic constituent of the verb. If so, the gapping is blocked owing to this incompatibility between the semantic requirements of gapping and the inherently syntactic nature of raising, which not only blocks LDs from semantics but also maps a portion of an LD (or LDs) to semantics from a union of syntax, lexicon and morphology. This explains why (226) is fine, since it involves the dropping of the verb 'tried' in a control construction where the semantic link between the subject of the dropped verb and the subject of the following infinitival clause remains preserved.

There are also other linguistic structures that instantiate the integration or coalescence of further forms from syntax or lexicon or morphology. Passivization is another such case. Passivization is an operation that does not so much prevent a portion of an LD (or LDs) from being mapped onto semantics from a union of syntax, lexicon and morphology semantics, as block LDs from semantics. Because of this, potential ambiguity is often blocked in passives, as in (227), or meanings are altered, as in (228).

(227) a. Everyone in this town speaks two languages.
b. Two languages are spoken by everyone in this town.

(228) a. Beavers build dams.
      b. Dams are built by beavers.

Recall that the examples in (228) have already been discussed in Chapter 2, whereas the case in (227) shows that quantificational scope ambiguities are often reduced or eliminated in passives. The passive version in (227b) has just one reading on which there exist two particular languages which are spoken by everyone in the town. Passivization consists in the demotion of the subject agent and the upgrade of the object to the grammatical subject status; different combinations of these two strategies play out in different languages. Both these strategies, in some way or other, introduce further forms from a union of syntax, lexicon and morphology. Readers may observe the commonality of expletive insertion (that is, the insertion of 'there') in (229) as well as in (230), which is not a passive construction per se but rather involves an (unaccusative) intransitive verb 'arrive' (the externalized AGENT is already defocused in (230), 'a dangerous giant' being the THEME).

(229) There were many pizzas eaten in his own backyard.

(230) Suddenly there arrived a dangerous giant from the cave.

Additional evidence exhibiting the same trait comes from impersonal passives across other languages. In impersonal passives the agent is *sort of* backgrounded, if not exactly demoted.

(231) er   wordt   gegeten
      there becomes eaten
      'There is eating.'   (Dutch)

(232) það   var ekki talað um   neitt   annað
      it-EXPLETIVE was not spoken about nothing other
      'People did not talk about anything else.' (Icelandic: from Maling 2006)

(233) sondha-i   nacha jai
      evening-LOCATIVE dancing go
      'Dancing can be done in the evening.'   (Bengali)

As can be observed above, the examples in (231)–(232) involve an expletive insertion, while the example from Bengali in (233) involves the insertion of a light verb 'jaoa' ('to go'). Apart from that, the blocking of LDs from semantics is also supported by the distinction between middles and passives which are both non-active voices. As Alexiadou and

Doron (2012) argue, the fundamental distinction between middles (as in 'This fruit cuts easily') and passives is that middles allow but do *not* require the participation of the agent argument, while passives require the participation of the agent argument. In fact, this falls straightforwardly out of the elastic nature of the language faculty; the participation of the agent argument is a semantic requirement subject to a constraint from $\mathscr{P}(\Phi)$, and the blocking of LDs from semantics makes this semantic requirement invisible to syntax.

More interestingly, since elasticity of the general architecture of language coheres with intentional projection, it would not be unreasonable to say that such projection realizes/instantiates what Dascal (1992) calls 'psychopragmatics' which also provides a basis for 'sociopragmatics'. For the intentional projection instantiates mental uses of the linguistic system (a matter of psychopragmatics), as well as making a space for the mental grounding of the linguistic system to be exploited in view of various sociocultural contexts and settings (a matter of sociopragmatics). In a way then, this extends the domain of psychopragmatics to mental *uses* of the linguistic system in a more general sense (not merely in reasoning, problem solving or dreams). It may also be mentioned that the intentional projection of the linguistic system of axioms and constraints can be interspersed with the interaction $(I(\chi))$ among the linguistic components at some subpersonal or non-intentional level. Another advantage that accrues from this is that any reference to any kind of logical form in pragmatic inferences that has to be mapped onto the semantic system for semantic interpretation is redundant. All pragmatic processes – whether primary or secondary (see Recanati 2004 for details) – can be realized/instantiated by the projection of the system of linguistic axioms and constraints onto cognitive processes. More evidence for this comes from passives in which grammatical relations of subjects and objects are not altered; rather, what is altered is the *ontological salience* of the participants in the event specified in the verb. The following example of *inverse passives* in the Algonquian language Plains Cree illustrates the point well.

(234) a. Ni- sekih -a   -nan atim
        1 scare theme DIRECT 1PL dog
        'We scare the dog.'
   b. Ni- sekih -iko   -nan atim
        1 scare theme INVERSE 1PL dog
        'The dog scares us.'   (Klaiman 1991) (PL = plural)

Such passives are called inverse passives because the ontological salience of a noun phrase reflecting its referent's relative importance in the concerns of the speaker and hearer is altered in passives. While both (234a) and (234b) rank 'we' higher than 'the dog' in ontological salience, (234b) says it all in an inverse manner with regard to (234a). The logical/semantic subject is 'we' and the logical/semantic object is 'the dog' in (234a), but this is reversed in (234b) in that the logical/semantic subject is now 'the dog' and logical/semantic object is 'we'. The marker '-iko' in (234b) expresses this morphologically.

Caution needs to be exercised in this connection. Under the current conception, pragmatic inferences need *not* be rules in the sense specified in Axiom 1, but rather are instantiated by the intentional projection of the system of rules and constraints as governed by the axioms. This leaves much for a rapprochement between pragmatics and semantics – a distinction which is again conceptually valid, but ontologically weak.

7.3 Summary

This chapter has underlined the importance of explanation in linguistic theory as it relates to concerns about the role the meta-theoretical proposal can play in locating linguistic competence at the centre of discussions on linguistic explanation. Though a lot has certainly been left out because of space considerations, significant threads that may be helpful in linguistic inquiry have been pinpointed. Issues of learnability will be the prime concern in the next chapter.

8
Linguistic Theory, Learnability, Mind and Computation

We may now gear up for the last issue to be taken up in this book. It is the issue of learnability as it relates to explanatory adequacy which is what has driven much of the linguistic theorizing in the Generative tradition. So remaining silent on this issue may not be fair. Besides, the question of how UG determines the specification of a particular grammar of a specific language was raised in Chapter 3, but much has not been articulated with regard to the issue of language acquisition. This chapter will point out the connections between the emerging reconceptualization of the relationship between grammar, mind and computation, and issues of learnability. As we shall see, the questions of language acquisition can be further sharpened and refined within the new proposal. It will be argued that it is best to abandon the prevailing conception of the relation between grammar, mind and computation, if the question of how UG determines the specification of a particular grammar of a specific language needs to be addressed.

In what follows the role of learnability in linguistic theory will be described with its links to the emerging new understanding. It is important to emphasize that the ramifications for the issue of learnability that will be highlighted will be at least tentative suggestions for possible lines of inquiry, and the discussion will not be exhaustive. There is a vast literature on computational learning theory, and it would be risky to make hasty generalizations (see for some interesting discussions, Shimansky 2004; Clark and Lappin 2012). Hence this chapter will simply clarify only those issues that readily mesh with the concerns raised in the present book. Questions about the effectiveness of learning algorithms or about the design problems in building models of learning theory will not be dealt with. It is not because they are uninteresting; rather, this goes way beyond the scope of the present book.

8.1   Linguistic theory and language learnability

Linguistic theory has not always gone hand in hand with learnability theories. One of the reasons has to do with the pronouncement within Generative Grammar that natural languages are not learnt, and that language acquisition is a genetically enveloped process of growth. This apparently justifies the rejection of anything that proves to be incompatible with the axioms of Generative Grammar. What if the axioms are in themselves wrong? If anything, the present book has tried to show that it is better that we think otherwise. One of the results from learnability theory that many linguists have appealed to comes from Gold's (1967) learnability model, which has demonstrated that the finite class of recursive languages is *identifiable in the limit* on the basis of positive data alone, and that the supra-finite class of languages cannot be *identified in the limit* on the basis of positive data alone. This has encouraged many linguists to believe that this proves that natural languages are not learnable on the basis of positive data because natural languages belong to the class of super-finite languages. And if natural languages are not so learnable, then UG must make language acquisition possible. Clark and Lappin (2011, 2012) have laid bare a number of unfounded assumptions that underlie the supposition that UG must be responsible for language acquisition. First, in Gold's model *identifiability in the limit* means converging on the right grammar class[1] after a presentation of a language over a finite but unbounded amount of time. The presentation of a language is simply a sequence of strings from the language in question, and Gold's framework assumes that for every presentation of a language the learner will converge on the target such that every language is *identified* to belong to the inferred grammar class. This is the central theme of the notion of *identifiability in the limit*. The problem this gives rise to is that natural languages are not in actual circumstances presented to children in a manner that can even remotely ensure every possible presentation of a language. That Gold's framework makes this idealization in a formal setting is something too often ignored or simply forgotten. Second, the assumption that natural languages belong to the class of supra-finite languages also has a tenuous link to actual properties of natural language grammars, for the exact computational property of natural languages is not yet known (see Mondal 2010). The class of recursive grammars such as context-free grammars[2] can also generate infinite languages, and if so, it is not clear in what sense the assumption above can be valid, as Clark and Lappin (2012) argue. Third, assumptions about the availability of only positive linguistic data and the absence of any negative linguistic data (parental corrections, for example) in the presentation of language children are exposed to are also a moot point of debate (see Sampson 2005; Pullum and Scholz 2002). Plus children also do not learn languages over a finite but unbounded period of time, for, after all, 2 billion years approximates a finite yet unbounded period of time. Even here Gold's idealization does not fit the realistic scenario.

The next section will weigh up many other assumptions about the relationship between grammar, mind and computation that are hidden in learnability-theoretic arguments that are aimed at advancing dubious theories of language acquisition. That is, if assumptions about the relationship between grammar, mind and computation wither away, there is no sense in which learnability-theoretic arguments supported by such assumptions can gain ground.

8.2   What language learnability tells us about the mind and computation

Learnability concerns specifying the conditions under which grammar classes are learnable by some learning procedure on the basis of linguistic data presented to the learning procedure. The learning procedure is a computable function that can be specified by some algorithm and then implemented in machines. If the learning procedure learns a grammar after a finite amount of time, the learning procedure must have constructed a correct representation of the grammar that can generate the sentences of the language falling under the grammar. Implicit in such a learnability framework is the assumption that the learning procedure can draw inferences from linguistic data, and then make the desired generalizations that help the procedure arrive at the correct construction of a hypothesis about the target grammar. The learning procedure is also supposed not to change the hypothesis about the target grammar once the hypothesis is observed to apply over all subsequent presentations of language. This implies that the learning procedure can also preserve or simply internalize the representation of a hypothesis about the target grammar. Now, if the rules as specified in Generative Grammar are to be learned in such a formal setting, the representation of a hypothesis about the target grammar would be neither effective nor viable, simply because natural language grammars cannot be represented in the mind in a manner that guarantees their computational manipulation. No learning procedure can validly incorporate any assumption about the representation of a hypothesis about the target grammar, if the prevailing conception of the relation between grammar, mind and computation is taken for granted. For the learning procedure is ultimately patterned on human learners, although in idealized configurations.

Wexler and Culicover's (1980) work is perhaps the most comprehensive study of the learnability of generative grammars, and their work has argued for the imposition of strong restrictions and conditions on grammars so that the learning procedure can converge on or approximate the correct generative grammar. In this connection, they have also cautioned that any restrictions imposed on learning procedures may also become a part of the grammar itself. This means that both learning procedures and grammars have to be sufficiently restricted for learnability to obtain, but the exact notion of sufficiency remains tenuous. Regardless of how grammars or learning procedures are restricted, learnability cannot get off the ground if the restrictions are defined in terms that make reference to properties of linguistic computation which cannot be both mental and computational. In other words, if restrictions on grammars or learning procedures are defined in terms of the properties of linguistic computation, no learning procedure for language learning that may be assumed to be working with Merge operations and other interface conditions can be constructed. Furthermore, there is also no reason why the inferential capacities of learning procedures cannot be more powerful than is currently conceived; the inferential capacities of learning procedures can also make analogical inferences which have the potential to make language learning much easier (see Itkonen 2005). But the dilemma, again, is that if the intentional processes have no access to the mental grammar, there is no sense in which analogical processes can even be seen to be implemented in learning procedures. One may now raise the objection that the construction of a learning procedure is entirely independent of a linguistic theory, inasmuch as learning procedures need not reflect all the properties ascribed to the faculty of language. If this is so, this objection itself undermines the prospect of being informed by and interfacing with learnability theory. So we end up exactly with what we started with at the beginning of this section.

However, on the present proposal, the formulation of learnability relevant to natural language acquisition/learning can reliably exploit features and properties of the representational/descriptive level of axioms, rules and constraints of grammar as well as aspects of the level of the general architecture of language. But computational models of learnability cannot themselves be identified with any part of the general architecture of language, and thus do not on their own inherit translational transparency between operations in a general architecture of language and a system of axioms, rules and constraints of grammar/ language. But there are possibilities the two levels of description offer which can open up new insights into the learnability of natural languages. We will say more on this in the next section.

8.3   What the mind and computation tell us about language learnability

The emerging conception of the relation between grammar, mind and computation can tell us much about the learnability of natural languages. This is what we now turn to. In the current context linguistic form does not have any atomic conception by virtue of the fact that linguistic form is distributed across domains/components of grammar, that is, syntax, lexicon, phonology and morphology. Hence linguistic form is not a monolithic entity. Meaning has, on the other hand, been restricted to the domain of semantics. This is necessitated by the observation that whatever is linguistically conceptualized can certainly be represented at different levels – lexical, phrasal and sentential (or even discoursal), but the differences between such levels of meaning – however represented – are not as ontologically marked as they are in a condition in which, say, syntax is contrasted with phonology (syntactic rules cannot be reduced to phonological rules and vice versa), or phonology is contrasted with morphology (phonological rules cannot be reduced to morphological rules and vice versa). So in the present context we have multiple possibilities of mapping between different types of linguistic form (namely, syntax, lexicon, phonology and morphology) and meaning (that is, the domain of semantics). This may raise a learnability problem, given that the space of all such possibilities of mapping between types of linguistic form and meaning may well prove computationally intractable in view of limitations on resources and the impossibility of defining computable functions on some mappings. Under this scenario, the constraints on the interaction among the domains of language $\Phi = \{C_1 \dots C_n\}$ come to the rescue. These constraints reduce a lot of possibilities of mapping between different types of linguistic form and meaning. We may thus think of this space as a *hypothesis space* which is a subset of the space of all possibilities of mapping between different types of linguistic form and meaning. Let us call the latter the *mapping space*.

Now from a learnability-theoretic perspective, the important point is that a *hypothesis space* may not always coincide with the learnable class of languages (Clark and Lappin 2011). Thus it seems more appropriate to say that the learnable class of languages in the current context *may* but need *not* be characterized so as to correspond to the hypothesis space that obtains only after the application of constraints that reduce all possible mappings between different types of linguistic form and meaning to a much smaller set. Therefore, the learnable class of languages in the current context may vary depending on what *kind* of constraints is imposed on what principles or procedures or systems concerned. For example, in the Gold (1967) framework of learnability significant restrictions are put on the inference procedure in order that an algorithm can converge on the target grammar upon the text presentation of the language data from which the inference procedure can make out whether a string belongs to the target language (or the class of learnable languages) or not. Likewise, restrictions can also come from the linguistic data on which a probability measure is imposed such that a measure of the distance between the target grammar and the hypothesized grammar may not always be equal to 0. We are also aware that real computational constraints on resources such as memory – human or whatever – and on time may also affect the characterization of the learnable class of languages. So do theoretical assumptions regarding the nature of learners, learning procedures, etc. Suffice it to say, neutrality on the issue of computation can be an advantage.

In the current context, we may safely assume that in any text presentation (which by its very nature does not contain any negative evidence) in any natural language-learning scenario that *may* not involve the presentation of negative evidence, both positive and negative evidence may come from different possible mappings between different types of linguistic form and meaning, given that $\Phi = \{C_1 \ldots C_n\}$ and global constraints of linguistic function, representation and processing operate as they do. It is the splitting of linguistic form among different domains of language and the variable mapping of types of linguistic form onto meaning, given $\Phi = \{C_1 \ldots C_n\}$, that can change the exact type of the learnable class of languages. For instance, take a language like Chinese, which barely has any morphology; in such a case the text presentation may not include any relevant information about morphological cues including agreement, etc. which are otherwise significant for the learning of the grammar of Chinese. In the current framework, such cues may come from other types of linguistic form such as phonology, and/or from relevant mappings of types of linguistic form onto meaning constituting a constrained space out of the overall hypothesis space. And this may change the class of learnable languages, insofar as the type of the learnable grammar type may be context-free grammars or context-sensitive grammars depending on the restrictions arising out of possible mappings between different types of linguistic form and meaning, given $\Phi = \{C_1 \ldots C_n\}$, even though the hypothesis space may well define recursively enumerable sets. This is not surprising given that the conditions under which a certain class of learnable languages qualifies as learnable vary with certain definitional assumptions and other restrictions (Savitch 1987). In addition, it is also the case that certain assumptions – however explicit or implicit – about (computational) models of language processing underlie the formulation of learnability in computational learning theory when applied to natural language. In such a scenario, if it turns out that properties of representation of the grammar type which qualifies as learnable matter to a conception of learnability, the formulation of learnability as it applies in natural language acquisition/learning can be made either at the level of the general architecture of language or at the representational/descriptive level. The choice is open.

8.4   Summary

This chapter has suggested some lines on which the question of language acquisition can be pursued from a learnability-theoretic perspective. Overall, the meta-theoretical proposal can overhaul and thus salvage much of the foundational system of linguistic theory, if the goal is followed in the direction indicated. With this, we come to the conclusion of what the book has made an attempt to convey. We shall make some final observations in the last chapter.

9
Conclusion

The discussion in the present study has perhaps offered a glimpse into the complex structure of the relation obtaining between language, mind and computation. In doing so, it has also made an attempt to show that the relationship is far more convoluted than is generally supposed. One of the important threads emerging out of the discussion is that many of the assumptions and presuppositions underlying the structure of the relation between language, mind and computation that forms the bedrock of linguistic theory are singled out for complete elimination or for potentially gradual revision. As we have seen, one of corollaries stemming from some of these assumptions is that grammar cannot be mental if it is construed to be computational (in its intrinsic sense). On the other hand, grammar cannot be computational, if it is to be mentally represented in a linguistically relevant way. In a way, it transpires that intentionality is the theoretically unacknowledged link that appears to tie together the set of assumptions underlying the two corollaries. The notion of intentionality is still an elusive notion in the philosophy of mind. It is often thought to be the property of what it is to be mental, on the grounds that the aboutness or directedness of mental states towards entities, propositions, etc. is conceived of as an inherent property of mentality. This notion, however, is not ripe enough for a full-fledged theory of how intentionality *really* functions or how it mediates the connection established between the mental state itself and the entities and propositions the mental state is directed at. Hence no theory of intentionality, or rather of intentional mediation, has been attempted in Chapter 6, where the meta-theoretical reformulation speaks of intentional projection. Needless to say, a well-formulated account of the very character of intentional projection is certainly desirable, although we have a very faint grasp of what it can be taken to be in the fullest possible detail.

Be that as it may, there is still a lot that the present exercise unfolds. A way towards dissolution of the perplexities that the assumptions and presuppositions underlying the relation between language, mind and computation unmask is also shown. A meta-theoretical reconceptualization of linguistic theory along lines that can help ground grammar in the mind without thereby inviting fiendish hidden inconsistencies covers much of the territory that the new proposal encompasses. It is believed that this can clarify the role of linguistic methodology with respect to the ontological place of language as much as it can illuminate the nature of language learning/acquisition. Nevertheless, it may be acknowledged that this endeavour is fraught with certain other difficulties. A meta-theory of the kind proposed in Chapter 6 may border on a unifying theory, which is what it is not. Even though the meta-theoretical reformulation, by being superimposed on other theoretical frameworks, encapsulates the aspects and features of different linguistic theories, it surely does not attempt to reduce aspects of certain theories to those of another theory. It is because the most synthesized theory may actually turn out to be the most reductive theory – which ultimately vitiates the prospect of having a theory that answers to the complexities expressible within a single theory. The other difficulty bears upon the question of whether it is necessary to have a meta-theory for linguistic theory. That is, what justifies the postulation of a meta-theory since a meta-theory is ultimately a theory? In this connection, we may not simply state the obvious by merely saying that the meta-theory is for drawing up certain otherwise overlooked consequences and ramifications concerning the nature of linguistic explanation and language acquisition. There is indeed more to be sketched out.

It may be noted that the meta-theoretical reformulation expresses a set of axiomatic statements about the relationship between grammar, mind and computation from which certain consequences *necessarily* follow. Both the set of axiomatic statements and the consequences are bound to encapsulate meta-theoretical or trans-theoretical generalizations, inasmuch as the set of axiomatic statements along with the necessary consequences identify properties of grammar (in its broader sense including syntax as well as phonology, semantics and morphology) which are instantiated in linguistic theories and/or frameworks anyway. Furthermore, the meta-theoretical proposal is such that it makes a conjecture about the relation between language, mind and computation which is observed, in its existing form, to be suspect on purely logical and linguistic grounds. Therefore, the meta-theoretical proposal is a theoretical outcome ensuing from the observation of a number of deleterious puzzles, paradoxes and inconsistencies surrounding the relationship between language, mind and computation. It is thus expected that other ways of conceptualizing the relationship of grammar to mind and computation may be integrated into the current proposal. This is another way of saying that there may be other possible ways of thinking about the relation between language, mind and computation. In fact, various plausible criticisms of the relationship between language and mind or between language and computation have been noted in the relevant chapters of this book, and they may well be expressed in terms that exploit aspects of the present proposal, although such criticisms barely scratch the surface of the deeper issues dealt with in the current book. Overall, it appears that the inherent nature of language must permit language capacity to be in tune with its biological grounding: language must be represented in the mind, language must be usable by humans, languages must be learnt by both children and adults, and finally, language(s) must evolve. Anything that has been proposed in this book does not militate against this. Rather, the present conception enriches the view of the relationship between language, mind and computation. It is hoped that this may mesh with a more fruitful discussion on the significant aspects of the biological grounding of language. Given that space considerations do not permit a more detailed formulation of the new view which is somewhat sketchy, a lot has to be worked out.

We conclude by making the following points that leave open further problems and challenges, as well as suggesting future directions for research.

- Many other linguistic phenomena, especially from morphology and phonology, have not been taken into consideration for the relevant discussions in this book. It is not because they are uninteresting; rather, it is because issues in syntax and semantics readily relate to issues of the mind and computation. However, important insights into the relationship between language, mind and computation can also be projected by examining a number of interesting phenomena from morphology and phonology such as agreement marking, incorporation, case marking, prosody, focus marking, etc.
- Many intricate aspects of other linguistic theories have not been discussed in detail. The way these theories may or do handle linguistic phenomena has also not been a part of the discussion here. This is

partly because of the focus of this book – which is to examine the relationship between language, mind and computation in mainstream linguistic theory. And it is the framework of mainstream Generative Grammar which incorporates in it most of the assumptions about such a relationship. Hence this has figured high in our discussion. It is not certainly due to any bias. If other theoretical frameworks aim to clarify the role of computation and the mind in connection with natural language, new proposals are certainly welcome.

- No comprehensive inspection of any empirical linguistic phenomenon has been attempted. However, this is not to deny that a single linguistic phenomenon probed in great depth would also offer valuable and useful insights when we aim at figuring out what can be discerned about the relationship between language, mind and computation.
- We have also not explored the possibility of how the meta-theoretical proposal can be made subject to experimental investigations. Any such investigation is empirically welcome.

Finally, a warning needs to be issued before we conclude this book as we near the end of this chapter. Any temptation to get entangled in the net of ideas of popular appeal (such as computation) is to be avoided at best, or at least taken with a grain of salt. It is often comforting to get a hypothesis hooked onto such populist ideas of appeal. Nevertheless, it is better to play it all safely. From a different perspective, the conception of the mental is complex enough, and the issue of mentality needs to be cautiously handled to see which features and aspects of the mind harmonize well with natural language grammar and which are discordant with the properties of natural language. Admittedly, this is a formidably difficult task. But the benefit to be accrued from this exercise is worth the price to be paid in accomplishing this task.

If the present work stimulates any fruitful way of doing linguistics, it can be, maybe reasonably enough, hoped that the book has served its purpose. Deeper and perhaps more fundamental inquiry into the nature of natural language itself can be the source of enormously enthralling and profoundly beautiful insights into the nature of the human mind, which can in turn illuminate the character of computation as well. This is a hope for the future though.

Notes

2 Language and Linguistic Theory

1. But see Bergen (2004) for an interesting discussion on phonaesthemes (such as English 'gl-' in words like 'glisten', 'glitter', 'gleam', 'glow', etc.) which, by virtue of not being a morpheme, seem to defy the *Principle of Compositionality* at the morphological level.

3 How Language Relates to the Mind

1. It needs to be highlighted that it is pointless to appeal to the theoretical and methodological success of certain theoretical constructs in other disciplines such as biology or physics in order to justify their incorporation into linguistics, inasmuch as the goal is to adapt such constructs for linguistic theory only to unjustifiably hide unfounded assumptions. Further, the notion of representation is as problematic even in neuroscience as it can be elsewhere, irrespective of whether (neuro)biologists glibly use it or not. If our current understanding of intentionality is not amenable to theoretically motivated formulations, so is our understanding of interface conditions (which are supposed to be imposed on the core system of the language faculty), legibility and so on. And if notions of interface conditions and legibility entail the notion of intentionality anyway, it makes no sense whatsoever to avoid dealing with intentionality. In the face of this dilemma, one may well assert, as Chomsky does, that intentionality and its associated terms do not make sense but those of interface conditions and legibility do, by being rendered in terms that refer to well-defined formal linguistic operations. If this argument goes through, it follows that interface conditions and legibility and a host of related concepts including the notion of representation become empty of substance, on the grounds that these terms remain merely terminological without any substantive value. The whole argument thus becomes self-terminating.
2. External Merge is equivalent to the ordinary concatenation of syntactic objects, while internal Merge can be reckoned as displacement/movement of items from where they were originally externally Merged.
3. An intensional description is different from an extensional description in that an intensional description encapsulates a generalization about something which may need a formidable space if described in extensional terms. For example, the set of odd numbers is extensionally specified as {1, 3, 5, 7, 9...} which will be countably infinite as we go on including odd numbers, whereas the intensional description would make a compact description: {x: x is not divisible by 2}. Thus an intensional description minimizes information.
4. In any phrase XP, the SPECIFIER and the complement are not a part of the projection of a phrase. That is, in the hierarchical organization of a phrase

XP the SPECIFIER can be something called *y* and the complement can be something called *z*. This looks like: [$_{XP}$ *y* [$_X$ X *z*]].

5. Note that each rule is defined here as a set which may or may not be a singleton set – that is, Ri→ {R1...Ri-1} or Ri→ {Ri}. To avoid getting into the area of contention on whether the mentally represented rules are propositional in form or not, I have used the union notation rather than the usual logical connective for propositional conjunction. Irrespective of whether Chomsky has really meant mental rules to be interpreted in the propositional sense, the logic of the present argument remains unaffected. But as far as I know, Chomsky (1985: 265–72) has indeed talked of propositional knowledge when talking about the cognizing of mental rules, although he asserts that one does not know that the rules recognized as such obtain or hold. To deny that is dishonest.

6. I assume that all the examples in (58)–(63) are cases of mismatch of the *Wh*-form and the associated meaning on the surface structure of sentences. Whether some of the cases are instances of movement or base generation is a theory-internal matter that I shall leave open. For example, free relatives (as in (61) rather than in (60)) are analysed by Bresnan and Grimshaw (1978) as instances involving the base insertion of *Wh*-elements in the positions where they appear.

7. As an anonymous reviewer points out, the basic evidence for the detection of gaps in *Wh*-questions and possibly in other constructions involving movement comes from a diagnostic ambiguity-resolution strategy. For instance, the sentence 'How often did he say she reported they left?' has got the *Wh*-adjunct 'how often' displaced, but the gap from which it has been displaced depends on whether the questioner wants to know how often he said something or how often she reported something or even how often they left.

8. Once again a reference to the Theta Criterion cannot save it from the trouble. One may obviously say that in the case of R1 the displaced/moved subject bears the theta-role assigned by the predicate adjacent to the gap, whereas in R2 the base-inserted subject bears the theta-role of a complex predicate. Even if this is granted, it does not explain why we *should not* interpret in (65), for instance, the subject 'this dog' as the THEME of 'handle' even when 'difficult to handle' is the complex predicate. Apart from that, theta-roles are, formally speaking, just roles; they are interpreted as such only at the C-I interface. If so, it does not make sense to pull in theta-roles since they too will ultimately engage the interpretative conceptual system anyway.

4   How Language Relates to Computation

1. The functional category symbol T has been used here uniformly for both tensed and non-tensed clauses. One may well argue over whether it is appropriate to use T uniformly in this way. In the present context, it is wholly immaterial whether the category symbol should be T or I (Inflection) or even something like T^N (denoting a non-finite T), because the tree diagram drawn is merely for an expository purpose. But I leave the theory-internal debate on this issue in Generative linguistics open.

2. Careful readers may recognize affinities between many of the paradoxes and inconsistencies uncovered in this book and versions of the Liar's Paradox.

3. At this point, one may appeal to oracle machines to circumvent this problem for the generative procedure of the language faculty. Oracle machines are an

extension of Turing machines with an oracle tape along with two states for oracle inputs and outputs that fall within the domain and range of an oracle function. Simply put, oracle machines take a query for a problem and output an answer when Turing machines connected to an oracle pass such queries to the oracle. In this sense, oracle machines are deterministic machines having answers to queries posed by Turing machines. However, it is not clear how one has to make sense of the idea of an oracle algorithm inside the putative computational system of the language faculty. The lexical system instantiated in the mind/brain, for example, may instantiate an oracle function and can thus answer membership queries about N, but it cannot say anything (*at least* in YES or NO) about whether the generative procedure of the language faculty will ever halt on N or not, precisely because it does not by itself instantiate the generative procedure of the language faculty and it has to be an intentional system to do that. This is nonsensical, on the grounds that such micro-intentional systems will pervade the putative computational system of the language faculty, which is supposed to be a non-intentional object of the human mind, and hence this can also invite the problem of an infinite hierarchy of intentional systems within the putative computational system of the language faculty. Moreover, any extension of the generative procedure of the language faculty in order to incorporate an abstract specification of an oracle needs to be put to the test of empirical adequacy that scrutinizes the linguistically significant aspects in terms of descriptive and explanatory adequacies of any such abstract specification of an oracle, in the absence of which any reference to such an oracle is utterly meaningless.

4. The idea that the computational system of the human language faculty can have N compiled throughout the entire syntactic derivation so that N can be accessed more than once (Stroik 2009) makes the *halting problem* with the generative procedure of the language faculty more severe. It is because the *halting problem* is now more distributed throughout the computational system of the language faculty so that any syntactic derivation at any stage can be subject to the *halting problem* with frequent but otherwise abrupt as well as absurd crashes that do not originate from anything linguistic per se.

5. That C also has φ-features has been motivated by Miyagawa (2010), who has shown that discoursal properties determined by Topic and Focus also trigger movement in languages such as Japanese, Korean and Chinese. For that reason, he proposes that C in such languages must have φ-features analogous to those of T or little v.

6. The problem of the combinatorial explosion of complexity was also explored by Church (1980) in his MS thesis, which an anonymous reviewer has brought to my notice. It was demonstrated there that the adjunction of preposition phrases (PP) to noun phrases (NP) in phrase structure rules such as NP$\rightarrow$ NP PP, PP$\rightarrow$ P NP leads to a combinatorial explosion of analyses on the order of n^4 structures to strings with n PPs following the first NP.

7. Frampton and Gutmann's (2006) crash-proof model of linguistic computation even without N cannot shrug off this problem, since the applications of the operations called Select and Attract run a local search for the right target (Goal) that takes part in feature sharing, and for some target to be found in the local computational space the relevant targets must have to be detected and thus scanned. This procedure thus inherits the problem of enormous growth of computational complexity which the crash-proof model is supposed

to eliminate. Moreover, treating the mechanisms of narrow syntax as the interface conditions themselves – which is what Frampton and Gutmann (2006) have argued for – puts the paradoxes of interpretation back into the computational system of the language faculty. So in this way too, Frampton and Gutmann's (2006) model does not obviate the formidable computational complexity problem, contrary to what they believe to be the case.

8. Computation in a purely abstract sense invites the problem of computational panpsychism – that is, the idea that everything in the universe executes computations, which is so trivial as to be practically meaningless. A notion of computation that avoids this problem is outlined in Mondal (2014a).

9. It needs to be stressed that this notion of computationality is an *intrinsic* notion of computationality in the sense that grammar is intrinsically a version of the Turing machine. In contrast, the *extrinsic* notion of computationality is trivial, and hence allows for the possibility of virtually everything (life, mind, universe, etc.) being computational.

5   Putting it all together: the Relation between Language, Mind and Computation

1. One may complain that this is a kind of pseudo-psychologizing which purports to ground whatever linguistic computation is construed to be in the mind, but as a matter of fact this does not have the adequate psychological import which the condition deserves. This complaint is misguided, on the grounds that the pseudo-psychologizing frame itself is implicit in the framework which postulates that linguistic rules and constraints as part of the mentally represented grammar are computed in the mind at some level of abstraction. So the onus is on those who espouse such a framework to provide proof required for an adequate psychological import of the mentally represented grammar. In fact, it is this kind of pseudo-psychologizing – which a research programme takes for granted by fiat – that is the source of the paradoxes and inconsistencies. The framing of the argument in the current context – which is aimed at uncovering the hidden paradoxes and inconsistencies – is designed to test just this pseudo-psychologizing with all the concomitant assumptions preserved in order to see how this fares within the constraints of its own framework. And the result of the test is laid bare for those who want to see the whole exercise through.

2. One may argue that the second major conjunct (C2) in this test sentence is not appropriate for a gapping construction, since the structure of C2 can be adequately described as a case of what is called *right node raising*, which raises the common structure across clauses to the rightmost edge of a clause. Even if it is true that gapping and right node raising are subtly different in many respects, the former being mainly restricted to verb phrases and the latter to noun phrases, prepositional phrases, adjective phrases, etc. Additionally, they are differently constrained across languages. However, there is a lot in common between gapping and right node raising in that both reduce materials across conjoined clauses and raise some (portion of) structure to another position (see for details, Hudson 1976). Besides that, if the gapped structure – whether in gapping per se or in right node raising – is always a semantically formed constituent (Steedman 1990), this semantic similarity which

underscores both gapping and right node raising is sufficient for the present argument. Moreover, the putative computational system of the language faculty cannot be assumed to be configured in a way that prejudges the question of inclusion of different linguistic phenomena in terms of different categories. That is, the generative procedure of the language faculty cannot be assumed to run gapping-only operations at some point, and then right node raising-only operations at some other point, and so on. This is profoundly bizarre.

3. It should be noted that the form of interaction of the *Economy Constraint* with choice function interpretations *need* not be similar across languages. Generally, Bangla is a language that has a fixed surface scope in most constructions involving QNPs. But there are a few complications that require attention.

A. (i) ekti   chhele proteyk meye-ke bhalobase
      a/one boy   every   girl-ACC love
      'A boy loves every girl.'

  (ii) proteyk bharotio ekti   despremik-ke manya   kare
      every   Indian   a/one patriot-ACC   obedience do
      'Every Indian respects a patriot.'

B. (i) ekti/ekjon chhele proteyk shikhok-ke   shroddha kare ebong ekti/ekjon
      Some/a   boy   every   teacher-ACC respect   do   and   some/a
      meye-o tai kare
      girl-too so do
      'Some boy admires every teacher and a girl does too.'

  (ii) proteyk chhele ekjon adhyapak-ke   shrodhdha kare ebong mari-o
      every   boy   some professor-ACC admiration do   and   Mary-too
      tai kare
      so do
      'Every boy admires a certain professor and Mary does too.'
                        (ACC = accusative case marker)

The sentence (i) in A is not ambiguous, but (ii) of A is, because (ii) can have a wide scope reading of the QNP 'ekti despremik' (a patriot) with respect to 'proteyk bharotio' (every Indian). What is important here is that *Ellipsis Scope Generalization* does not hold in (i) of B because of surface scope rigidity, whereas the first conjunct in (ii) of B is ambiguous just like its English counterpart, and so a choice function interpretation seems suitable in (ii) of B if the generalization that Bangla has a fixed surface scope in most constructions involving QNPs is to be preserved. To sum, the facts in A and B cannot be adduced to establish that quantificational scope relations in Bangla obtain through displacement/movement, given that (i) of B is unambiguous despite the structural context present in it. In fact, Chinese, Korean, Hungarian, etc. also behave in similar ways.

4. In the examples above, I have used the by now familiar category symbol TP instead of IP (Inflectional Phrase) which has been used by Aoun and Li. TP is the modern version of IP, but anything discussed here does not depend on any distinction, however construed, between IP and TP.

5. However, Mondal (2011) has demonstrated that all these approaches to quantificational scope readings are mutually inconsistent with each other and often produce conflicting results when applied to the same set of empirical data.

6. This possibility arises simply because the putative computational system of the language faculty cannot in itself block a pragmatically deviant interpretation (see Fox 1999b for relevant examples of such a kind).

7. This reading is not outright impossible, especially if we imagine a scenario in which many buildings are situated in such a spatial configuration that a single flag can be seen as the flag that happens to be in front of a number of buildings when viewed from the perspective of each of the buildings in that spatial configuration.

8. Such an approach to lexical structures has been endorsed by Hale and Keyser (2002). This view broadly conceived is called *lexicalism*. Borer (2005) differentiates such an approach, which she calls an *endo-skeletal* approach, from an *exo-skeletal* approach, which traces the syntactic–semantic and morphological properties of lexical items to the internal syntax in those lexical items. Such internal syntax simply reduces to structure-building principles similar to those in larger linguistic constructions, thus involving operations of Merge. Hence the name *exo-skeletal*, as structures formed outside of a listed item in the lexicon which gives rise to a skeletal configuration constitute elements of syntax which is sort of 'internalized', with the operations of Merge generalizing within the structural domains of lexical items. That is, the direction of explanatory fit is from structure-building principles in larger linguistic constructions to those in lexical items, while the converse is true for the *endo-skeletal* approach. A more radical version of the *exo-skeletal* approach appears in Starke (2011).

9. The notion of semantic interpretation that LF contributes to within the framework of Generative Grammar is, in subtle ways, different in Montague Grammar. Any natural language expressions in Montague Grammar are translated into expressions of Intensional Logic (IL), which constitutes an intermediate logical form that represents semantic structures, and these expressions in IL are then given model-theoretic interpretations. Most importantly, this translation into IL does not exactly parallel the role played by LF in Generative Grammar. The translation into IL expressions is immaterial, but model-theoretic interpretations are *real* semantic interpretations (Dowty et al. 1981).

10. First-order logic is a theory of logic that specifies individual entities (names and variables) and predicates that take those entities as arguments, as in [Sad(j)] for 'John is sad'. Thus first-order logic is countable and deductively complete because deduction of a consequence from the premises is always possible, while second-order logic, which specifies properties, relations, etc. (as in 'John's being polite is a good thing' where 'John's being polite' is not an individual entity of the kind the name 'John' is; rather, it is a property), is not so. In this connection one should also bear in mind that the procedure for the verification of the validity of the formulas of first-order logic may never terminate at all. That is, effective procedures for the verification of the validity of the formulas of first-order logic do not exist; only verification can be done but with no hope of ever observing the termination of the task. The impossibility of having an algorithmic solution to the verification of the validity of the formulas of first-order logic was first found by Alonzo Church and Alan Turing. See Higginbotham (1998) for more details on higher-order logic in natural language.

11. Here some readers can get a flavour of the Chierchian notation. The $^\cup x$ notation converts a nominal (an entity e) into an adjectival *property* (a type of a predicate $<e{\rightarrow}t>$, as in 'Blue is my favourite colour', for example).

12. Barsalou's (1999) theory of perceptual symbols is exactly such a possibility.

13. Even if some pictorial or visual representation is used in theoretical physics, it is never meant to be an independently alternative description of the physical reality that can replace the mathematical expressions which a pictorial or visual representation recodes. Thus, for example, Feynman diagrams represent the interactions of fundamental particles in particle physics, but this diagrammatic representation is not meant to be an alternative to the mathematical expressions. Rather, Feynman diagrams are an aid in the understanding of the mathematical expressions that describe the interactions of fundamental particles in particle physics. Hence one cannot understand Feynman diagrams ignoring the mathematics that underlies Feynman diagrams.

14. This problem can also be phrased in terms that make reference to the Peircian view of semiosis in which the semiotic object interpretative processes operate on and the interpretative processes oscillate between each other.

6 The Emerging Connection

1. In structures with the expletive 'there …', which are also called *existential structures*, quantifiers such as 'every', 'most', 'all' are blocked, while quantifiers such as 'a few', 'few', 'a/an', 'some', 'two/three/…' etc. are okay. This observation is credited to Milsark (1977). Note that the latter class includes cardinal determiners/quantifiers, but the former class contains universal determiners/quantifiers.

2. It is also important to underline the difference between the model-theoretic approaches to natural language grammar (see Pullum 2013) and the present meta-theoretical formulation. While many aspects of the former can be seen to be reflected in the present meta-theoretical formulation as *part* of the specification of the system of axioms, rules and constraints, the present conception differs in having something substantive to say about the *grounding relation* that links an axiomatic system of natural language to the language faculty instantiated in the mind. Mature formulations of views on the relationship between grammar, mind and computation exist (as in Boas and Sag 2012), and the present meta-theoretical view may be taken to be largely complementary to such theoretical ventures.

3. Readers may now get a flavour of the algebraic treatment of lexical structures from the lexicon, despite the fact the ingredients for the lexical conceptual structures are taken from Pustejovsky's *generative lexicon theory*, which aims to account for many productive (or predictive) aspects of conceptual structures in lexical processes. The question of whether the lexicon contains generative rules of the kind proposed within *generative lexicon theory* may be left open. The present proposal is compatible with whatever choice one makes; the uniform nature of LDs that may be shared among lexicon, syntax and semantics makes a space for generative rules.

4. Note that the properties of semantic structures described in both Cognitive Grammar and formal semantics are all considered to be important, insofar as they are independently recognizable and have different formal consequences. Since the intentional projection of the linguistic system coheres with the description of the system of axioms, rules and constraints, the oscillation between any semantic property and mental processes of semantic interpretation is part of the description itself.
5. Note that the term 'event' in Jackendoff's notation (2002) is used in a more general sense that designates states as well.
6. That an LD of syntax in the tuple <LD_1,..., LD_i> is different from the one in the tuple <LD_1,..., LD_j> is based on the assumption that the sentence 'Who came after what?', for example, is a different syntactic–semantic object from the grammatically deviant version '*What did who come after?', which can be given a representation by means of the tuple <LD_1,..., LD_i>, but not through the tuple <LD_1,..., LD_j>. The structural possibilities become apparent when we consider echo-questions like 'John came after what?' in English or even structural configurations of the type [$_S$ *Wh*-Phrase *Wh*-Phrase...] in a language like Hungarian.
7. This point was noted in Bierwisch (1999).

7 Linguistic Theory, Explanation and Linguistic Competence

1. Adger designates this by the symbol ₚ, and it is immaterial for the present purpose of mere illustration whether we use **P** or ₚ.

8 Linguistic Theory, Learnability, Mind and Computation

1. A grammar class is determined in terms of Chomsky's hierarchy of formal grammars: unrestricted grammars generating recursively enumerable languages are ranked highest, then comes the class of context-sensitive grammars, then the class of context-free grammars, and at bottom, the class of regular grammars.
2. Context-free grammars are grammars the rules of which are defined in the following manner: A→ B C, for example. Note that the instruction that A can be replaced by B and C is independent of any specification of the context in which this replacement is to be executed. Hence the name *context-free grammar*. Context-free grammars are also equivalent to what is familiarly known as phrase structure grammars.

References

Adger, D. (2013). A *Syntax of Substance*. Cambridge, Mass.: MIT Press.

Agbayani, B. and Zoerner, E. (2004). Gapping, pseudogapping and sideward movement. *Studia Linguistica* 58(3): 185–211.

Alexiadou, A. and Doron, E. (2012). The syntactic construction of two non-active voices: Passive and middle. *Journal of Linguistics* 48(1): 1–34.

Anderson, J. M. (2006). Structural analogy and universal grammar. *Lingua* 116: 601–33.

Anderson, J. M. (2011). *The Substance of Language*, Vol. 3. Oxford: Oxford University Press.

Antony, L. M. and Hornstein, N. (eds) (2003). *Chomsky and his Critics*. Oxford: Blackwell.

Aoun, J. and Li, Y. A. (1993). *Syntax of Scope*. Cambridge, Mass.: MIT Press.

Aoun, J. and Li, Y. A. (2003). *Essays on the Representational and Derivational Nature of Grammar*. Cambridge, Mass.: MIT Press.

Bach, E. and Marsh, W. (1987). An elementary proof of the Peters–Ritchie theorem. In Savitch, W. J., Bach, E., Marsh, W. and Safran-Naveh, G. (eds) *The Formal Complexity of Natural Language*, 41–55. Dordrecht: Kluwer.

Bach, K. (2013). The lure of linguistification. In Penco, C. and Domaneschi, F. (eds) *What is Said and what is not: The Semantics/Pragmatics Interface*, 87–98. Stanford: CSLI Publications.

Barsalou, L. (1999). Perceptual symbol systems. *Behavioral and Brain Sciences* 22(4): 577–660.

Barton, G. E., Berwick, R. C. and Ristad, E. V. (1987). *Computational Complexity and Natural Language*. Cambridge, Mass.: MIT Press.

Beck, S. (1996). Quantified structures as barriers for LF-movement. *Natural Language Semantics* 4: 1–56.

Beck, S. (2006). Intervention effects follow from focus interpretation. *Natural Language Semantics* 14: 1–56.

Beghelli, F. and Stowell, T. (1997). Distributivity and negation: The syntax of *each* and *every*. In Szabolcsi, A. (ed.) *Ways of Scope Taking*, 71–107. Dordrecht: Kluwer Academic Press.

Bergen, B. K. (2004). The psychological reality of phonaesthemes. *Language* 80(2): 290–311.

Berwick, R. C. (1991). Computational complexity theory and natural language: A paradox resolved. *Theoretical Linguistics* 17(1–3): 123–58.

Berwick, R. C., Pietroski, P., Yankama, B. and Chomsky, N. (2011). Poverty of the stimulus revisited. *Cognitive Science* 35(7): 1207–42.

Berwick, R. C. and Weinberg, A. S. (1984). *The Grammatical Basis of Linguistic Performance*. Cambridge, Mass.: MIT Press.

Bierwisch, M. (1999). How much space gets into language? In Bloom, P., Peterson, M. A., Nadel, L. and Garrett, M. F. (eds) *Language and Space*, 31–76. Cambridge, Mass.: MIT Press.

Bishop, J. M. (2009) A cognitive computation fallacy? Cognition, computations and panpsychism. *Cognitive Computation* 1: 221–33.

Bittner, M. and Hale, K. (1995). Remarks on definiteness in Warlpiri. In Bach, E., Jelinek, E., Kratzer, A. and Partee, B. (eds) *Quantification in Natural Language*, 81–106. Dordrecht: Springer.

Bloomfield, L. (1933). *Language*. New York: Henry Holt.

Boas, H. C. and Sag, I. (eds) (2012). *Sign-Based Construction Grammar*. Stanford: CSLI Publications.

Boeckx, C. and Hornstein, N. (2004). Movement under control. *Linguistic Inquiry* 35(3): 431–52.

Borer, H. (2004). The grammar machine. In Alexiadou, A., Anagnostopoulou, E. E. and Everaert, M. (eds) *The Unaccusativity Puzzle*, 288–331. New York: Oxford University Press.

Borer, H. (2005). *In Name Only: Structuring Sense*, Vol. I. New York: Oxford University Press.

Borg, E. and Lepore, E. (2002). Symbolic logic and natural language. In Jacquette, D. (ed.) *A Companion to Philosophical Logic*, 86–102. Oxford: Blackwell.

Bowers, J. (2010). *Arguments as Relations*. Cambridge, Mass.: MIT Press.

Bresnan, J. (1982). *The Mental Representation of Grammatical Relations*. Cambridge, Mass.: MIT Press.

Bresnan, J. (2001). *Lexical Functional Syntax*. Oxford: Blackwell.

Bresnan, J. and Grimshaw, J. (1978). The syntax of free relatives in English. *Linguistic Inquiry* 9(3): 331–91.

Bromberger, S. (1992). *On what we Know we don't Know: Explanation, Theory, Linguistics, and how Questions Shape them*. Chicago: University of Chicago Press.

Burton-Roberts, N. (2011). On the grounding of syntax and the role of phonology in human cognition. *Lingua* 121(14): 2089–102.

Cable, S. (2010). *The Grammar of Q: Q-Particles, Wh-Movement and Pied-Piping*. New York: Oxford University Press.

Cann, R., Kempson, R. and Wedgwood, D. (2012). Representationalism and linguistic knowledge. In Kempson, R., Fernando, T. and Asher, N. (eds) *Philosophy of Linguistics*, 357–401. Oxford: Elsevier.

Carlson, G. (2003). On the notion 'showing something'. In Moore, J. and Polinsky, M. (eds) *The Nature of Explanation in Linguistic Theory*, 69–82. Stanford: CSLI Publications.

Carlson, G. (2006). 'Mismatches' of form and interpretation. In Geenhoven, V. van (ed.) *Semantics in Acquisition*, 19–35. Dordrecht: Springer.

Cattell, R. (1976). Constraints on movement rules. *Language* 52: 18–50.

Chalmers, J. D. (2012). A computational foundation for the study of cognition. *The Journal of Cognitive Science* 12(4): 323–57.

Chaves, R. P. (2013). An expectation-based account of subject islands and parasitism. *Journal of Linguistics* 49(2): 285–327.

Chierchia, G. (2013). *Logic in Grammar: Polarity, Free Choice, and Intervention*. New York: Oxford University Press.

Chomsky, N. (1957). *Syntactic Structures*. The Hague: Mouton de Gruyter.

Chomsky, N. (1965). *Aspects of the Theory of Syntax*. Cambridge, Mass.: MIT Press.

Chomsky, N. (1975a). *Questions on Form and Interpretation*. Berlin: Mouton de Gruyter.

Chomsky, N. (1975b). *The Logical Structure of Linguistic Theory*. New York: Plenum Press.

Chomsky, N. (1977). On *wh*-movement. In Culicover, P., Wasow, T. and Akmajian, A. (eds) *Formal Syntax*, 71–132. New York: Academic Press.

Chomsky, N. (1980). *Rules and Representations*. New York: Columbia University Press.

Chomsky, N. (1981). *Lectures on Government and Binding*. Holland: Floris Publications.

Chomsky, N. (1985). *Knowledge of Language: Its Nature, Origin, and Use*. New York: Praeger.

Chomsky, N. (1995). *The Minimalist Program*. Cambridge, Mass.: MIT Press.

Chomsky, N. (2000a). *New Horizons in the Study of Language and Mind*. Cambridge, Mass.: MIT Press.

Chomsky, N. (2000b). Minimalist inquiries: The framework. In Martin, R., Michaels, D. and Uriagereka, J. (eds) *Step by Step*, 89–156. Cambridge, Mass.: MIT Press.

Chomsky, N. (2001). Derivation by phase. In Kenstowicz, M. (ed.) *Ken Hale: A Life in Language*, 1–52. Cambridge, Mass: MIT Press.

Chomsky, N. (2004). Beyond explanatory adequacy. In Belletti A. (ed.) *Structures and Beyond: The Cartography of Syntactic Structure*, Vol. 3, 104–31. Oxford: Oxford University Press.

Chomsky, N. (2005). Three factors in language design. *Linguistic Inquiry* 36: 1–22.

Chomsky, N. (2007). Biolinguistic explorations: Design, development, evolution. *International Journal of Philosophical Studies* 15(1): 1–21.

Chomsky, N. (2008). On phases. In Freidin, R., Otero, C. P. and Zubizarreta, M. L. (eds) *Foundational Issues in Linguistic Theory*, 133–66. Cambridge, Mass.: MIT Press.

Christiansen, M. H. and MacDonald, M. C. (2009). A usage-based approach to recursion in sentence processing. In Ellis, N. C. and Larsen-Freeman, D. (eds) *Language as a Complex Adaptive System*, 126–61. Language Learning 59: Supplement.

Church, K. (1980). On memory limitations in natural language processing. MS thesis, MIT.

Cinque, G. (1999). *Adverbs and Functional Heads: A Cross-Linguistic Perspective*. New York: Oxford University Press.

Cinque, G. and Rizzi, L. (2010). The cartography of syntactic structures. In Heine, B. and Narrog, H. (eds) *Oxford Handbook of Linguistic Analysis,* 51–65. New York: Oxford University Press.

Clark, A. and Lappin, S. (2011). *Linguistic Nativism and the Poverty of the Stimulus*. Oxford: Blackwell.

Clark, A. and Lappin, S. (2012). Computational learning theory and language acquisition. In Kempson, R., Asher, N. and Fernando, T. (eds) *Handbook of the Philosophy of Science*, Vol. 14: *Philosophy of Linguistics*, 445–75. Oxford: Elsevier.

Collins, C. (1991). Why and how come. *MIT Working Papers in Linguistics* 15: 31–45. Cambridge: MIT.

Collins, C. (1997). *Local Economy*. Cambridge, Mass.: MIT Press.

Collins, J. (2004). Faculty disputes. *Mind and Language* 19(5): 503–33.

Collins, J. (2007). Review of Devitt's *Ignorance of Language*. *Mind* 116: 416–23.

Cooper, C. (2013). *Languages and Machines*. Notes for Math 237, 5th edn. http://web.science.mq.edu.au/~chris/langmach/.

Crain, S. (2012). *The Emergence of Meaning*. Cambridge: Cambridge University Press.

Cresswell, M. J. (1985). *Structured Meanings: The Semantics of Propositional Attitudes*. Cambridge, Mass.: MIT Press.

Culicover, P. and Jackendoff, R. (2003). The semantic basis of control in English. *Language* 79: 517–56.

Culicover, P. and Jackendoff, R. (2005). *Simpler Syntax*. New York: Oxford University Press.

Danon, G. (2006). Caseless nominals and the projection of DP. *Natural Language & Linguistic Theory* 24(4): 977–1008.

Danon, G. (2011). Agreement and DP-internal feature distribution. *Syntax* 14(4): 297–317.

Dascal, M. (1992). Why does language matter to artificial intelligence? *Minds and Machines* 2: 145–74.

Dascal, M. (2003). *Interpretation and Understanding*. Amsterdam: John Benjamins.

Devitt, M. (2006). *Ignorance of Language*. Oxford: Oxford University Press.

Devitt, M. (2013). Three methodological flaws of linguistic pragmatism. In Penco, C. and Domaneschi, F. (eds) *What is Said and what is not: The Semantics/Pragmatics Interface*, 285–300. Stanford: CSLI Publications.

Dodwell, P. (2000). *Brave New Mind: A Thoughtful Inquiry into theNature and Meaning of Mental Life*. New York: Oxford University Press.

Dowty, D. (1979). *Word Meaning and Montague Grammar*. Dordrecht: Springer.

Dowty, D., Wall, R. and Peters, S. (1981). *Introduction to Montague Semantics*. Dordrecht: Kluwer.

Elman, J., Karmiloff-Smith, A., Bates, E., Johnson, M., Domenico, P. and Plunkett, K. (1996). *Rethinking Innateness: A Connectionist Perspective on Development*. Cambridge, Mass.: MIT Press.

Epstein, S. and Seely, T. D. (eds) (2002). *Derivation and Explanation in the Minimalist Program*. Oxford: Blackwell.

Epstein, S. and Seely, T. D. (2006). *Derivations in Minimalism*. Cambridge: Cambridge University Press.

Fiengo, R. and May, R. (1996). Interpreted logical forms: A critique. *Rivista di Linguistica* 8: 349–74.

Fillmore, C. J. (1970). Subjects, speakers, and roles. *Synthese* 21(3): 251–74.

Fodor, J. (1975). *The Language of Thought*. Cambridge, Mass.: Harvard University Press.

Fodor, J. (1983). *The Modularity of Mind: An Essay on Faculty Psychology*. Cambridge, Mass.: MIT Press.

Fodor, J. (2000). *The Mind does not Work that Way*. Cambridge, Mass.: MIT Press.

Fodor, J., Bever, T. G. and Garrett, M. F. (1974). *The Psychology of Language*. New York: McGraw-Hill.

Forbes, G. (2001). Intensional transitive verbs: The limitations of a clausal analysis. Unpublished manuscript.

Forbes, G. (2006). *Attitude Problems: An Essay on Linguistic Intensionality*. New York: Oxford University Press.

Foster, C. L. (1992). *Algorithms, Abstraction and Implementation: Levels of Detail in Cognitive Science*. San Diego: Academic Press.

Fox, D. (1999a). *Economy and Semantic Interpretation*. Cambridge, Mass.: MIT Press.

Fox, D. (1999b). Reconstruction, binding theory, and the interpretation of chains. *Linguistic Inquiry* 30(2): 157–96.

Fox, D. (2002). Economy and scope. *Natural Language Semantics* 3(3): 283–341.

Fox, D. (2003). On logical form. In Hendrick, R. (ed.) *Minimalist Syntax*, 82–123. Oxford: Blackwell.

Fox, D. and Nissenbaum, J. (1999). Extraposition and scope: A case for overt QR. In Bird, S., Carnie, A., Haugen, J. D. and Norquest, P. (eds) *Proceedings of 18th West Coast Conference in Formal Linguistics*, 132–44. Somerville, Mass.: Cascadilla Press.

Frampton, J. and Gutmann, S. (2002). Crash-proof syntax. In Epstein, S. D. and Seely, T. D. (eds) *Derivation and Explanation in the Minimalist Program*, 90–103. Oxford: Blackwell.

Frampton, J. and Gutmann, S. (2006). How sentences grow in the mind. In Boeckx, C. (ed.) *Agreement Systems*, 121–57. Amsterdam: John Benjamins.

Fresco, N. (2011). Concrete digital computation: What does it take for a physical system to compute? *Journal of Logic, Language and Information* 20: 513–37.

Frixione, M. (2001). Tractable competence. *Mind and Machines* 11: 379–97.

Gärdenfors, P. (2004). *Conceptual Spaces: The Geometry of Thought*. Cambridge, Mass.: MIT Press.

George, A. (1989). How not to be confused about linguistics. In George, A. (ed.) *Reflections on Chomsky*, 90–111. Oxford: Blackwell.

Gold, E. M. (1967). Language identification in the limit. *Information and Control* 10: 447–74.

Goldreich, O. (2008). *Computational Complexity: A Conceptual Perspective*. Cambridge: Cambridge University Press.

Golumbia, D. (2010). Minimalism is functionalism. *Language Sciences* 32(1): 28–42.

Gross, S. (2005). The nature of semantics: On Jackendoff's arguments. *The Linguistic Review* 22: 249–70.

Gruber, J. S. (1965). Studies in lexical relations. PhD dissertation, MIT.

Hale, K. and Keyser, S. J. (2002). *Prolegomenon to a Theory of Argument Structure*. Cambridge, Mass.: MIT Press.

Halliday, M. A. K. (1973). *Explorations in the Functions of Language*. London: Edwin Arnold.

Hallman, P. (2004). NP-Interpretation and the structure of predicates. *Language* 80(4): 707–47.

Harris, R. A. (1993). *The Linguistic Wars*. New York: Oxford University Press.

Hauser, M. D., Chomsky, N. and Fitch, T. (2002). The faculty of language: What is it, who has it and how did it evolve? *Science* 298: 1569–79.

Hehner, E. C. R. (2010). Problems with the halting problem. Unpublished manuscript, University of Toronto.

Heim, I. and Kratzer, A. (1998). *Semantics in Generative Grammar*. Oxford: Blackwell.

Hengeveld, K., Jan Rijkhoff, J. and Siewierska, A. (2004). Parts of speech systems and word order. *Journal of Linguistics* 40(3): 527–70.

Higginbotham, J. (1998). On higher-order logic and natural language. In Smiley, T. (ed.) *Proceedings of the British Academy 95: Philosophical Logic*, 1–27. Oxford: Oxford University Press.

Hintikka, J. (1977). Quantifiers in natural languages: Some logical problems. *Linguistics and Philosophy* 1(2): 53–72.

Hinzen, W. (2006). *Mind Design and Minimal Syntax*. New York: Oxford University Press.

Hinzen, W. (2009). Successor function + LEX = human language? In Grohman, K. (ed.) *InterPhases: Phase-Theoretic Investigations of Linguistic Interfaces*, 25–47. New York: Oxford University Press.

Hockett, C. F. (1958). *A Course in Modern Linguistics*. New York: Macmillan.

Hofmeister, P., Arnon, I., Jaeger, T. F., Sag, I. A. and Snider, N. (2013). The source ambiguity problem: Distinguishing the effects of grammar and processing on acceptability judgments. *Language and Cognitive Processes* 18(1–2): 48–87.

Hopcroft, J. E. and Ullman, J. D. (1979). *Introduction to Automata Theory, Languages and Computation*. Reading, Mass.: Addison-Wesley.

Hornstein, N., Lasnik, H. and Uriagereka, J. (2006). The dynamics of islands: Speculations on the locality of movement. *Linguistic Analysis* 33(1–2): 149–75.

Hudson, R. A. (1976). Conjunction reduction, gapping, and right-node raising. *Language* 52(3): 535–62.

Huizing, C., Kuiper, R. and Verhoeff, T. (2010). Halting still standing-programs versus specifications. In Qin, S. (ed.) *Unifying Theories of Programming*, 226–33. Lecture Notes in Computer Science. Berlin: Springer.

Hymes, D. H. (1972). On communicative competence. In Pride, J. B. and Holmes, J. (eds) *Sociolinguistics: Selected Readings*, 269–93. Harmondsworth: Penguin.

Itkonen, E. (2005). *Analogy as Structure and Process*. Amsterdam: John Benjamins.

Jackendoff, R. (1971). Gapping and related rules. *Linguistic Inquiry* 2(1): 21–35.

Jackendoff, R. (2002). *Foundations of Language: Brain, Meaning, Grammar, Evolution*. New York: Oxford University Press.

Jackendoff, R. (2007). *Language, Consciousness, Culture*. Cambridge, Mass.: MIT Press.

Jackson, B. (2007). Beyond logical form. *Philosophical Studies* 132: 347–80.

Janssen, T. M. V. (1997). Compositionality. In van Benthem, J. F. A. K. and Ter Meulen, A. (eds) *Handbook of Logic and Language*. Amsterdam: Elsevier.

Janssen, T. M. V. (2001). Frege, contextuality and compositionality. *Journal of Logic, Language and Information* 10(1): 115–36.

Jespersen, O. (1924). *The Philosophy of Grammar*. London: Allen & Unwin.

Johnson, D. and Lappin, S. (1997). A critique of the Minimalist Program. *Linguistics and Philosophy* 20(3): 273–333.

Johnson, K. (2009). Gapping is not (VP-) ellipsis. *Linguistic Inquiry* 40(2): 289–328.

Joseph, J. E. (2002). *From Whitney to Chomsky: Essays in the History of American Linguistics*. Amsterdam: John Benjamins.

Katz, J. and Postal, P. (1964). *An Integrated Theory of Linguistic Descriptions*. Cambridge, Mass.: MIT Press.

Katz, M. (2008). Analog and digital representation. *Minds and Machines* 18: 403–8.

Kayne, R. (1994). *The Antisymmetry of Syntax*. Cambridge, Mass.: MIT Press.

Keenan, E. L. (2005). In situ interpretation without type mismatches. Manuscript, UCLA.

Keenan, E. and Stabler, E. (2010). On language variation and linguistic invariants. UCLA Working Papers in Linguistics No. 15.

Kempson, R., Meyer-Viol, W. and Gabbay, D. (2001). *Dynamic Syntax: The Flow of Language Understanding*. Oxford: Blackwell.

Klaiman, M. H. (1991). *Grammatical Voice*. Cambridge: Cambridge University Press.

Kornai, A. (2008). *Mathematical Linguistics*. Berlin: Springer.

Kornai, A. (2010). The algebra of lexical semantics. In Ebert, C., Jäger, G. and Michaelis, J. (eds) *The Mathematics of Language*, 174–99. Berlin: Springer.

Kracht, M. (1998). On reducing principles to rules. In Blackburn, P. and de Rijke, M. (eds) *Specifying Syntactic Structure*, 25–53. Stanford: CSLI Publications.

Krifka, M. (1991). Some remarks on polarity items. In Zaefferer, D. (ed.) *Semantic Universals and Universal Semantics*, 150–89. Dordrecht: Foris.

Kuno, S. (1976). Gapping: A functional analysis. *Linguistic Inquiry* 7: 300–18.

Lakoff, G. (1971). On generative semantics. In Steinberg, D. and Jakobovits, L. (eds) *Semantics: An Interdisciplinary Reader in Philosophy, Linguistics and Psychology*, 232–96. New York: Cambridge University Press.

Lakoff, G. (1987). *Women, Fire and Dangerous Things*. Chicago: Chicago University Press.

Landau, I. (2008). Movement-resistant aspects of control. In Davis, W. D. and Dubinsky, S. (eds) *New Horizons in the Analysis of Control and Raising*, 293–326. Dordrecht: Springer.

Langacker, R. (1987). *Foundations of Cognitive Grammar*. Stanford, Calif.: Stanford University Press.

Langacker, R. (1999). *Grammar and Conceptualization*. Berlin: Mouton de Gruyter.

Langendoen, D. T. and Postal, P. (1984). *The Vastness of Natural Languages*. Oxford: Basil Blackwell.

Larson, R. and Ludlow, P. (1993). Interpreted logical forms. *Synthese* 95: 305–55.

Larson, R., den Dikken, M. and Ludlow, P. (1997). Intensional transitive verbs and abstract clausal complementation. Unpublished manuscript.

Levin, B. and Grafmiller, J. (2013). Do you always fear what frightens you? In King, T. H. and de Paiva, V. (eds) *From Quirky Case to Representing Space: Papers in Honor of Annie Zaenen*, 21–32. Stanford: CSLI Publications.

Ludlow, P. (2011). *The Philosophy of Generative Linguistics*. New York: Oxford University Press.

Luuk, E. and Luuk, H. (2011). The redundancy of recursion and infinity for natural language. *Cognitive Processing* 12(1): 1–11.

McCawley, J. D. (1987). Review of *The Vastness of Natural Languages*. *International Journal of American Linguistics* 53(2): 236–42.

Maling, J. (2006). From passive to active: Syntactic change in progress in Icelandic. In Lyngfelt, B. and Solstad, T. (eds) *Demoting the Agent: Passive, Middle and Other Voice Phenomena*, 197–224. Amsterdam: John Benjamins.

Marr, D. (1982). *Vision: A Computational Investigation into the Human Representation and Processing of Visual Information*. San Francisco: W. H. Freeman.

Matthews, R. (2006). Knowledge of language and linguistic competence. *Philosophical Issues* 16(1): 200–20.

May, R. (1985). *Logical Form: Its Structure and Derivation*. Cambridge, Mass.: MIT Press.

May, R. (1989). Interpreting logical form. *Linguistics and Philosophy* 12: 387–435.

Miller, P. (1999). *Strong Generative Capacity: The Semantics of Linguistic Formalism*. Stanford: CSLI Publications.

Milsark, G. (1977). Toward an explanation of certain peculiarities of the existential construction in English. *Linguistic Analysis* 3: 1–29.

Miyagawa, S. (2010). *Why Agree? Why Move: Unifying Agreement-Based and Discourse Configurational Languages*. Cambridge, Mass.: MIT Press.

Moltmann, F. (2008). Intensional verbs and their intentional objects. *Natural Language Semantics* 16: 239–70.

Moltmann, F. (2013). *Abstract Objects and the Semantics of Natural Language*. Oxford: Oxford University Press.

Mondal, P. (2010). Exploring the N-th dimension of language. *Research in Computing Science* 46: 55–66.

Mondal, P. (2011). Quantificational scope and the syntax–semantics interface. Unpublished manuscript, Indian Institute of Technology Delhi.

Mondal, P. (2012). Can internalism and externalism be reconciled in a biological epistemology of language? *Biosemiotics* 5: 61–82.

Mondal, P. (2013a). Logical form vs. logical form: How does the difference matter for semantic computationality? In Pfeiffer, H. D., Ignatov, D. I., Poelmans, J. and Gadiraju, N. (eds) *Conceptual Structures for STEM Research and Education.* Lecture Notes in Computer Science, Vol. 7735, 254–65. Berlin: Springer.

Mondal, P. (2013b). Intensional emotive constructions and the nature of linguistic meaning: Towards an architecture of the language–emotion interface. Unpublished manuscript, Indian Institute of Technology Delhi.

Mondal, P. (2014a). Does computation reveal machine cognition? *Biosemiotics* 7: 97–110.

Mondal, P. (2014b). How does the faculty of language relate to rules, axioms and constraints? *Pragmatics and Cognition* 21(2): 270–303.

Mondal, P. and Mishra, R. S. (2013). Does (linguistic) computation need culture to make cognition viable? *Procedia: Social and Behavioral Sciences* 97: 464–73.

Montrul, S. (2011). Multiple interfaces and incomplete acquisition. *Lingua* 121(4): 591–604.

Moortgart, M. (1997). Categorial type logics. In van Benthem, J. F. A. K. and Ter Meulen, A. (eds) *Handbook of Logic and Language*, 95–171. Amsterdam: Elsevier.

Motomura, M. (2001). Formal approaches to Japanese linguistics 3: Proceedings from FAJL 3. *MIT Working Papers in Linguistics* 41: 309–23.

Mulder, R. and den Dikken, M. (1992). Tough parasitic gaps. *Annual Meeting of the North East Linguistic Society* 22: 303–17.

Munakata, T. (2009). The division of C-I and the nature of the input, multiple transfer, and phases. In Grohmann, K. (ed.) *InterPhases: Phase-Theoretic Investigations of Linguistic Interfaces*, 48–81. New York: Oxford University Press.

Nanni, D. (1980). On the surface syntax of constructions with *easy*-type adjectives. *Language* 56(3): 568–81.

Ndayiragije, J. (2012). On raising out of control. *Linguistic Inquiry* 43(2): 275–99.

Neelman, A. and Weerman, F. (1998). *Flexible Syntax: A Theory of Case and Arguments.* Dordrecht: Kluwer.

Neeleman, A. and van de Koot, H. (2010). Theoretical validity and psychological reality of the grammatical code. In Everaert, M., Lentz, T., De Mulder, H., Nilsen, Ø. and Zondervan, A. (eds) *The Linguistics Enterprise: From Knowledge of Language to Knowledge in Linguistics*, 183–212. Amsterdam: John Benjamins.

Nunes, J. (2004). *Linearization of Chains and Sideward Movement.* Cambridge, Mass.: MIT Press.

Nunes, J. and Uriagereka, J. (2000). Cyclicity and extraction domains. *Syntax* 3: 20–43.

O'Brien, G. and Opie, J. (2011). Representation in analog computation. In Newen, A., Bartels, A. and Jung, E. (eds) *Knowledge and Representation*, 109–28. Stanford: CSLI Publications.

Ohala, J. J. (1990). There is no interface between phonology and phonetics: A personal view. *Journal of Phonetics* 18(2): 153–72.

Ohala, J. J. (2005). The marriage of phonetics and phonology. *Journal of Acoustical Science and Technology* 26(5): 418–22.

Ohala, J. J. (2010). The relation between phonetics and phonology. In Hardcastle, W. J., Laver, J. and Gibbon, F. E. (eds) *The Handbook of Phonetic Sciences*, 2nd edn, 653–77. Oxford: Blackwell.

Partee, B. (1977). John is easy to please. In Zampoli, A. (ed.) *Linguistic Structures Processing*, 281–312. Amsterdam: North Holland Publishing.

Partee, B. and Rooth, M. (1983). Generalized conjunction and type ambiguity. In Bauerle, R., Schwarze, C. and von Stechow, A. (eds) *Meaning, Use and Interpretation of Language*, 361–83. Berlin: Mouton de Gruyter.

Peacocke, C. (1989). When is a grammar psychologically real? In George, A. (ed.) *Reflections on Chomsky*, 111–31. Oxford: Blackwell.

Penrose, R. (1994). *Shadows of the Mind: A Search for the Missing Science of Consciousness*. Oxford: Oxford University Press.

Pesetsky, D. (2000). *Phrasal Movement and its Kin*. Cambridge, Mass.: MIT Press.

Pesetsky, D. and Torrego, E. (2004). The syntax of valuation and the interpretability of features. Manuscript, University of Massachusetts, Boston.

Peters, S. and Ritchie, R. W. (1973). On the generative power of transformational grammars. *Information Sciences* 6: 49–83.

Piccinini, G. and Scarantino, A. (2011). Information processing, computation and cognition. *Journal of Biological Physics* 37:1–38.

Pollard, C. and Sag, I. (1994). *Head-Driven Phrase Structure Grammar*. Chicago: University of Chicago Press.

Pollard, C. and Xue, P. (2001). Syntactic and nonsyntactic constraints on long-distance reflexives. In Cole, P., Hermon, G. and Huang, C. T. J. (eds) *Long-Distance Reflexives*, 317–40. New York: Academic Press.

Postal, P. (1972). The best theory. In Peters, S. (ed.) *Goals of Linguistic Theory*, 131–79. New Jersey: Prentice-Hall.

Postal, P. (1974). *On Raising*. Cambridge, Mass.: The MIT Press.

Postal, P. (1998). *Three Investigations of Extraction*. Cambridge, Mass.: MIT Press.

Postal, P. (2004). *Skeptical Linguistic Essays*. New York: Oxford University Press.

Potts, T. C. (1975). Model theory and linguistics. In Keenan, E. L. (ed.) *Formal Semantics of Natural Language*, 241–50. Cambridge: Cambridge University Press.

Prince, A. and Smolensky, P. (1993). *Optimality Theory: Constraint Interaction in Generative Grammar*. New Jersey: Rutgers University Center for Cognitive Science.

Pritchett, B. (1992). *Grammatical Competence and Parsing Performance*. Chicago: Chicago University Press.

Pullum, G. K. (2013). The central question in comparative syntactic metatheory. *Mind and Language* 28(4): 492–521.

Pullum, G. and Scholz, B. (2002). Empirical assessment of stimulus poverty arguments. *The Linguistic Review* 19: 9–50.

Pullum, G. K. and Scholz, B. (2010). Recursion and the infinitude claim. In van der Hulst, H. (ed.) *Recursion in Human Language* (Studies in Generative Grammar 104), 113–38. Berlin: Mouton.

Pustejovsky, J. (1995). *The Generative Lexicon*. Cambridge, Mass.: The MIT Press.

Putnam, H. (1961). Some issues in the theory of grammar. In Jakobson, R. (ed.) *Structure of Language and its Mathematical Aspects*, 25–42. Providence, RI: American Mathematical Society.

Putnam, H. (1988). *Representation and Reality*. Cambridge, Mass.: MIT Press.

Pylyshyn, Z. (1984). *Computation and Cognition: Toward a Foundation for Cognitive Science*. Cambridge, Mass.: MIT Press.

Pylyshyn, Z. (1991). Rules and representations: Chomsky and representational realism. In Kasher, A. (ed.) *The Chomskyan Turn*, 231–51. Cambridge, Mass.: Blackwell.

Quine, W. V. O. (1970). Methodological reflections on current linguistic theory. *Synthese* 21(3–4): 386–98.

Rado, T. (1962). On non-computable functions. *Bell System Technical Journal* 41 (3): 877–84.

Rappaport Hovav, M. and Levin, B. (2005). *Argument Realization*. Cambridge: Cambridge University Press.

Rappaport Hovav, M. and Levin, B. (2008). The English dative alternation: The case for verb sensitivity. *Journal of Linguistics* 44: 129–67.

Recanati, F. (2004). *Literal Meaning*. Cambridge: Cambridge University Press.

Reinhart, T. (1997). Quantifier scope: How labor is divided between QR and choice functions. *Linguistics and Philosophy* 20(4): 35–97.

Rezac, M. (2006). On tough-movement. In Boeckx, C. (ed.) *Minimalist Essays*, 288–325. Amsterdam: John Benjamins.

Richards, N. (2001). *Movement in Language: Interactions and Architectures*. New York: Oxford University Press.

Ristad, E. V. (1993). *The Computational Complexity Game*. Cambridge, Mass.: MIT Press.

Ross, J. (1986). *Infinite Syntax*. New Jersey: Ablex.

Ruys, E. and Winter, Y. (2010). Scope ambiguities in formal syntax and semantics. In Gabbay, D. and Guenthner, F. (eds) *Handbook of Philosophical Logic*, 2nd edn, 1–60. Amsterdam: John Benjamins.

Sabel, J. (2002). A minimalist analysis of syntactic islands. *The Linguistic Review* 19: 271–315.

Sadock, J. (1991). *Autolexical Syntax: A Theory of Parallel Grammatical Representations*. Chicago: University of Chicago Press.

Sadock, J. (2012). *The Modular Architecture of Grammar*. Cambridge: Cambridge University Press.

Sag, I. A. and Wasow, T. (2011). Performance-compatible competence grammar. In Borsley, R. D. and Börjars, K. (eds) *Non-Transformational Syntax: Formal and Explicit Models of Grammar*, 359–77. Oxford: Blackwell.

Sampson, G. (2005). *The 'Language Instinct' Debate*. London: Continuum.

Sauerland, U. (1999). Relativized minimality effects with quantifier raising. Unpublished manuscript, Tübingen University.

Savitch, W. (1987). Theories of language learnability. In Manaster-Ramer, A. (ed.) *Mathematics of Language*, 61–72. Amsterdam: John Benjamins.

Schütze, C. T. (1996). *The Empirical Base of Linguistics: Grammatical Judgments and Linguistic Methodology*. Chicago: Chicago University Press.

Searle, J. (1992). *The Rediscovery of the Mind*. Cambridge, Mass.: MIT Press.

Selkirk, E. (2006). Contrastive focus, givenness and phrase stress. Unpublished manuscript, University of Massachusetts, Amherst.

Seuren, P. A. M. (2004). *Chomsky's Minimalism*. New York: Oxford University Press.

Seuren, P. A. M. (2009). *Language in Cognition*, Vol. I. New York: Oxford University Press.

Seuren, P. A. M. (2013). *From Whorf to Montague: Explorations in the Theory of Language*. New York: Oxford University Press.

Shapiro, L. (2008). Symbolism, embodied cognition, and the broader debate. In De Vega, M., Glenberg, A. M. and Graesser, A. C. (eds) *Symbols and Embodiment: Debates on Meaning and Cognition*, 57–74. New York: Oxford University Press.

Shieber, S. M. (1987). Separating linguistic analyses from linguistic theories. In Whitelock, P., Wood, M. M., Somers, H. L., Johnson, R. and Bennett, P. (eds) *Linguistic Theory and Computer Applications*, 1–36. London: Academic Press.

Shieber, S. M. (1992). *Constraint-Based Grammar Formalisms*. Cambridge, Mass.: MIT Press.

Shimansky, Y. P. (2004). The concept of a universal learning system as a basis for creating a general mathematical theory of learning. *Minds and Machines* 14(4): 453–84.

Siegel, M. E. (1984). Gapping and interpretation. *Linguistic Inquiry* 15(3): 523–30.

Simpson, A. (2000). *Wh-Movement and the Theory of Feature-Checking*. Amsterdam: John Benjamins.

Slezak, P. (2009). Linguistic explanation and 'psychological reality'. *Croatian Journal of Philosophy* 9: 3–21.

Smolensky, P. and Legendre, G. (2006). *The Harmonic Mind*. Cambridge, Mass.: MIT Press.

Soames, S. (1984). Linguistics and psychology. *Linguistics and Philosophy* 7: 155–79.

Soames, S. (2008). *Philosophical Essays*, Vol. 1: *Natural Language: What it Means and how we Use it*. New Jersey: Princeton University Press.

Sperber, D. and Wilson, D. (1995). *Relevance: Communication and Cognition*. Oxford: Blackwell.

Stabler, E. (1987). Kripke on functionalism and automata. *Synthese* 70(1): 1–22.

Stabler, E. (2010). Recursion in grammar and performance. Presented at the 2009 University of Massachusetts Recursion Conference, 1–18.

Starke, M. (2011). Towards an elegant solution to language variation: Variation reduces to the size of lexically stored trees. Unpublished manuscript, Barcelona.

Steedman, M. (1990). Gapping as constituent coordination. *Linguistics and Philosophy* 13(2): 207–63.

Steenbergen, M. V. (1991). Long distance binding in Finnish. In Koster, J. and Reuland, E. (eds) *Long-Distance Anaphora*, 231–44. Cambridge: Cambridge University Press.

Stroik, T. (2009). The numeration in Survive-minimalism. In Putnam, M. T. (ed.) *Towards a Derivational Syntax: Survive-minimalism*, 21–38. Amsterdam: John Benjamins.

Ter Meulen, A. G. B. (1997). *Representing Time in Natural Language: The Dynamic Interpretation of Tense and Aspect*. Cambridge, Mass.: MIT Press.

Tesniére, L. (1959). *Eléments de Syntaxe Structurale*. Paris: Klincksieck.

Truswell, R. (2011). *Events, Phrases, and Questions*. New York: Oxford University Press.

Turing, A. M. (1936). On computable numbers with an application to the Entscheidungs problem. *Proceedings of the London Mathematical Society* 42(2): 230–65.

Uriagereka, J. (2008). *Syntactic Anchors: On Semantic Structuring*. New York: Cambridge University Press.

Uriagereka, J. (2012). *Spell-Out and the Minimalist Program*. New York: Oxford University Press.

Valin Van, R. D. (2003). Minimalism and explanation. In Moore, J. and Polinsky, M. (eds) *The Nature of Explanation in Linguistic Theory*, 281–97. Stanford: CSLI Publications.

Van Valin, R. D. (2005). *Exploring the Syntax–Semantics Interface*. Cambridge: Cambridge University Press.

Warglien, M. and Gärdenfors, P. (2013). Semantics, conceptual spaces, and the meeting of minds. *Synthese* 12(190): 2165–93.

Watumull, J. (2012). A Turing program for linguistic theory. *Biolinguistics* 6(2): 222–45.

Wexler, K. and Culicover, P. W. (1980). *Formal Principles of Language Acquisition*. Cambridge, Mass.: MIT Press.

White, L. (2011). Second language acquisition at the interfaces. *Lingua* 121(4): 577–90.

Index